The Irony of Identity

The Irony of Identity

Self and Imagination in the Drama of Christopher Marlowe

Ian McAdam

DELAWARE

Newark: University of Delaware Press
London: Associated University Presses

Associated University Presses
440 Forsgate Drive
Cranbury, NJ 08512

Associated University Presses
16 Barter Street
London WC1A 2AH, England

Associated University Presses
P.O. Box 338, Port Credit
Mississauga, Ontario
Canada L5G 4L8

The paper used in this publication meets the requirements of the American National Standard for Permanence of Paper for Printed Library Materials Z39.48-1984.

Library of Congress Cataloging-in-Publication Data

McAdam, Ian 1960–
    The irony of identity : self and imagination in the drama of Christopher Marlowe / Ian McAdam.
      p.   cm.
    Includes bibliographical references and index.
    ISBN 0-87413-665-2 (alk. paper)
    1. Marlowe, Christopher, 1564–1593—Knowledge—Psychology.
2. Identity (Psychology) in literature.   3. Psychoanalysis and literature—England—History—16th century.   4. Drama—Psychologocal aspects.   5. Irony in literature.   6. Self in literature.
7. Imagination.   I. Title.
PR2677.I35M37   1999
822'.3—dc21
                                    98-36997
                                       CIP

To my parents

Contents

Acknowledgements

This study began as a doctoral thesis at Dalhousie University, Halifax, Nova Scotia. I am grateful to my supervisor, Ronald Huebert, for his guidance, advice, and support. I would also like to thank my readers, John Baxter and Christina Luckyj, for their thorough review of the dissertation and for their valuable suggestions. After experiencing my own busy teaching schedules in the years since leaving Halifax, I have come to realize that I did not at the time properly acknowledge the effort made by these three professors; I take this opportunity to correct the oversight and express my appreciation. Since the work has, through a series of revisions, undergone substantial alterations in tone and treatment, I must add that no one can, or should, take responsibility for the final version except myself.

I would also like to thank Ingrid Hotz-Davies, fellow doctoral candidate at Dalhousie University, and Goran Stanivukovic, fellow sessional instructor at the University of Calgary, for their friendship and support over the years; both have demonstrated to me that colleagues and friends can entertain ideological differences and still respect each other's humanity, and both have offered me more love than I probably deserved.

An abridged version of Chapter 5 has previously appeared as "Carnal Identity in *The Jew of Malta*," in *English Literary Renaissance* 26, no. 1 (1996): 46–74; an earlier version of Chapter 7 has appeared as "*Edward II* and the Illusion of Integrity" in *Studies in Philology* 92, no. 2 (1995): 203–29. I gratefully acknowledge permission to republish this material.

The Irony of Identity

1

Introduction

In Donne's "Good Friday, 1613: Riding Westward," the speaker's conflict is paradigmatic of a central paradox in Renaissance literature. Though his "soul's form bends towards the east," where he should see Christ crucified, he, the erring human, is carried by "pleasure or business" toward the west. He admits he is almost glad to "not see / That spectacle [the cross] of too much weight for me," since "Who sees God's face, that is self life, must die." The speaker realizes he is not yet ready for the final surrender to God, but consoles himself by hoping that his act of disobedience, turning his back on Christ, will begin a process of transformation ("Burn off my rusts, and my deformity") which will eventually restore the divine image within him. West paradoxically becomes east, but the circle may be completed only because the speaker insists first on asserting his own identity. Self-assertion becomes the first step toward self-surrender.

In the case of Donne's speaker the journey westward is further justified by the fact that he keeps the images of Christ's sacrifice "present yet unto my memory." But the poet does more than remember the passion; the poem itself is an act of imagination that gives meaning to the journey of self-assertion and gives hope for the future possibility of self-surrender. The conflict between self-assertion and self-surrender that Donne's poem seems to resolve so neatly recurs as a major source of tension in other Renaissance works, though of course the conflict is not always easily resolved, and the imaginative response is often concerned with more than simply the transformation of sin in the sense of personal purgation. In a devotional lyric the parameters are necessarily limited—God, the human self, and the battle of wills between them—but much of the epic and dramatic literature of the period examines more fully the act of self-assertion, and sees it as a heroic and sometimes tragic endeavor. In this literature self-assertion becomes more than simply an act of rebellion against the Godhead. It becomes a process and a project that, thanks largely to Stephen Greenblatt, has come to be known as "self-fashioning." Among other examples, Greenblatt quotes Calidore's statement from *The Faerie Queene* 6.9.31: "in each mans self . . . / It is, to fashion his owne lyfes estate" (although Greenblatt does not pause to observe it, this assertion may be, ironically but interestingly, an overly optimistic misreading by Calidore of Meliboe's philosophy); the critic argues that in the sixteenth century *"fashion* seems to come into wide currency as a way of designating the forming of a self."[1] Much of the literature of the period is indeed concerned with this struggle to achieve and maintain personal identity. Yet certain Renaissance writers—Spenser and Milton are prime examples—retain, even while they stress the need for the establishment of individual identity, a belief that the energies of the self remain subordinate to a greater power. Even at their most humanistic they experience an intimation that could be called in the broadest sense mystical: the self that must be fashioned so heroically is in a sense illusory—it creates itself only in the end to surrender itself. These writers thus seem haunted by Augustine's admonition, also quoted by Greenblatt: "Hands off yourself. Try to build up yourself, and you build a ruin."[2] Nevertheless, the heroic effort is recognized as necessary, inescapable, for much of this literature intimates an idea succinctly voiced by a modern psychiatrist and writer: "An identity must be established before it can be transcended."[3]

While my quotation from a contemporary popular writer intimates my belief that psychological aspects of Renaissance experience have a transhistorical significance for readers today, I do not wish to ignore the special philosophical and ideological conditions that attended the heroic effort of self-fashioning in a Renaissance context. William Kerrigan and Gordon Braden in *The Idea of the Renaissance* discuss among other thinkers the importance of Pico della Mirandola, "an uncanny figure whose rightness for the period far outweighs the empirical question of his direct influence."[4] In Pico's *Oration on the Dignity of Man* God tells Adam, "We have made you a creature neither of heaven nor of earth, neither mortal nor immortal, in order that you may, as the free and proud shaper of your own being, fashion yourself in the form you may prefer." Pico summarizes:

upon man, at the moment of his creation, God bestowed seeds pregnant with all possibilities, the germs of every form of life. Whichever of these a man shall cultivate, the same will mature and bear fruit in him. If vegetative, he will become a plant; if sensual, he will become brutish; if rational, he will reveal himself a heavenly being; if intellectual, he will be an angel and the son of God. And if, dissatisfied with the lot of all creatures, he should recollect himself into the center of his own unity, he will there, become one spirit with God, in the solitary darkness of the Father, Who is set above all things, himself transcend all creatures.[5]

Here we find even more clearly than in the Donne lyric the pattern of establishing/fashioning and then transcending identity: man transcends all creatures only after embracing all creation. Kerrigan and Braden make much of what they call the "Piconian moment" in terms of Renaissance ambition: "Genesis has been rewritten to accommodate our new parity with God."[6] Yet it is important here to recognize, with Patrick Grant, that while the *Oration* "has all the hallmarks of enlightenment humanism," these enlightenment attitudes are paradoxically "expressed from within a traditional framework, and the *Oration*, like all of Pico's writings (and so much else in the Renaissance), maintains a traditional Augustinian and guilt-culture focus."[7] There is certainly a sense in the *Oration* of the corrupting influence of physicality and earthbound thought—man is criticized for being "bedazzled by the empty forms of the imagination" and praised for being "unmindful of the body"[8]—which makes it so different from later forms of humanism.

In the present critical climate Patrick Grant's formulation of the Renaissance as an encounter between medieval guilt culture, with its emphasis on the Augustinian sense of inherited sin and the need for divine grace, and an emerging emphasis on enlightenment and individual achievement, may appear unfashionable; yet it remains, I believe, a helpful initial tool in understanding the period: "The conflict between a deeply rooted mythology of fallenness and inherited guilt, against which human behavior must be judged, and an ethical endeavor toward an autonomy of reason admired but still feared produces in the Renaissance both profound and disturbing theology and literature."[9] While Greenblatt as well acknowledges that Augustine's view was "influential" down through the centuries, he and other critics of the last two decades underestimate the impact of Augustinian thought on Renaissance literature. Greenblatt, Catherine Belsey, and Jonathan Dollimore, at the forefront of the historicist/materialist movement in Renaissance studies during the eighties, are certainly all at pains to attack the idea that there exists an essential, universal human nature, yet their primary aim is to reveal that human identity is no more than a "cultural artifact." Thus Greenblatt in his *Renaissance Self-Fashioning* "perceived that fashioning oneself and being fashioned by cultural institutions—family, religion, state—were inseparably intertwined." For Greenblatt the end result of this realization of the "fictiveness" of the human self seems to be to halt suddenly on the precipice of a metaphysical void and suck in his breath: "to let go of one's stubborn hold upon selfhood, even selfhood conceived as a fiction, is to die."[10] Belsey, in *The Subject of Tragedy: Identity and Difference in Renaissance Drama*, is more obviously political in her attacks on the repressive ideology of "liberal humanism": subjectivity is "not natural, inevitable or eternal; on the contrary, it is produced and reproduced in and by a specific social order and in the interests of specific power-relations."[11] In Belsey's view even the most earnest and sophisticated inquiries into the nature of the inner self—psychoanalysis, for example—primarily serve "to keep us off the streets,"[12] and she asserts in her study of Milton that "meaning is for us now no longer a metaphysical mystery, like Milton's Incarnation, but a site of struggle, a place to lay claim to the possibilities we want to realize."[13] Some may disagree with Belsey's exclusions from the list of possibilities "we" want to realize, although there is certainly no denying that there is now an intense struggle between essentialist and constructionist, between idealist and materialist, over—or on the site of—meaning. Although Dollimore is more sensitive to humankind's desire, even down to the present day, to cling to essentialist belief,[14] his dismissal of religion is no less complete than Belsey's. He does, however, encounter some difficulty in his argument that the "decentring of man" in the early-seventeenth century—occurring after the decline of what he calls "Christian essentialism" and before the emergence of the "essentialist" humanism of the Enlightenment—resulted in an "emphasis on the extent to which subjectivity was to be socially identified."[15] The difficulty arises since he must refute any suggestion that the instability or "discontinuity" of the self in the literature of the period may be related to the very religious philosophies whose impact or importance he wishes to downplay. He does admit at one point that "in general terms essentialism might at least be qualified by . . . Augustinian [theology] . . . because of its emphasis on man's helpless depravity." Moreover, he suggests a little later that Calvinism, because of its similar emphasis on depravity, created "a destabilising tendency all its own," which presumably also had a major influence on a literature in which "man is decentred to reveal the social forces that both make and destroy him."[16]

Yet how far is the human individual "decentered," and does this literature retain any vision of an "essence" behind the image of humankind as a composite of social forces? Such vision varies greatly from writer to writer. Middleton, for example, comes close to the type of Renaissance writer Dollimore envisages: one who "transposes" theological contexts for socially subversive reasons. Marlowe, on the other hand, though also remarkably subversive, seems much more personally engaged in the theological issues he explores, and more deeply concerned with man's "essential" nature. Marlowe, in fact, seems obsessed with religious ideas to a greater degree than any other major dramatist of the period. Though Paul Kocher may exaggerate when he argues that "criticism of Christianity . . . appears in all the biographical documents as the most absorbing interest of [Marlowe's] life,"[17] he nevertheless underlines a very important element in Marlowe's life and work. What particularly needs emphasizing is that the intensity of the attack strongly suggests a peculiar religious temperament within Marlowe himself. We can speculate that growing up in Canterbury, the "mother-city of the Church of England, the seat of the Primate and centre of national ecclesiastical affairs of state,"[18] may have had an impact on a sensitive and intellectually acute youth, and we know for certain that a condition of the Archbishop Parker scholarship under which Marlowe studied for six years at Cambridge was that its recipients were expected to enter the ministry. The fact that Marlowe did not might simply indicate either that he discovered his first love for poetry and playwrighting, or that he cynically misrepresented his intentions to take advantage of the scholarship—were it not for the other evidence in hand that suggests a continuing interest in religious ideas, an interest of a most radical kind.[19] The Baines Note, for example, remains an intriguing account of Marlowe's unusual thought and behavior. Earlier referred to as the Baines Libel, it lost this designation some time in midcentury, when critical opinion swayed in favor of its validity. Recent historical scholarship, especially with respect to its author, has perhaps raised the question whether the "Baines Libel" is in fact a more accurate description. Charles Nicholl in *The Reckoning* points out that Baines's "denouncing of Marlowe's blasphemy is not done in a mood of prim-mouthed disapproval, as is often implied."[20] In 1583, at the English Catholic seminary at Rheims where he (like Marlowe, perhaps, a few years later) was a spy, Baines wrote and signed a long confession that suggests he may have shared many of Marlowe's "monstrous opinions." Roy Kendall examines the confession in detail and remarks, "Marlowe's and Baines's hobby-horses were—if not identical—very similar: except that Baines was running a string of them at least half a decade before Marlowe is known to have mounted his first one. It is as if Baines was both Marlowe's Judas and Marlowe's John the Baptist."[21] Moreover, the note seems to have been written under some duress, since "a government agent, Thomas Drury, actively sought out Baines to obtain information from him, tracking him down not without some difficulty as Drury himself avers."[22] Yet in spite of this new evidence, neither of these scholars has chosen to dismiss the note. Nicholl's "personal belief is that the 'Note' does contain genuine Marlowe attitudes, but that it presents them in a heavily debased form."[23] Kendall concludes that "the assertions in [his] essay regarding the mirror image of Baines and Marlowe do not necessarily mean the Baines Note does not reflect the private views of Marlowe as expressed in his table talk and perhaps in his underground lecture."[24] He does, however, warn that "great caution must be used when turning the 'master key to the mind of Marlowe,'" the metaphor Paul Kocher applied to the Baines Note. Kocher in fact examined the Baines Note in detail[25] and demonstrated, in J. B. Steane's opinion, "'an essential unity of design,' showing how the accusations in the note can be grouped so as to summarize a broad and coherent attack on religion."[26] While we must use it cautiously, it is my opinion as well that the Baines Note does provide us with important evidence concerning Marlowe's thought and character, and that Kocher's reading remains a valuable, if now qualified, contribution to Marlowe studies.

Yet another piece of historical evidence deserves more attention than it has received. We know that the "atheistic" material found among Kyd's papers in May 1593 consisted of a copy of part "of an anonymous treatise quoted in full for purposes of confutation by John Proctor in 1549 in a book called *The Fal of the Late Arrian*."[27] The "late Arrian" was probably John Assheton, who had attempted to deny the divinity of Jesus Christ and had afterward recanted. Frederick Boas comments that "It is surprising evidence of the range of Marlowe's reading that he had once in his possession these portions of a heretical treatise more than thirty years old by an obscure parish priest."[28] This fact suggests, however, not so much an extraordinary range of reading as a strong interest in Arian doctrine.[29]

It is worth inquiring, therefore, into the reasons for this particular interest, and to do so requires a closer examination of the Arian treatise. William Dinsmore Briggs informs us that "the sheets of the original MS. are bound up in reverse order, and that when properly arranged their contents is [sic] practically continuous, so that the document is not made up of a series of fragments, but is, though incomplete, perfectly coherent. It will be seen, also, that we possess something more than the first half of the document."[30] Briggs then reprints the entire Arian treatise paragraph by paragraph, presumably supplying the second half from Proctor's book. That the Marlowe copy originally contained the entire Arian treatise is likely, judging from Kyd's claim that "amongst those waste and idle papers . . . wch vnaskt I did deliuer vp, were founde some fragments of a disputation tochinge that opinion, affirmd by Marlowe to be his, and shufled wth some of myne vnknown to me by some occasion of o^r wrytinge in one chamber twoe yeares synce."[31] The doctrine expounded in the treatise is, as Briggs points out, heretical but in no sense atheistical. I reproduce selected passages:

> What the scriptures do witnes of God, it is cleere and manyfest ynoughe: for fyrst Paule to the Romans declareth that he is euerlastynge, and to Tymothie inuisible and immortall, to the Thessaloniens lyuing and true. . . . We therfore cal God (whiche onelye is worthy this name and appellacion) euerlastynge, inuisible, incommutable, incomprehensible, immortall, &c.

> And if Iesus Christ, euen he whiche was borne of Marye, was God, so shal he be a visible God, comprehensible, and mortall, which is not counted God with me, *quoth* great Athanasius of Alexandrye, &c.

> For if we be not able to comprehend nor the angels, nor our own soules which are thynges creat, to wrongfully then and absurdly we make the Creatour of them comprehensible, especially contrary to so manifeste testimonyes of the scriptures, &c.

> For howe may it be thought true religion whiche vnitethe in one subiecte contraryes, as visibilitie, and inuisibilitie, mortalitie and immortalitie, &c.[32]

The divinity of Christ is thus denied, not through an atheistical denial of the Godhead, but through what seems a profound respect for it. What is perhaps the most interesting passage of the treatise occurs near the end:

> But not to trouble your lordship any lenger with my rude & barberous talke, shortly thus I thinke of Iesus Chryst. Verely that he was the most electe vessel, the orgen or instrument of the deuine mercy, a Prophet and more then a Prophete, the son of God, but according to the spreete of Sanctificacion, the fyrst begotten but emongest many brothers.[33]

A doctrine that insists strongly on human limitation paradoxically suggests humankind's potential spiritual glorification; by denying divinity to Jesus Christ, it seems to promise quasi-divinity to all humankind.

Marlowe's possession of such a document not only proves his fascination with unorthodox theological ideas (if the Baines Note leaves us in doubt of this), but also encourages us at least to wonder about his link to the kind of "atheistical" thought associated with Raleigh's School of Night. Evidence for the existence of the School has been sifted through by various scholars, mainly in the first half of the twentieth century; the idea has recently received much less attention, probably due to a general realization that, given the amount of evidence, the School of Night's existence can never be absolutely proven or disproven. M. C. Bradbrook[34] and Eleanor Grace Clark[35] come out in favor of such a School; Kocher[36] attempts to cast serious doubts on its existence. In the sixties A. D. Wraight again treated the idea of the School seriously, and devoted part of her discussion to the influence of the thinkers of this group exerted by Giordano Bruno.[37] More recently, Hilary Gatti has again explored the connection between Marlowe and Bruno.[38] Even John Bakeless, who finds the evidence for the School of Night "rather slender," remarks: "it seems probable that the Italian philosopher's visit helped produce a general atmosphere of religious speculation which both Marlowe and Raleigh found congenial."[39] The possibility of Bruno's influence on Marlowe has been most thoroughly explored by James Robinson Howe in *Marlowe, Tamburlaine, and Magic*.[40] Although Howe's central hypothesis—that the warrior Tamburlaine is a completely admirable "metaphoric figure" representing the Renaissance magus or ideal man—remains doubtful, and though his discussion of *Tamburlaine* is full of questionable assumptions, he does, I think, persuasively argue that the "neo-Platonic-Hermetic line of thought" put forward by Bruno and other Re-

naissance philosophers such as Ficino and Pico significantly influenced Marlowe and his intellectual milieu. Howe quotes the
modern scholar Eugenio Garin's description of the Renaissance
magus figure:

> Among all human activities, magical work actually comes to assume
> a central position, so much so that in itself it expresses almost in the
> manner of an example that divine power of man which Campanella
> exalts in his justly famous verses. The man at the center of the cosmos
> is the man who, having grasped the secret rhythm of things, becomes
> a sublime poet but, like a God, does not limit himself to writing words
> of ink on perishable paper; on the contrary, he writes real things in
> the grand and living book of the universe.[41]

This description would seem to be inspired by Ficino's assertion,
also quoted by Howe, that "not only does the human intelligence
claim for itself as a divine right the ability to form and fashion
matter through the medium of art, but also to transform the nature of existence by its own power."[42] The promise of almost unlimited personal power no doubt "inspired" Marlowe on some
level, but my immediate qualification indicates my belief that,
from the very beginning of his artistic career, Marlowe's interest
was combined with an unsettled cynicism, and that he was keenly
aware of how many of these aspirations must remain limited to
the realm of the imagination; indeed, the relative power, or pow-
erlessness, of the human imagination is a major theme of his
writing.[43] This dual viewpoint of course makes him a profoundly
ironic writer, but by now there is general agreement that he cannot be characterized as a complacent and detached moralist
calmly exposing the follies of the human race. It is true that his
work exposes human limitation and the folly of striving for unre-
stricted personal power; thus a moral critical approach to the
plays often provides valuable insights. But it is also true that
Marlowe identifies closely with his protagonists, that he "is
deeply implicated in his heroes," as Greenblatt[44] and earlier critics
taking a "romantic" approach have argued. I contend that this
close identification arises from the fact that Marlowe embraced
the necessity of self-assertion, even while he could never fully
escape the belief in, or suspicion of, its ultimate futility. In the
terms, then, of the humanist critical debate, neither a moral nor
a romantic approach to Marlowe's plays fully elucidates their
meaning.

This by no means superseded or irrelevant debate in Marlowe
criticism has certainly been complicated by more recent new his-

toricist and materialist approaches. A recent study by Emily Bartels, for example, contains the central thesis

> that Marlowe's plays, in bringing alien types to center stage, subversively resist that exploitation and expose the demonization of an other as a strategy for self-authorization and self-empowerment, whether on the foreign or the domestic front. To understand the historical and ideological import of his representations is vital to an understanding of the cultural and individual self-fashioning of the Renaissance. For the plays provide one of the most visible, most popular, and most radical voices of resistance to a dominant discursive trend, which was shaping ideas of self and state.[45]

While I do not propose a systematic refutation or analysis of this approach, my ideological assumptions take my exploration of Marlowe in a very different direction. I must admit here that I am partly appropriating Greenblatt's term "self-fashioning" for my own uses, assuming a sense that implies a greater degree of personal responsibility, although there is, in spite of his final emphasis on contingency, a real ambiguity in how even Greenblatt employs this term.[46] But contrary to Bartels, I do not find the central significance of Marlowe's plays is to reveal the exploitative nature of various strategies of self-authorization; rather, Marlowe seems to be searching for or testing strategies of self-authorization that may become, in a radically changing society, personally and socially legitimate. There is an interesting moment in Bartels's argument when she finds it necessary to acknowledge "that in some cases these strategies break down and encourage rather than refute [cultural] biases . . . . The problem . . . suggests that Marlowe, despite the radicality of his position, was nonetheless conditioned by his era and partially subject to the prejudicial tendencies he was otherwise subverting."[47] Yet this "problem" may arise partly from the prejudicial ideological assumptions of current criticism. As part of her thesis Bartels makes the following assertion, one typical of cultural materialism: "all that can be known for sure about the 'other' points to where the self/other binarism leads: to the idea of the other as abstractly but unquestionably negative."[48] Those who do not share materialist assumptions may wonder if this constitutes a central axiom of human interaction, or instead a limited and indeed relatively immature process of identity formation. I contend that our increased historical and cultural sensitivity need not preclude recourse to a formulation in which human "otherness" is construed positively or constructively—that is, an ideological framework recognizing "others" to which or for which the self is responsible, and with which, through a dialectical process of interaction, the self grows and matures: (a mature conception of) God, a social structure commanding loyalty or commitment, family, loved one(s). In the context of the more radical materialist discourse, the self never seems to grow at all, except in its awareness of its own ideological oppression.

I do not, however, want naively to claim that the demonizing of the other is an uncommon phenomenon in self-fashioning, that it can be safely ignored, or that there are simple social means of overcoming this tendency. But I do wish to question whether we have recently overemphasized the negative other as a kind of central principle of our social interaction and organization, as well as our critical methodology. Twentieth-century intellectual life has of course grappled, and continues to grapple, with this problem. To take a significant example, the inevitability of cultural demonization receives support from Freud in his discussion of the aggressive instinct in *Civilization and Its Discontents*:

> The advantage which a comparatively small cultural group offers of allowing this instinct [aggression] an outlet in the form of hostility against intruders is not to be despised. It is always possible to bind together a considerable number of people in love, so long as there are other people left over to receive the manifestations of their aggressiveness. . . . In this respect the Jewish people, scattered everywhere, have rendered most useful services to the civilizations of the countries that have been their hosts; but unfortunately all the massacres of the Jews in the Middle Ages did not suffice to make that period more peaceful and secure for their Christian fellows. When once the Apostle Paul had posited universal love between men as the foundation of his Christian community, extreme intolerance on the part of Christendom towards those who remained outside it became the inevitable consequence.[49]

The passage is noteworthy for its ambivalence. What begins as an assertion of a useful method for encouraging social cohesion modulates into an ironic recognition of the horrible suffering of Freud's own people. While the confusion of complacent cynicism and implicit moral outrage might incline us to reconsider aspects of Freud's own ontological assumptions, an adequate exploration of these issues would constitute the subject of another study, perhaps beyond the scope of literary criticism. Nevertheless, I will venture to voice a suspicion here that, by embracing historically recurrent patterns of cultural pathology as inevitable or paradigmatic, we run the danger of ironically institutionalizing the behavior we intellectually and emotionally deplore. Moreover, and more to the point of this study, through our ongoing theoretical eradication of the humanist subject, we have recently vastly underestimated the role of individual ethical and moral choice, and individual responsibility, in the process of personal and social self-fashioning.

Marlowe, as Bartels claims, is certainly aware of the oppressive nature of various strategies of cultural self-authorization, a theme which emerges most clearly in *The Jew of Malta*. But as I suggested above, the emphasis in the plays is not so much on the external abuses of cultural self-fashioning as on the internal anxieties involved in the striving toward successful self-integration. It is true that Marlowe's plays are subversive, but what they tend to subvert are ideologies and belief systems—primarily religious ones—that interfere with the project of achieving "manliness" or personal cohesiveness. In general it may be claimed that the plays are heterodox in their treatment of traditional religious doctrine, but orthodox in their exposure of human limitation. The project of legitimate or practical self-fashioning is disrupted in the plays by a fantasy of absolute control (in part fueled by Marlowe's Hermetic interest), which continually threatens to collapse into its binary opposite, an almost absolute loss of (self-)control (which in part seems to confirm the Augustinian passivity he was resisting). Proper manliness would seem to exist in the dialectical resolution of these two extremes.

The plays, however, offer no facile resolution to the tensions they embody, which of course is one reason for their richness as works of literature. The collapsing binary I have identified is certainly meaningful in a psychoanalytic context, and I wish to adopt a broadly psychoanalytic base for this study, with important qualifications. To begin in the most general terms, supplied conveniently by Stephen Frosh, "Society drives the most personal parts of us—our desires—into deeply protected guerrilla positions, whence they continue their sniping into everyday life. 'The infantile conflict between actual impotence and dreams of omnipotence . . . is also the basic theme of the universal history of mankind.'"[50] This is also a major theme or pattern in Marlowe's plays, which reveal, in psychoanalytic terms, a regressive tendency or arrested development along the axis of individuation. In other words, the struggle toward manhood and adulthood is inhibited by a failure to negotiate successfully the phase of infantile narcissism. Relevant to my purpose here are the theories of the post-Freudian ego psychologists. According to these theories a young man's masculinity "represents his separation from his mother. . . . The principal danger to the boy is not a unidimensional fear of the punishing father but a more ambivalent fantasy-fear about the mother. The ineradicable fantasy is to return to the primal maternal symbiosis. The inseparable fear is that restoring the oneness with the mother will overwhelm one's independent selfhood."[51] While this approach tends to eschew an Oedipal configuration, I believe a religious belief in a Heavenly Father may become another version, or equivalent of, the "primal maternal symbiosis," or represent for the individual a dangerously tempting source of narcissistic completeness. I therefore share Debora Kuller Shuger's intuition that "fathers, and especially divine fathers, are deeply endowed with what we call maternal attributes."[52]

That the concept of narcissism can be fruitfully applied to Marlowe's work has I think been clearly demonstrated by Peter S. Donaldson, whose essay "Conflict and Coherence: Narcissism and Tragic Structure in Marlowe"[53] applies the psychoanalytic work of Heinz Kohut to Marlowe's plays, primarily *Tamburlaine*. As Frosh points out, Heinz Kohut, whose theories and practice are referred to as self psychology or the psychology of the self, articulates many current ideas regarding narcissistic pathology "with considerable power and with a focus on the development of the 'self' as an active centre of psychological experience that links him with humanistic as well as psychoanalytic thinkers."[54] The aspect of Kohut's work that Donaldson emphasizes involves the "shift from a model of the mind based on conflict to one in which the coherence of the self is regarded as prior to any conflicts in which the self engages."[55] Kohut's exploration of the pre-Oedipal stages of human development suggests that "castration anxiety, penis envy or other aspects of the Oedipus complex may be merely a mask for deeper fears concerning the cohesion or reality of the self."[56] Applying this theory to Renaissance tragedy, Donaldson argues: "Interpersonal, even Oedipal conflict provides a frame for the inner drama in plays like *Hamlet, King Lear, Edward II*, and *Dr. Faustus*, but the point here is that such conflict *is* merely a frame, a structure which, like the outwardly Oedipal symptoms of Kohut's narcissistic patients, first masks and then reveals far deeper and more primitive terrors."[57] Although there is a remarkable variety among theories of pre-Oedipal pathology,[58] I propose to make use most closely of Kohut's formulations concerning the psychology of the self, partly because I find them the most cogent and accessible. However, since I do not believe that human beings, or the literary texts that help them come to terms with human experience, can be reduced to any single theoretical description, my study will not claim that Marlowe or his work should be explained completely in Kohutian or indeed in psychoanalytic terms. In fact, one of the most attractive features of Kohut, as opposed to the egomaniacal Freud, is that he maintained an extremely open mind and believed his field was "too young to be concerned with issues of orthodoxy."[59] Nevertheless, having acknowledged these theories as useful tools, the question that needs to be asked is, how can we apply psychoanalytic theories that have been constructed from evidence concerning the experience of modern or postmodern individuals to the early modern period?

It is perhaps time to state more directly that this study is governed by certain transhistorical assumptions. I am, for example, ready to endorse John Russell's assertion in *Hamlet and Narcissus* that "the conflicts that fundamentally inform individual historicity cannot be narrowly confined to those identified by critics of the poststructuralist persuasion. Prior to conflicts structured according to gender, race, or class are the conflicts that emerge out of the individual's essential historicity."[60] Such conflicts, as Russell indicates, inform and structure later conflicts in the larger social arena. But in addition to Russell's assertion of the universality of life cycles, I wish also to acknowledge without embarrassment an interiority of self informed by conscious choice, memory, and will. Questions of cultural coercion ultimately fascinate me less than the exploration of individual assertion and survival in the face of not only social and cultural but physical and temporal limitation. Admittedly, the suggestion of "authenticity" remains unpopular, even in discussions that admit interiority. The recent reassertion of the importance of "inwardness" in the Renaissance is perhaps best exemplified by Katharine Eisaman Maus's study *Inwardness and Theater in the English Renaissance*. Maus recognizes that since "the idea of 'inward truth' in early modern England is intimately linked to transcendental religious claims, antagonism to those claims perhaps contributes to the recent tendency to underestimate the conceptual importance of personal inwardness in this period." Yet Maus admits she shares the "religious incredulity" of many recent scholars, and proceeds to universalize our postmodern attraction to the "notion that selves are void."[61] Whether or not we as scholars share this "religious incredulity," Maus's historicized readings of "inwardness" seem ultimately limited by the homologies she adopts. For example, her linking of *Othello* with English juridical practices, while intriguing, has psychological implications that serve to reactivate or revalidate the psychoanalytic paradigm that Maus claims she found "increasingly irrelevant."[62] A similar claim can be made concerning her treatment of other dramatic texts by Shakespeare, Marlowe, and Kyd; in many of these discussions the critical conclusions strongly invite clarification and expansion in psychoanalytic terms, in particular the terms of pre-Oedipal development and pathology. While for Maus the "developmental" concerns of psychoanalysis came to seem unrelated to her primarily "epistemological" concerns, the complexity of self-fashioning and the interrelatedness of self-formation and personal and social interaction make this distinction or methodological separation questionable. Moreover, in spite of the complexity of self-fashioning, I also wish to assert my agreement with historian Lyndal Roper that "it does not endanger the status of the historical to concede that there are aspects of human nature which are enduring,"[63] and that it is perhaps time to overcome the embarrassment of universalizing. The concept of the integrated self as a "meaningful" construct offered by some (non-Lacanian) psychoanalytic theory still holds attraction to those scholars who resist the "notion that selves are [completely] void."

There has, in any case, been a tendency in recent materialist discourse to project our own present concerns into our readings of the past. It is not uncommon now to draw parallels between the early modern and postmodern eras because both periods involve rapid social change and intense ideological conflicts. This parallel sometimes takes the form of a comparison of the time when humanism, as an inherently oppressive "essentialist" ideology, was struggling into being during the birth of the Enlightenment, to the present time, when it is clearly crumbling. This formulation, it should be noted, involves reductive and crude essentialist assumptions about "humanism." Thomas Greene in his essay "The Flexibility of the Self in Renaissance Literature" includes the following passage: "'Homines non nascuntur, sed finguntur,' Erasmus wrote—men are fashioned rather than born—a formula which might be taken as the motto of the Humanist revolution."[64] A closer examination of the meaning of humanism may lead us as well to a reevaluation of gender stereotypes. In the face of the assumption that humanism means a complacent reassurance of a given essence, which has in particular privileged and naturally empowered male individuals in Western society, it is worth noting, with anthropologist David D. Gilmore, "the often dramatic ways in which cultures construct an appropriate manhood—the presentation or 'imaging' of the male role. In particular, there is a constantly recurring notion that real manhood is different from anatomical maleness, that it is not a natural condition that comes about spontaneously through biological maturation but rather is a precarious or artificial state that boys must win against powerful odds."[65] The humanist subject is neither as simple, nor as simply achieved, as is sometimes supposed; since it is not simply a "given" of patriarchal social structures, our interest in its construction need not be a reaffirmation of oppressively patriarchal values. With the recent attempts to increase opportunities of self-realization for all individuals in society, we have naturally become intensely interested in exactly how and why we personally and socially construct human identities, and have grown less willing to accept traditional formulations. These interests have increased our fascination with the Renaissance, when these formulations were partly consolidated. Donaldson argues that "there is a sense in which the Renaissance was [a] decisive period in the emergence of characteristically Western attitudes toward the self, in which outward confidence, assertiveness, and independence are so often attended by fears of inner emptiness, nullity, or incoherence."[66] It is worth considering therefore what historical and personal factors in Marlowe's life might have contributed to uncertainty and instability in the formation of selfhood.

Keith Wrightson observes that in the late sixteenth century "interrelated demographic and economic developments brought an enhanced prosperity to the upper and middling ranks of society, a prosperity based upon exploitation of the opportunities provided by an expanding national market. They also brought about a marked polarization of living standards and a massive growth in poverty and deprivation."[67] L. G. Salingar provides a similar description of the effects of this new economic exploitation: "Capitalism, in a century of steeply rising prices, brought about radical changes in the composition of society. Spending habits of 'excess' upset the customary standards founded on old routines of farming the soil. And a new spirit of competition loosened the whole social hierarchy."[68] An era of increased social mobility raises personal anxiety, especially for young men eager to make their way in a patriarchal society, since the possibility of rising into wealth and success is always attended by the danger of falling into poverty and degradation. Marlowe, as the son of a shoemaker, was obviously dependent on scholarships to pursue an education; his first priority was thus to excel intellectually. But he seems to have been unusally ambitious for fame and fortune, and willing to take unusual risks. By about his fourth year at Cambridge he was involved with the Elizabethan intelligence service, and probably remained active in espionage till the end of his life. While I find some aspects of Charles Nicholl's argument doubtful, this writer has done Marlowe (and Renaissance) studies an immense service by detailing the situations and circumstances of the men caught up in the nightmarish underside of Elizabethan politics. Relevant to the whole question of the uncertainty of self and identity is Nicholl's exploration of mistrusted agents and double agents and agents provocateurs:

> John Le Carré calls espionage a "secret theatre," and I find this applying, time after time, to Elizabethan espionage. So much was concocted, so much was unreal. . . .
> We are in the familiar "wilderness of mirrors"—another phrase from Cold War espionage that is entirely apt for the Elizabethans. A Catholic may be turned, but he is still a Catholic. Perhaps he is playing the double game, so that his role as informer is just another layer of cover. This was a problem for the spymaster, and it is a problem for anyone trying to investigate this business four hundred years later. These people have left behind a paper-chase of documents and records, but the things they did and said are always open to diametrically opposed interpretations. Is he a genuine conspirator or an *agent provocateur*? Is he a purveyor of information or disinformation?[69]

There is, however, according to Nicholl one certainty about Marlowe's motivations: "We find Marlowe in the company of spies and swindlers because, regrettably, he was one himself. Our regret has no real claim on him. Posterity prefers poets to spies, but this young man could not be so choosy. He lived on his wits or else went hungry, and he was probably rather better rewarded for spying than he was for the poetry we remember him by."[70] Economic necessity does, I believe, go far in explaining Marlowe's involvement in the "secret theatre," and probably as well the unsettled cynicism I have already identified. These pressures may explain the more sordid and cynical elements in the plays that Nicholl draws attention to, such as Spencer's speech to Baldock in *Edward II* : "You must be proud, bold, pleasant, resolute— / And now and then stab, as occasion serves" (2.1.42–43). And yet it is impossible to ignore the other side of Marlowe's character, the drive toward and obsession with absolutes, which he expresses through his central rather than his peripheral characters.

This drive toward absolutes, which also feeds the uncertainty or instability of selfhood in the plays, is at least partly a function of the theological bent of Marlowe's thinking. Returning to the question of Hermetic influence on Marlowe, I quote a passage from Bruno's *De Immenso et Innumerabilis:* "Hence it is clear that every spirit and soul has a certain continuity with the spirit of the universe, so that it has its being and existence not only there where it perceives and lives, but it is also by its essence and substance diffused throughout immensity as was realised by many Platonists and Pythagoreans."[71] Wraight sees a connection between Bruno's thought and the Arian heresy[72] and adds that "even Raleigh is in essence a deist."[73] John Aubrey's account of Raleigh's speech before his execution is interesting in its implications:

> I remember the first Lord Scudamore sayd 't was basely said of Sir Walter Ralegh to talk of the anagram of Dog [and that] in his speech on the scaffold I heard my cousin Whitney say (and I think 't was printed) that he spake not one word of Christ, but of the great and incomprehensible God with much zeal and adoration, so that he concluded that he was a-Christ not a-theist.[74]

Given Marlowe's probable sympathy with this kind of religious thought—in light of the Arian treatise in his possession—we may speculate on the effect it had on his life and work. It is likely that Marlowe shared with Raleigh an assertive, even aggressive, desire to eradicate the need for an Intercessor or Mediator. Marlowe as an aspiring young poet and playwright would naturally be attracted on one level to the philosophies of Pico, Ficino, and Bruno, since they would serve as an inspiration and a justification of his own creative abilities. As Dollimore remarks, "Humanists like Ficino and Pico, under the influence of neoplatonism, advocate man's spiritual self-sufficiency and even come close to suggesting an *independent* spiritual identity: 'With his super celestial mind he transcends heaven. . . . man who provides generally for all things both living and lifeless is a *kind* of God' (Ficino, *Platonic Theology* . . .)."[75] Yet "come close to suggesting" is a crucial qualification, since an "independent spiritual identity" is in a sense a contradiction in terms; what the "humanism" of Ficino and Pico does, in effect, is to attempt to appropriate or incorporate the divine "other" into the self. This failure to accept the natural limitations of humankind's physicality might produce psychological tension for various reasons: a difficulty in dealing with the burden of responsibility imposed by such godlike powers, a destabilizing fantasy of unlimited control, and an exaggerated concern for, or dependency upon, or indeed *doubt* about, this supposed divine presence. In the latter case, the anxiety induced may resemble the more strictly Protestant and Calvinist fear of reprobation, which Marlowe may have entertained, although I do not find the critique of religion evident in the plays to be specifically an attack on predestination, but rather to involve a more general attempt to free the human consciousness from any sense of spiritual dependency. I am not sure that the reasons for psychic instability I have given are in fact mutually exclusive, and I admit that I accept the potential for psychopathology in religious belief, in the sense that it continually disrupts the striving for humanist or personal integrity, and that this "dis-ease" of the mind is evident in Marlowe's plays.

My reference to the natural limitations of human physicality also takes me into dangerous waters with respect to current radical discourse. I take heart at Lyndal Roper's recent publication, *Oedipus and the Devil: Witchcraft, Sexuality and Religion in Early Modern Europe*. Roper argues that the reality of the physical body, including sexual difference, cannot be denied in intellectual inquiry; she is courageously honest in her introduction:

> That a distinction looks different in different historical periods does not show that it is entirely contingent. . . .
> Sexual difference is not purely discursive nor merely social. It is also physical. The cost of the flight from the body and from sexual difference is evident in what much feminist historical writing has found impossible to speak about. . . .
> I do not think I was untypical in seeking to escape femininity by a flight from the body and a retreat to the rational reaches of discourse. The pain, the frustration, and the rage of belonging to the sex which does not even yet have its own history, and which is so often in the role of outsider in any intellectual context, make it tempting to deny sexual difference altogether— or to attempt to design one's sexual identity in any way one chooses. This is a wild utopianism.[76]

Perhaps we can see here the beginnings of a more positive and open cooperation between male and female scholars; younger male scholars can certainly empathize with the pain, frustration, and rage arising from intellectual and professional exclusion on the basis of sex. I must make clear that I am reasserting an essential conception of the body not in support of any patriarchal notions of natural domination, but as a plea for greater honesty about how our bodies affect our responses and partly determine our choices of action. But my primary interest in the above passages involves their attitude toward language and discourse. The flight from the body that Roper refers to is oddly parallel to the flight from the body I have identified in Hermetic philosophy. Admittedly, the motivating ideologies are radically different: Hermeticism posits a "free" (although highly developed, skilled, and disciplined) conscious agent, while radical materialism or constructionism posits consciousness as completely dependent on social and ideological context. Yet curiously, both may, in the final analysis, be termed magical thinking, reflecting a belief that one can, through the proper incantation or discursive manipulation, attain absolute control over one's physical circumstances and environment. Both are, finally, a wildly excessive estimation of the power of human language and discourse.

The overestimation of the power of language, particularly poetic language, has certainly been noted in Marlowe before, and it will be worth further examination in the chapters to follow, but I wish here to point out that this particular feature of Marlowe's art again may be related to religious and ideological conflicts within the playwright himself. We have seen in the quotations treating Hermetic and Neoplatonic ideas that the "sublime poet . . . like a God, does not limit himself to writing words of ink on perishable paper" but "writes real things in the grand and living book of the universe." Such a claim takes us back into the "Piconian moment," and William Blackburn points out that Pico's concept of magic was "far more ambitious than the natural or astrological magic practised by such humanists as Ficino . . . which relied on the *spiritus mundi* for its efficacy." Pico combined Hermetic magic with practical cabalism, which involves "tapping the magical power of Hebrew, a language of supreme efficacy in magic because, according to scriptures, God created the world by speaking."[77] However, such striving for absolute control has dark consequences, partly because, as Kerrigan and Braden suggest, there is no such thing as a human being (among other human beings) with *absolute* control: "The rhetorical structure of the Piconian moment becomes a scenario for villainy when the infinite must be won from other men."[78] Marlowe's plays, after exploring various Hermetic fantasies involving absolute rhetorical control, ultimately substantiate what may be termed the Augustinian position of limited referentiality. This position may be connected to the influence of Calvinism, which we know was the main mediator of the Augustinian revival in England in the sixteenth century.[79] Richard Waswo informs us that Calvin, in the final version of the *Institutes*, attempts strenuously

> to deny the authority of Augustine to the "literalists" and to claim it for himself, on the precise basis of the linguistic/sacramental analogy. They cannot use Augustine's references to Christ's "flesh and blood" in the Eucharist to support their "real" presence, Calvin insists, because the Saint "explains himself, saying that sacraments take their names from their likeness to the things they signify." Calvin thus goes to the heart of the matter, opposing the Lutheran demand for semantic unity with the authority of the most prestigious thinker to have naturalized the whole vocabulary of signification in Christianity. The crucial question was whether this vocabulary applied equally to the operation of both words and sacraments, whether both were "signs." Luther had said no, finding in the performative and creative power of the Word a kind of operation (different only in degree from that of ordinary words) distinct from "signifying." Calvin, and most other Protestants, said yes. Although all accepted, contra the Catholics, Luther's distinction between sacrament and Word in terms of power, none saw this power, as he did, as differentiating sacraments from words in terms of semantic operation.
>
> Calvin thus repeats, with the help of Augustine, that the faith-creating Word is alone efficacious, that without the promise, the "visible sign" in the sacrament is meaningless.[80]

Humankind fails, in Calvin and in Marlowe's plays, to successfully appropriate the mediating creative Word, and though Marlowe in his career eventually attempts to turn his back on all kinds of spiritual mediation and dependency, Christian belief continues, I will argue, to haunt him. This obsession is evident not only in his confirmation of the limited referentiality of language (in which the Calvinist viewpoint probably blends with Marlowe's acceptance of a more limited, "nonmagical" humanist position) but in the recurring biblical and theological motifs and images throughout the plays. There is certainly some element of truth in Kocher's remark that, however desperate Marlowe's desire to be free, "he was bound to Christianity by the surest of chains—hatred mingled with reluctant longing, and fascination much akin to fear."[81]

There is another "destabilizing" facet of Marlowe's personal life that creates as well this tension between fear and reluctant longing: his homosexuality. This subject has undergone two major developments in Marlowe criticism. The first is that it has simply come to be talked about freely, without reluctance or the combination of abhorrence and condemnation that occurred in the past.

William Godshalk's 1971 discussion of *Dido Queen of Carthage*, for example, contains moral assumptions that the author no doubt regrets today:

> The action begins rather shockingly with the discovery of "lupiter *dandling* Ganimed *vpon his knee.*" . . . The viewer can hardly sympathize with what he sees and hears. As Don Cameron Allen remarks, the "affair of Jupiter with Ganymede is an example of *amor illegitimus et praeternaturalis*" . . . and we must stress the meaning of "unnatural" in *praeternaturalis.* Marlowe's initial presentation invites, or even demands, this emphasis, and it is from this tainted framework that we are introduced to the love story of Dido and Aeneas. . . . Homosexual love is, by common judgment, completely without worth.[82]

J. B. Steane, in his 1969 introduction to the Penguin *Complete Plays*, refutes A. L. Rowse's assertion that "Marlowe was a well-known homosexual": " . . . for that there is no *evidence* at all. . . . Baines says that Marlowe said that 'all they that love not tobacco and boys were fools' and homosexuality plays a part in three of his works, in two of them very incidentally: these things are hardly evidence."[83] The sexual and cultural liberation of the past twenty years has done much to dismiss both the moral condemnation by critics and their denial of strong homosexual impulses on the part of the writer. Certainly Marlowe's work suggests at the least an unusually strong interest in homosexual desire. The whole induction to *Dido Queen of Carthage*, as Harry Levin points out, is "elaborated *con amore* out of a half a line from the *Aeneid.*"[84] As Claude J. Summers argues, Marlowe's presentation in *Edward II* "of homosexual love in casual, occasionally elevated, frequently moving, and always human terms is unique in sixteenth-century English drama."[85] The Neptune episode in *Hero and Leander* is intensely, hauntingly erotic. But perhaps the best literary "evidence" of all is the contrasting descriptions of Hero and Leander at the beginning of the poem, the former so detached and artificial, the latter so warm and physically appreciative.

Yet an increased attention to sexual history and sexual behavior in the Renaissance, as well as a widespread acceptance of Michel Foucault's constructionist theory of sexuality, have raised the question of whether it is not completely anachronistic to talk of homosexuals or homosexual identity in the Renaissance. Alan Bray, in his influential book *Homosexuality in Renaissance England*, gives us a clear warning:

> To talk of an individual in this period as being or not being "a homosexual" is an anachronism and ruinously misleading. The temptation

to debauchery, from which homosexuality was not clearly distinguished, was accepted as part of the common lot, be it never so abhorred. For the Puritan writer John Rainolds homosexuality was a sin to which "men's natural corruption and viciousness is prone"; when the governor of Plymouth colony, William Bradford, mused in his history of the colony why "sodomy and buggery (things fearful to name) have broken forth in this land," the first answer he gave was all-embracing: "our corrupt natures, which are so hardly bridled, subdued, and mortified."[86]

While in the early eighties this was a clear correction in the face of the evolving view of homosexuals as constituting a distinct personality type and a distinct subculture in society, more recent developments in sexual theory may raise for some the question of whether the modern reality of homosexual identity—in the sense of its universality—is all that different from the Renaissance situation. I am thinking of the current emphasis on the "homosocial" and its relation to the "homosexual." Eve Sedgwick in *Epistemology of the Closet* thus describes her project in her earlier book: "*Between Men* tried to demonstrate that modern, homophobic constructions of male heterosexuality have a conceptual dependence on a distinction between men's *identification* (with men) and their *desire* (for women), a distinction whose factitiousness is latent where not patent."[87] I cannot imagine this to be the last word on the debate concerning male sexual identity. While I do not propose entering full tilt into this particular debate, in general I find the recent emphasis on the *precariousness* of male (heterosexual) identity of great interest, indeed of transhistorical interest, and therefore relevant to a study of Marlowe, where I believe it is intimately connected to the precariousness of the humanist identity in the face of Augustinian Christianity. Put in the simplest terms, the demand inherent in the traditional male role to be consistently strong, heroic, and assertive places a burden on the male individual that makes him long for self-surrender, the opportunity to be weak; makes him long, in fact, for a Christian heaven where, as Northrop Frye points out, Christ is the only male.[88] Lyndal Roper's observations on Reformation gender relations may be relevant here as well, though she considers a German rather than an English context. "Protestant clergy," she observes,

tended to cast the Catholic cleric as a particular kind of man because the doctrinal battle engaged two different kinds of manliness. . . . When Protestant clergy joined the ranks of the other heads of house-

hold, becoming men like them, it is not surprising that the figure
of the hated Catholic priest took on a kind of psychic necessity for
evangelicals, as he began to represent aspects they wished to obliter-
ate from their own masculine identity. Time and again evangelicals
termed the Catholic monks whores of the Devil, painting the Pope as
the arch-whore. Monks and priests were thus women of the most
lustful kind, beings who were to be excoriated partly because they
stood for the clergy's own too recent past.
    . . . Catholic clergy are represented as women and as sodomitical
partners: by implication their Protestant peers, who take the active
position, are real men.[89]

In general it can be claimed that, in spite of its roots in the Augustinian revival, the paradoxical Protestant development of individualism and eventual securalization put more pressure on
males to act like properly assertive men.[90] They had, after all,
broken free from the "mother" Church.

However, I am not endorsing a theory of homosexuality as an
unsuccessful resolution of the Oedipus complex, and I assert my
commitment to the essentialist view with respect to questions of
individual sexuality. Sedgwick in *Epistemology of the Closet* remarks
that it would seem compulsory for any recent "gay-oriented"
book to mediate on or attempt to adjudicate "constructivist versus
essentialist views of homosexuality."[91] She herself "demurs,"
since "any such adjudication is impossible to the degree that a
conceptual deadlock between the two opposing views has by now
been built into the very structure of every theoretical tool we have
for undertaking it."[92] Nevertheless, Bruce R. Smith in *Homosexual
Desire in Shakespeare's England: A Cultural Poetics* attempts to mediate between the "Scylla and Charybdis" of the essentialist/
constructionist debate (two versions of the latter term seem to be
in use). Presumably under the pressure of recent widespread
critical acceptance, Smith dutifully summarizes Foucault's constructionist theory of sexuality, providing key quotations from *The
History of Sexuality:*

> Sexuality must not be thought of as a kind of natural given which
> power tries to hold in check, or an obscure domain which knowledge
> tries gradually to uncover. It is the name that can be given to a histori-
> cal construct: not a furtive reality that is difficult to grasp, but a great
> surface network in which the stimulation of bodies, the intensification
> of pleasures, the incitement to discourse, the formation of special
> knowledges, the strengthening of controls and resistances, are linked
> to one another, in accordance with a few major strategies of knowl-
> edge and power.[93]

Smith's book is in fact useful to the students of literature unfamil-
iar with current debates over sexuality, since it offers references
to a great many recent discussions of sexual theory and history.
However, those who follow up some of the articles dealing with
the essentialist/constructionist debate may quickly develop sympathy with Sedgwick's "demurral." Gays and lesbians in particular are liable to recognize the sensibleness of Sedgwick's remark:
"But I am additionally eager to promote the obsolescence of 'es-
sentialist/constructivist' because I am very dubious about the ability of even the most scrupulously gay-affirmative thinkers to
divorce these terms, especially as they relate to the question of
ontogeny, from the essentially gay-genocidal nexuses of thought
through which they have developed."[94] Smith in fact does not
appear to negotiate this particular controversy very successfully,
and by the end of his introductory chapter has slid well over to
the essentialist side, as the statement of his "political purpose"
makes clear: "it is an attempt to consolidate gay identity in the
last decade of the twentieth century, to help men whose sexual
desire is turned toward other men realize that they have not only
a present community but a past history."[95]

I am therefore prepared to admit or assert what Smith (in my
opinion) is simply reluctant to: I am not convinced by Foucault's
theories. In fact, while Foucault's writings on the whole are no
doubt seductively appealing stylistically, I find them deeply problematic morally: for example, the desire for a political philosophy
not constructed around the problem of sovereignty and the complete theoretical rejection of the constituent subject lead in my
opinion to highly questionable assertions, indeed value judg-
ments, concerning the incorporation of social power and the internalization of discipline. This admission does not mean that I
am completely out of sympathy with the new historicist emphasis
on the way human identity is to a large extent shaped by social
and cultural forces; however, such approaches have raised ethical
issues that have yet to be adequately addressed. Valerie Traub,
for example, observes that "many of the repressions which Freud
argues were necessary to culture in *Civilization and Its Discontents*
are necessary only within the context of patriarchal and hetero-
sexist ideologies,"[96] and few will be anxious to disagree. But it is
significant that Traub must recognize a certain resistance to her
materialist reading of sexuality and sexual behavior as ideologically constructed, when the constructions in question, such as
marriage and monogamy, are regarded as "benign."[97] I find an
oddness in the insistence in some materialist discourse that proof

of the constructed nature of certain human "ideals," such as romantic love, necessarily involves our acceptance of their spuriousness,[98] when many regard the disciplined ordering of desire within predictable or consistent frameworks of behavior to be a valuable goal within society. Thus, while I admire both the perceptiveness and honesty of Traub's *Desire and Anxiety*, I reject her materialist assertions that the unconscious is (completely) a social product and that the "separation between the psychic and the material" is a "false dichotomy."[99] Taking into account all the factors that shape personal identity—the external pressures of culture, social and familial environment, and the internal and individually specific determinants such as personal history, the physical body, the patterns of conscious choice over time (where choice is possible)—I cannot accept Foucault's assertion that sexuality is superficial, not an "obscure domain." That is, while sexuality is no doubt determined to an extent by social forces (moral and cultural structures and strictures), it is complex and varied enough to indeed be "deep"—or at least so unidentifiable and so completely beyond the realm of practical social control that whatever happens between the polymorphously perverse infant and the sexually functioning adult might as well be regarded as essential, if it is not in many cases biologically so. Moreover, I cannot escape the suspicion that the current bias in favor of constructionist readings of sexuality among academics arises in some cases from a "practical" desire to embrace the position that promises the most discursive mileage, rather than from purely "altruistic" political motivations regarding the world at large. While in literary studies an essentialist approach may seem to offer only an opportunity for brief and idle speculation about where an author falls with respect to Kinsey's scale, I believe evidence for essential sexual motivation contextualized with other psychological factors can lead to subtle and complex analyses. I find it reasonable therefore to assume that human individuals are essentially motivated by various degrees of bisexuality, which partly determines their responses to their specific social and cultural context.

In Marlowe's case the plays suggest a strong homosexual component in the author, which is the source of considerable personal conflict. In his essay "Marlowe and Renaissance Self-Fashioning," Greenblatt remarks that while the "family is at the center of most Elizabethan and Jacobean drama as it is the center of the period's economic and social structure," in Marlowe "it is something to be neglected, despised, or violated." The effect is to "dissolve the

structure of sacramental and blood relations that normally determine identity in this period and to render the heroes virtually
autochthonous, their names and identities given by no one but
themselves."[100] While these assertions perhaps offer a partially
inaccurate generalization about Renaissance drama as a whole,
the remarks nevertheless point to an interesting aspect of Marlowe's work, which likely resulted from a subconscious intimation
that he would have to achieve his own self-fashioning without
the supporting "structure" described by Greenblatt. I use the
term "subconscious" since I believe that Marlowe only gradually
recognized or admitted homosexual desires as he matured, without ever fully embracing their reality; in fact, Traub's linking of
psychoanalytic displacement with the new historicist notion of
containment does have special applicability for Marlowe, for the
artistic treatment of homosexuality in the plays partially but never
fully escapes a tendency toward displacement and containment.
In early plays such as *Dido* and (especially) *Tamburlaine*, we find
a great resistance to sexual surrender since, as in Spenser, it is
seen as interfering with heroic endeavor and encouraging effeminacy. Mary Beth Rose's claim in *The Expense of Spirit* is pertinent
here (though, like many critics, she offers an extremely reductive
reading of *Dido*): "Elizabethan tragedy . . . represents a heroism
of public action that highlights the protagonist's will to power,
treating women and eros either as potentially destructive or as
subliminally idealized, but always peripheral to the represented
action of a play."[101] Thus Tamburlaine checks the temptation to
succumb to Zenocrate's beauty with terms that resemble Atin's
castigation of Cymochles in the Bower of Bliss: "Up, up, thou
womanish weake knight, / That here in Ladies lap entombed art, /
Unmindful of thy praise and prowest might"(*The Faerie Queene*
2.5.36). Yet there is, as I have argued, sufficient evidence throughout Marlowe to strongly suggest that "Ladies lap" was not, for
him, where the greatest temptation lay. The Spenserian resistance
to romantic surrender is thus intensified by Marlowe's own aversion to heterosexual involvement, as well as a reluctance to admit
longings that contradicted the sexual mores of his society. Alan
Bray has clearly outlined the severity of the official morality of
the Renaissance with respect to homosexual behavior:

Attitudes to homosexuality had hardly changed since the thirteenth
century; it was in the Renaissance as it was then, a horror, a thing to
be unreservedly execrated.

It is difficult to appreciate the weight of that condemnation if one
has not had to read through—as the researcher must—the constant
repetition of expressions of revulsion and horror, of apologies for
the very mention of the subject that it was felt necessary to express
whenever was mentioned the "detestable and abominable sin,
amongst Christians not to be named."[102]

It is true that Bray describes as well a "tacit acceptance of homosexual prostitution and of institutionalised homosexuality in the
household and educational system" of the Renaissance, and observes that "prosecutions for homosexuality were very rare occur-
rences," but he is careful to conclude that this "was not tolerance"
but "rather a reluctance to recognise homosexual behaviour, a
sluggishness in accepting that what was being seen was indeed
the fearful sin of sodomy."[103] Bray outlines social, legal, and economic reasons why this was so. In Marlowe's case the need to
challenge the hypocrisy of his society was strong, presumably
partly because of the strength of his forbidden desires. But again
I doubt that this challenge was a completely fearless one, and a
young man of Marlowe's unorthodox but nevertheless strongly
religious nature would be more than usually sensitive to the theologically grounded moral condemnation. The homoerotic elements in his writing do not prove necessarily that Marlowe
accepted or celebrated his own sexual nature. According to
Baines, Marlowe said not only "That all they that love not tobacco
& Boies were fooles," but also "That St John the Evangelist was
bedfellow to Christ and leaned alwaies in his bosome, that he
vsed him as the sinners of Sodoma."[104] Though it could be argued
that Marlowe in the latter case was simply relying on the shock
value that any reference to homosexuality would carry in his society, elsewhere the Baines Note indicates such contempt for Christ
on Marlowe's part that it seems unlikely the playwright would
attribute to this figure a characteristic he had come to regard as
a positive aspect of his own personality. It is indeed a curious
contradiction. There is, however, a curious contradiction in the
orthodox position itself: Augustinian or mystical passivity may
be seen to discourage manly assertiveness and encourage effeminacy, and yet it is the Christian moral code that most strenuously,
savagely denouces homosexuality. The intense conflicts evident
in Marlowe's plays therefore do not reflect solely his personal
confusion.

The above reasoning, it may be objected, attempts to connect
effeminacy with homosexuality, which admittedly, as Bruce Smith

points out, is inherently problematic in a Renaissance context: a man was often called effeminate because "he like[d] women only too much." However, Smith also remarks that if "we take at face value what Stephen Gosson, Phillip Stubbes, and other Puritan attackers of stage-plays have to say, sodomy is the ultimate in a Babylonian school of abuses. . . . To play the sodomite is, in these writers' eyes, to play the female."[105] Although Smith argues that in this context the distinction between male and female must be understood as between sexual moderation and sexual excess, I believe that Constance Kuriyama's suggestion that Marlowe strove to deny homosexuality in the form of "'feminine' weakness and submission"[106] remains convincing. It is likely, since homosexuality was not recognized as a distinct personality type in the Renaissance, that the temptation to surrender sexually to another man would have been perceived in such terms as Kuriyama suggests, that is, not just as a failure of manly assertion, but also as the fear of becoming "like a woman," though it should be understood metaphorically, not literally.[107] There is abundant evidence in Marlowe to suggest that he saw the conflict at least partially in these terms; this fear and resistance constitutes the most damaging and destructive demonization of an "other" in the construction of the properly "masculine" self in Marlowe. It is probably significant as well that, according to Baines, Marlowe claimed that "all they that love not Tobacco & *Boies* were fooles," since the term "boy" may not suggest necessarily a very young male but a passive partner in homosexual intercourse.[108] It seems almost transhistorically true that resistance to this specifically *sexual* passivity very frequently predominates in the construction of male sexual identity, especially with respect to patriarchal concern with male power.[109]

Having claimed that both religious and sexual conflicts in Marlowe's psychology must be taken into account in an exploration of his work, and having suggested as well that there is some kind of development from early to later works, I must now address the issue of chronology. Very few Marlowe critics are foolhardy enough to claim absolute certainty about the order in which Marlowe composed his works, and I do not pretend here to offer incontrovertible proof for a definite chronology. I do intend, however, to discuss the plays in the order of *Dido Queen of Carthage*,[110] *Tamburlaine*, parts 1 and 2, *Doctor Faustus*, *The Jew of Malta*, *The Massacre at Paris*, and *Edward II*, in the belief that this probably represents the order of composition. This chronology was suggested by Ellis-Fermor, and in her essay "*Edward II:* Marlowe's

Culminating Treatment of Love," Leonora Leet Brodwin compares it with other suggested chronologies, offering several compelling reasons for accepting Ellis-Fermor's.[111] Kocher as well
accepts this chronology. The biggest bone of contention is of
course whether *Doctor Faustus* comes in the middle or at the end
of the canon. On this question I would side with J. B. Steane in
favor of an early date, for the general reasons given in the conclusion to his study.[112] Steane builds upon the argument offered by
M. M. Mahood in *Poetry and Humanism*, where she claims that in
Marlowe's tragedies "'the whole story of Renaissance humanism
is told,' its worship of life and pride in humanity suffering gradual diminution and impoverishment."[113] If we ignore for a moment the minor plays, there is indeed a "gradual diminution"
observable as we move from *Tamburlaine* through *Faustus* and *The
Jew* to *Edward II*. However, this decrease in the heroes' virtù represents something more complicated than a steadily increasing criticism of Renaissance humanism. *Tamburlaine*, itself a surprisingly
complicated play (or plays), does I believe illustrate quite definitely what Steane has called Marlowe's "remarkable contrasts of
mind: one cultivating a sharp, critical humour which is oddly
destructive of the rapt high-seriousness and idealism that marks
the other."[114] Thus the play, which seems an enthusiastic exploration of Hermetic idealism, serves in the end as a critique of such
philosophy, a critique that ultimately affirms humankind's subor-
dination to a greater power. In *Faustus* Marlowe attempts to rid
himself completely of the religious dependency that is expressed
(somewhat reluctantly) in *Tamburlaine*, by exorcising his personal
fears; the result is a devastating vision not of the tyranny, nor of
the absence of God (for Marlowe cannot yet free himself from a
poet's admiration of the glory and power of creation), but of His
supreme indifference. Meanwhile Marlowe's philosophical interest changes, from the Hermeticism that informs *Tamburlaine*
(though rather ironically), to the Machiavellianism of the later
plays. The self must now struggle more independently to fashion
an identity—usually in the face of a hostile society, since the
awareness of homosexual tendencies has become more conscious.
Yet in spite of this struggle to come to terms with the physical
and social aspects of human existence, the later plays remain
haunted by the Augustinian suggestion that humankind's ultimate, permanent identity can only be a spiritual one.

Thus it could be said that Marlowe's central artistic vision is
a realization of the individual's responsibility for his own self-
fashioning, but always with a concomitant awareness that such a

self is ultimately illusory. The sense of the fictiveness of the human self leads to a parallel between self-fashioning and artistic creation in the plays; that is, the characters become creative artists of their own selves and of their roles in the world. It is the purpose of this study to examine how the artistic imagination functions in this struggle toward creating and sustaining a viable human identity, as well as to explore the reasons why, in psychological terms, the tension arising from the conflict between self-assertion and self-surrender always leads to tragic results in Marlowe's plays—that is, to a failure of self-fashioning. Through their imaginative responses, the characters experience various degrees of conflict and anxiety in the process of testing the limits of the natural and social world. This struggle and anxiety can, I suggest, be related both to Marlowe's sexual and religious conflicts at his moment of history, and to our own concerns with what it means to create and maintain a self in an ideologically conflicted world.

2

Dido Queen of Carthage: Tenuous Manhood

MARLOWE WAS LIKELY DRAWN TO THE SOURCE MATERIAL FOR *DIDO Queen of Carthage*—books 1, 2, and 4 of Virgil's *Aeneid*—for reasons other than that the poem was well known to the Elizabethans and that these books were chosen for intensive study in the grammar schools and universities.[1] The conflict between self-assertion and self-surrender finds a reflection in Virgil's epic, a work structured partly around the tension between the Roman *pietas*, exemplified by Aeneas, and *furor*, exemplified by Dido and Turnus, although Aeneas himself demonstrates the latter as an inescapable component of his military prowess. Aeneas, I suggest, is the kind of ambivalent hero that would appeal to Marlowe's psychological concerns, both religious and sexual. Partly due to the nature of these conflicts, the play Marlowe produced has in turn given rise to ambivalent and varied critical responses.[2]

Marlowe's Aeneas, like Virgil's, is a man faced with a divinely ordained heroic project that has already caused him much suffering in the past and that promises more in the future; understandably he is tempted to abandon his struggle prematurely, taking refuge instead in the arms of Dido and behind the walls of Carthage, before the gods convince him he must resume his voyage. It is possible to view this archetypal narrative pattern in a more specifically psychological or Freudian sense, and Constance Brown Kuriyama, in a chapter of *Hammer or Anvil* entitled "Emasculating Mothers," sees the central conflict represented in the play as an attempt "to fulfill a predestined adult role [while] remaining hopelessly stagnated in a state of passive dependency by yielding to the wishes of . . . maternal characters."[3] While Kuriyama overemphasizes Aeneas's Oedipal conflict and the emasculating quality of the maternal characters, her discussion is up to a point illuminating since she sees the problem with which the play grapples as "essentially one of defining or confirming identity."[4] I wish to modify Kuriyama's approach by seeing the psychological aspects of the play primarily in pre-Oedipal rather than Oedipal terms, which need first to be established before turning to the text of the play.

In a chapter of *The Restoration of the Self* entitled "The Bipolar Self," Heinz Kohut argues that

> during early psychic development a process takes place in which some archaic mental contents that had been experienced as belonging to the self become obliterated or are assigned to the area of the nonself while others are retained within the self or are added to it. As a result of this process a core self—the "nuclear self"—is established. This structure is the basis for our sense of being an independent center of initiative and perception, integrated with our most central ambitions and ideals and with our experience that our body and mind form a unit in space and a continuum in time.[5]

Once these rudiments of the self have been laid down, there occurs a second group of processes that determine "whether, and, if so, in what form, the self will indeed be firmly established. . . . This group of processes makes its specific contributions to the formation of an ultimately cohesive self by compensating for a disturbance in the development of one of the constituents of the self via the especially strong development of the other." He continues:

> The two chances relate, in gross approximation, to the establishment of the child's cohesive grandiose-exhibitionistic self (via his relation to the empathically responding merging-mirroring-approving self-object), on the one hand, and to the establishment of the child's cohesive idealized parent-imago (via his relation to the empathically responding self-object parent who permits and indeed enjoys the child's idealization of him and merger with him), on the other. The developmental move frequently proceeds—especially in the boy—from the mother as a self-object (predominantly with the function of mirroring the child) to the father as a self-object (predominantly with the function of being idealized by the child). . . . From the point of view of the child, the developmental movement (in the majority of cases) leads from the self's greatness being mirrored to the self's active merger with the ideal—from exhibitionism to voyeurism . . . ; that is, the two basic constituents of the nuclear self which the child attempts to build up appear to have divergent aims. Still, insofar as concerns the whole nuclear self that is ultimately laid down, the strength of one constituent is often able to offset the weakness of the other.[6]

Kohut terms the "abiding flow of actual psychological activity that establishes itself between the two poles of the self, i.e., a person's basic pursuits toward which he is 'driven' by his ambitions and 'led' by his ideals" the "tension arc."[7] Kohut is careful to point out that the child does not need "continuous, perfect empathic responses from the side of the self-object nor unrealistic admiration" but "proper mirroring at least some of the time." It is in fact "the optimal frustration of the child's narcissistic needs that, via transmuting internalization [a kind of internalization of the self-objects], leads to the consolidation of the self and provides a storehouse of self-confidence and basic self-esteem that sustains a person throughout life."[8]

As Stephen Frosh summarizes then: "For Kohut, narcissism is a normal developmental phase and the grandiose and idealising tendencies that inform narcissism have a respectable place in every infant's life. However, when these tendencies are not negotiated successfully [because of failure of the self-objects], the self grows in a distorted or partial way, stuck in part or whole at the infant phase."[9] In cases of disturbed development "the early narcissistic self is experienced as under attack, and its grandiose and idealising inclinations become repressed rather than realistically modified—leading to vacillations of the ego between irrational overestimation of the self and feelings of inferiority"; other problems include "chronic manipulativeness" of later self-objects and "an inability to genuinely love anything, whether self or other."[10] In *The Restoration of the Self* Kohut observes that "the clinical manifestation of an exhibitionistic or voyeuristic perversion may arise in consequence of the breakup of those broad psychological configurations of healthy assertiveness vis-à-vis the mirroring self-object and of healthy admiration for the idealized self-object, to which—protractedly, traumatically, phase-inappropriately—the self-object did not respond."[11] Kohut's analytic method for self pathology "entails the slow internalization of missing psychic structure [that is, transmuting internalization]": in transference, a self/self-object relation appropriate to the earlier stage "spontaneously arise[s] between patient and analyst, and, by means of an empathic mode of observation . . . the analyst slowly helps the patient to a restoration of self."[12] But Kohut also expresses interest in artistic processes that parallel or resemble the analytic one. Referring to Proust, Kohut claims that this artist's "creative effort . . . held him together for many years after the loss of the parental self-objects (especially his mother) that had sustained the cohesion of his self. . . . The reconsolidation achieved by Proust . . . rested on a massive shift from himself as a living and interacting human being to the work of art he created."[13] Thus the artistic process can be viewed as a grand compensatory effort on the part of an artist to achieve, within his or her own cultural and social milieu, a sense of both independent cohesiveness and personal belonging in the face of the threats of psychic disintegration and alienation.

Returning to *Dido Queen of Carthage*, we recognize that certain anxieties regarding the attainment of a self-cohesion that can bear the responsibilities of manhood are expressed and uneasily explored by Marlowe through the character of Aeneas. The heroic project facing Aeneas is on a metaphoric level his own self-fashioning. It is therefore not wrong to see the play, at least as far as Aeneas is concerned, as "adolescent in its basic concerns."[14] Aeneas is experiencing the loss of the empathically responding merging-mirroring-approving self-object—his mother, Venus, whom he still needs in order to confirm his grandiose self as the son of a goddess and potential founder of the Roman Empire. His rhetoric in fact contains a momentary suggestion of Christhood that is of course absent in Virgil:

> Stay, gentle Venus, fly not from thy son!
> Too cruel, *why wilt thou forsake me thus?*
> Or in these shades deceiv'st mine eye so oft?
> Why talk we not together hand in hand
> And tell our griefs in more familiar terms?
> But thou are gone and leav'st me here alone,
> To dull the air with my discoursive moan.
>
> (1.1.242–48, my emphasis)

Though still under Venus's special protection, he must, after the fall of Troy, his birthplace, set out independently and establish a new sense of identity:

> *Dido.* What stranger art thou that dost eye me thus?
> *Aen.* Sometime I was a Trojan, mighty Queen;
> But Troy is not; what shall I say I am?
>
> (2.1.74–76)

Aeneas's response suggests the cultural component of his identity, which is to an extent a construct formed from the materials of his social environment: not who, but what am I. Because of his temporary uncertainty of identity, Aeneas is placed in some danger, for in Dido he is faced with a woman who, in response to her own needs, would impose an identity upon him, that of her dead husband:

> *Ilio.* Renowmed Dido, 'tis our General:
> Warlike Aeneas.
> *Dido.* Warlike Aeneas, and in these base robes?
> Go fetch the garment which Sichaeus ware.
>
> (2.1.77–80)

She thus poses an immediate threat to Aeneas's independence and integrity, and her unempathetic response suggests another version of narcissistic disturbance: she expresses a desire to establish Aeneas as a mirroring self-object replacement for her own unendurable loss, the death of her husband.

Dido's comparative forcefulness and Aeneas's weakness in their first exchange suggests the inversion of conventional male and female active and passive roles that critics have noted in their relationship.[15] While Virgil's Aeneas exhibits humility in his first encounter with Dido—

> Fit thanks for this are not within our power,
> Not to be had from Trojans anywhere
> Dispersed in the great world
>
> (1.818–20)[16]

—there is certainly nothing in the epic to suggest Aeneas's repeated refusal to sit beside Dido during their first meeting in Marlowe's play. When Aeneas, having finally seated himself, accepts Dido's pledge "In all humility" (2.1.99), she upbraids him: "Remember who thou art: speak like thyself; / Humility belongs to common grooms." Kuriyama finds the tone of this speech "distinctly maternal,"[17] yet Dido is not threatening Aeneas with emasculation; she is rather chiding him to take on a more assertive role—though, ironically, one wholly determined by her own expectations and desires.

In spite of Aeneas's apparent weakness in this scene, he takes center stage when he launches into his tale of the fall of Troy. There has been a striking disagreement over the impression Aeneas's narrative creates or was meant to create. Some argue that the Troy narrative deflates Aeneas by revealing his tendency to desert women.[18] John Bakeless, on the other hand, suggests that it places Marlowe's Aeneas, in comparison to Virgil's, in an admirable light.[19] Mary Elizabeth Smith quotes Bakeless's argument approvingly, but nevertheless concludes: "From Aeneas's own mouth we hear described feats of exaggerated boldness and strength, and so with his own words Marlowe cleverly mocks him."[20] The play indeed adopts a bewildering variety of tones, but it is difficult to believe that in a speech that J. R. Mulryne and Stephen Fender rightly claim "must be classed among Marlowe's most powerful, and most savage, dramatic writing,"[21] the playwright is simply mocking his speaker's credibility. Aeneas's manhood is certainly brought into question—he laments that "manhood would not serve" (2.1.272) and fails to save three women (Creusa, Cassandra, Polyxena) in a row—although a similar anxiety is also expressed in Virgil's poem, when Aeneas stands "unmanned" (2.731) after witnessing the murder of the patriarch Priam.

A psychoanalytic reading can shed light on the confusing ambivalence of Aeneas's Troy narrative. There are, as Kuriyama has noticed, certain Oedipal motifs in Aeneas's speech: images suggestive of castration anxiety—"Headless carcases piled up in heaps" (2.1.194)—and of Oedipal triumph—"Old men with swords thrust through their aged sides, / Kneeling for mercy to a Greekish lad, / Who with steel pole-axes dash'd out their brains" (197–99). And while Aeneas does, as Bakeless argues, attribute to himself a certain amount of heroic assertiveness—"Yet flung I forth and, desperate of my life, / Ran in the thickest throngs, and with this sword / Sent many of their savage ghosts to hell" (210–12)—his action seems marginal to the Oedipal struggle he observes. With the arrival of Achilles's son, Pyrrhus, "fell and full of ire" (213), Aeneas is conveyed to safety by his mother, Venus. Pyrrhus continues to the royal palace, where he first cuts off Priam's hands and then murders the old king:

> Then from the navel to the throat at once
> He ripp'd old Priam; at whose latter gasp
> Jove's marble statue gan to bend the brow,
> As loathing Pyrrhus for this wicked act.
>
> (255–58)

As Kuriyama has remarked, these actions are a good example of Oedipal conflict and potential Oedipal guilt, but it is significant that they are only observed or retold secondhand by the divinely protected Aeneas.[22] The psychology of the self suggests an explanation for this distancing from Oedipal strife. As Kohut argues, "The presence of a firm self is a precondition for the experience of the Oedipus complex. Unless the child sees himself as a delimited, abiding, independent center of initiative, he is unable to experience the object-instinctual desires that lead to the conflicts and secondary adaptations of the oedipal period."[23] Kohut's shift in emphasis to pre-Oedipal structures raises certain questions that he admits even he cannot answer; for example, "Does the new viewpoint lead us . . . to a different perception of the very content of the child's oedipal experiences?"[24] Kohut speculates that much of the anxiety of Oedipal development may in actuality be related to weaknesses in the nuclear self, and that more successfully integrated selves experience joy and a sense of increasing potential during the Oedipal transition. The Troy narrative can be regarded as Aeneas's, and perhaps more significantly Marlowe's, voyeuristic engagement in Pyrrhus's Oedipal struggle. It constitutes in fact a kind of voyeuristic pathology, evident in the disturbing tone in these passages. Kuriyama observes that "Aeneas certainly heaps a great deal of negative language on Pyrrhus, toward whom the overall attitude of the scene is distinctly ambivalent—more awestruck, perhaps, than admiring."[25] But there is a brutality in the narrative and its imagery that surpasses Aeneas's sense of awe:

> Not mov'd at all, but smiling at his tears,
> This butcher, whilst his hands were yet held up,
> Treading upon his breast, struck off his hands.
>
> . . . .
>
> At which the frantic Queen leap'd on his face,
> And in his eyelids hanging by the nails,
> A little while prolong'd her husband's life.
> At last, the soldiers pull'd her by the heels,
> And swung her howling in the empty air,
> Which sent an echo to the wounded King;
> Whereat he lifted up his bed-rid limbs,
> And would have grappled with Achilles' son,
> Forgetting both his want of strength and hands:
> Which he disdaining whisk'd his sword about,
> And with the wound thereof the King fell down.
>
> (2.1.240–54)

The narrative voice is not recounting a history of its own Oedipal conflicts and (potential) adaptations, but the voyeuristic enjoyment of another's heightened aggression, and there thus emerges at moments in the rhetoric and imagery a sadism, a savage glee, in this fantasy of Oedipal triumph, which is heightened by the incongruity created by Aeneas's otherwise deferential manner and attitude.

The other oddity of the Troy retelling concerns Dido's reactions. The power of Aeneas's narration moves her to the extent that she interjects emotionally several times: "O Hector, who weeps not to hear thy name!" (2.1.209); "Ah, how could poor Aeneas scape their hands?" (220); "O end, Aeneas, I can hear no more!" (243). Yet she also appears insensitive to his suffering—"Nay, leave not here; resolve me of the rest" (160)—and her final remark at the end of the scene deserves closer examination:

> O had that ticing strumpet ne'er been born!
> Trojan, thy ruthful tale hath made me sad.
> Come, let us think upon some pleasing sport,
> To rid me from these melancholy thoughts.

It is a curiously dismissive, inadequate response; she has been discomfited, and now seeks more pleasant distractions. In this respect she differs greatly from Virgil's Dido, who, in subsequent days we are told,

> wanted to repeat
> The banquet as before, to hear once more
> In her wild need the throes of Ilium,
> And once more hung on the narrator's words.
>
> (4.107–10)

Marlowe's Dido does not make that kind of emotional investment, nor does she display so deep an imaginative response. J. B. Steane notices this quality in Dido even before Aeneas has narrated his experiences: "When Dido commands him to describe the fall of Troy she does it with little imagination or sympathy, having only the curiosity of one who has heard several versions and now has the opportunity to hear an authentic account."[26]

Dido's lack of empathy seems the narcissistic correlative to Aeneas's tenuous self-cohesion—he appears almost too sensitive and reflective for the role of an epic hero. Outside Carthage's walls he "stands . . . amaz'd" (2.1.2) at the sight of a statue or image (critics have read the text both ways) of Priam. Aeneas's response initially suggests a complete evasion of heroic responsibility, for it seems he wants to become, like Marvell's nymph, an artifact of eternal grief:

> O my Achates, Theban Niobe,
> Who for her sons' death wept out life and breath,

> And, dry with grief, was turn'd into a stone,
> Had not such passions in her head as I.
> Methinks that town there should be Troy, yon Ida's hill,
> There Xanthus stream, because here's Priamus—
> And when I know it is not, then I die.
>
> (2.1.3–9)

Oddly, Aeneas in his identification with female Niobe thinks of her mourning for her sons but not for her daughters, the elision suggesting an unconscious longing for idealized male self-objects. Achates initially chooses to share Aeneas's fantasy, commiserating with him in his grief:

> And in this humour is Achates too.
> I cannot choose but fall upon my knees,
> And kiss his hand. O, where is Hecuba?
> Here she was wont to sit.
>
> (10–13)

Significantly, Achates seems less obsessed with the paternal self-object, and will accept the illusion of art only up to a point; he immediately proceeds to emphasize the reality of their situation:

> but, saving air,
> Is nothing here, and what is this but stone?
>
> (13–14)

Aeneas, however, chooses to continue the fantasy to the extent that it clearly alarms Achates, although Aeneas now sees the statue as an inspiration to heroic action rather than a source of paralyzing grief:

> *Aen.* O, yet this stone doth make Aeneas weep,
> And would my prayers, as Pygmalion's did,
> Could give it life, that under his conduct
> We might sail back to Troy, and be reveng'd
> On those hard-hearted Grecians which rejoice
> That nothing now is left of Priamus!
> O, Priamus is left and this is he!
> Come, come aboard, pursue the hateful Greeks!
> *Ach.* What means Aeneas?
> *Aen.* Achates, though mine eyes say this is stone,
> Yet thinks my mind that this is Priamus.
>
> (15–25)

The heroic impulse is finally subsumed in an act of self-sacrifice that involves a desire for merger with the self-object and for self-annihilation, denying all past and future suffering:

> And when my grieved heart sighs and says no,
> Then would it leap out to give Priam life.
> O, were I not at all, so thou mightst be!
> Achates, see, King Priam wags his hand;
> He is alive; Troy is not overcome!
> *Ach.* Thy mind, Aeneas, that would have it so
> Deludes thy eyesight: Priamus is dead.
>
> (26–32)

J. R. Mulryne and Stephen Fender claim that the treatment of Aeneas in this scene "involves a certain deflation of the hero" while at the same time "our regard for him remains undiminished; the feelings his delusion expresses are entirely praiseworthy."[27] Because of the deflation, "there enters into our relationship with [Aeneas] a distance that is also an uncertainty." This uncertainty may be related to the critical dispute concerning whether *Dido* should be regarded as a burlesque of Virgil or as a serious tragedy.[28] Mulryne and Fender, though they regard the play as a failure, assert that Marlowe was attempting something quite sophisticated:

> Marlowe's subject in *Dido* was the not entirely un-Virgilian one of men who choose, but do not choose, their destiny. Aeneas is at once the noble leader of a people and the victim both of a destiny chosen for him and of the wayward impulses of his own fancies and those of others. . . . The situation is an absurd one in that contrary estimates of every action are possible and patently self-cancelling.[29]

While an interesting description of Aeneas's dilemma, the suggestion that Marlowe consciously set out to establish this vision of existential "absurdity" throughout the play is questionable. Our ambivalent response is related to the difficult and uncertain nature of the individuation process we see portrayed, the seemingly "self-cancelling" process of simultaneous separation and identification. Aeneas strongly identifies with Priam, King of Troy, and has difficulty in now living without that source of identification, in a way that suggests dependency on a father or authority figure: "Ah, Troy is sack'd, and Priamus is dead, / And why should poor Aeneas be alive?" Significantly, when he is later asked to rename the city he plans to build at Carthage, he rejects suggestions that he name it after either himself or his son, insisting instead that it be given "my old father's name" (5.1.23). The emotional intensity involved in the attempt at identification cannot be dismissed as mere weakness. Virgil's Aeneas as well is deeply moved by the images of Troy he finds engraved on Carthage's walls:

> "What spot on earth,"
> He said, "what region of the earth, Achates,
> Is not full of the story of our sorrow?
> Look, here is Priam . . ."
> He broke off
> To feast his eyes and mind on a mere image,
> Sighing often, cheeks grown wet with tears.
>
> (1.624–34)

Moreover, Marlowe has precluded our passing judgment on Aeneas as a dreamer by having his hero, on first appearance, exhibit common sense and sound leadership, as Mary Elizabeth Smith points out.[30] It therefore seems likely that Marlowe did not intend the scene involving Priam's statue simply to parody or ridicule Aeneas, but that the playwright has here begun to explore a theme dear to his heart and central to his work: humankind's imaginative enhancement of experience, and the role of imagination in the process of personal and social self-fashioning. The ambivalence evident in this scene recurs in Marlowe's later treatment of this subject, for the imagination can help individuals come to terms with physical and social experience, as well as delude them into believing they can evade a dialectical engagement with the responsibilities and contingencies of human experience.

I suggest the statue scene involves an attempt at "transmuting internalization" of an idealized self-object by which Aeneas can fill in a missing psychic structure. The ambivalence of the scene does increase our sympathy, for we recognize at once both Aeneas's weakness and his attempts to compensate for it. However, this reading of the text arises from my concurrence with Kohutian theory on the validity and viability of an integrated selfhood, and I recognize that other psychoanalytic theories might produce very different readings. A Lacanian reading, for instance, might be tempted to see the statue scene in *Dido* as indeed heightening the burlesque element in the play. One could claim that Aeneas's obsession with the statue is a false identification, which shows a certain arrest in the Imaginary stage. Aeneas has failed to successfully enter the Symbolic order, the "domain of the signifier," where "the perpetual restructuring of the subject takes place."[31] The entry into the Symbolic order indicates a relinquishment of the infantile fantasy of absolute control, because the individual learns to live with language, with signs, which involves a deferral of absolute meaning and absolute desire (God/the mother's body). I am, however, uneasy with certain recent appropriations of Lacanian theory, particularly as they exploit his famous statement that "the ego is structured exactly like a symptom. At the heart of the subject, it is only a privileged symptom, the human symptom *par excellence*, the mental illness of man."[32]

Let me, to take one of many recent examples, turn for a moment to Garry Leonard's recent Lacanian reading of James Joyce. Leonard gives an admirably clear and helpful summary of Lacanian conditions of self:

> Lacan . . . makes consciousness richly problematical by positing the subject as decentered and self-alienated. He sees Freud's ego as consisting of a mirrored reflection of the outside world. The subject is split between a narcissistic, objectlike total being (*moi*) and a speaking subject (*je*) who tries to validate this (fictional) unity of being by seducing the objective world (the Other) into declaring it authentic. Thus the moi is inherently paranoid because its existence is dependent upon, and solicitous of, outside validation. The je is controlled more than it can afford to realize because the moi exerts constant pressure upon the je to complete the moi's story of self-sufficient autonomy. Beyond this split subject is the Real subject of the unconscious that cannot be represented in imagery or signified in language.[33]

Lacan's concept of the Real constitutes the most problematic component of his theory, because he himself apparently cannot define it clearly. Malcolm Bowie struggles with the concept, calling it finally "the vanishing point of the Symbolic and Imaginary alike."[34] The mystery tempts one to consider the religious, even mystical overtones inherent in the concept. Jonathan Dollimore's mystification is certainly evident in his remark, "if we were to ask which was the more metaphysical, divine law or the psychoanalytic unconscious, some might reply, 'the unconscious, though not by much.' Whatever, I do not find it surprising that Lacan admired Augustine."[35] What does seem clear is that we are emphatically warned not to identify the Lacanian Real with "objective reality." And yet one suspects that it is just this aspect of human experience that much recent appropriation of Lacanian theory (and other poststructuralist thought) fails adequately to engage with: humankind's physicality, its physical being in the world, its "incarnation." The reflection the child sees in the mirror is not just an image of illusory autonomy but the vehicle through which the self will and must continue to function for a lifetime, enduring first its dependency on other bodies and later accepting responsibility for other bodies.

Lacanian theory also, in my view, has given rise to intriguing but questionable readings of masculine and feminine subjectivity. I turn again to Leonard, who offers

> an admittedly oversimplified scenario of how the structure of the masculine subject generates the symptom of femininity: In the *Wizard of Oz* . . . Dorothy . . . sees Toto pull back a curtain . . . to expose the wizened wizard (the needy penis as opposed to Oz, the engorged phallic signifier). He is exposed as intently manipulating the tremendously hyperbolic machinery of the Phallic Order. "Pay no attention to the man behind the curtain" cries the little man. This is the pathetic credo of the masculine subject who finds himself at the center of a machine that castrates him to preserve the prior fantasy of his unified existence. This example of the self-denial of a masculine subject . . . highlights the paradox about the Phallic Order and the Name-of-the-Father, which . . . Lacan outlines . . . : men victimize others (exert power) precisely because their identity places them in an impossible gender construct in which they can never feel powerful enough.[36]

The first curiosity that strikes me in this account is the phrase "men victimize others (exert power)." Leonard, unintentionally perhaps, equates exerting power with making victims. Unintentional or not, this equation raises questions concerning necessary agency in social and personal experience. Individuals have to exert power, and often over other individuals (their children, their students, their employees, their constituents, to take four obvious examples), but we must insist that this does not always consist of victimization. It is also questionable that men can never feel powerful enough, and the kind of vicious circle Leonard identifies—"the more a masculine subject subscribes to Phallic Order in an attempt to deny . . . fear of dissolution . . . the more he is vulnerable to this precise effect"[37]—cannot be accepted as a universal condition. Kohut in fact identifies fear of dissolution as evidence that self-cohesion has not been achieved. The consolidation of self in fact leads to positive effects:

> Besides the increased self-esteem and strengthening of ambitions and purposes that result from the integration of the grandiose self, and

the strengthening of ideals, self-approval, and admiration for others that result from the integration of the idealized parent imago with the ego and superego, Kohut notes a greater capacity for empathy, creativity, humor, and for that wisdom which involves understanding and accepting human limitations.[38]

Leonard's Lacanian account of masculinity (as, I suggest, a paradigm of much recent analysis of human subjectivity) fails to distinguish between responsible and tyrannical, necessary and self-indulgent, healthy and pathological forms of self-assertion; moreover, I do not accept that language is intrinsically phallocentric, and I cannot believe that the arena of responsible adult assertiveness must be construed as a castrating hyperbolic machinery. To add one final observation of Leonard's account of masculinity: it might well be asked if a narrative moment from the puerile context of a Hollywood version of wish fulfillment (there's no place like home), based on a children's fairy tale, is the best basis for an analysis of adult gender roles. (Rather than as an archetype of universal gender roles, this particular narrative might more profitably be analyzed in terms of Frank Baum's personal and sexual problems.)

To recapitulate, while a psychoanalytic approach bent on regarding the ego as nothing but a symptom might well reinforce the burlesque interpretations of the statue scene by emphasizing Aeneas's delusionary state, Kohut's psychology of the self accounts instead for the ambivalent responses that have figured in interpretations of the play and of the male hero's character. In his identification with the statue, Aeneas does attempt to use his imaginative responses constructively, to bolster his self-cohesion. Admittedly, this potentially constructive or positive attempt at "transmuting internalization" is not often successfully completed by Marlowe's characters. There is a short exchange in act 3 that nicely contrasts Dido's imaginative response to experience with Aeneas's. As the hunting party traverses the wood in 3.3 Achates remarks to Aeneas:

> As I remember, here you shot the deer
> That sav'd your famish'd soldiers' lives from death,
> When first you set your foot upon the shore,
> And here we met fair Venus, virgin-like,
> Bearing her bow and quiver at her back.

Aeneas replies:

> O, how these irksome labours now delight
> And overjoy my thoughts with their escape!
> Who would not undergo all kind of toil
> To be well stor'd with such a winter's tale?
>
> (51–59)

In spite of his naïveté—which brings his response perilously close to narcissistic regression—Aeneas finds imaginative consolation in a narrative that mirrors the sufferings he has experienced. Imaginative reconstruction, whether a narrative or a statue, gives *meaning* to experience, potentially allowing Aeneas to reflect on his heroic project and accept the sacrifices he must make. While Priam's statue brought him close to despair, it also focused his heroic energies—"Come, come aboard, pursue the hateful Greeks" (2.1.22)—and now the prospect of accumulating "winter's tales"—records of "irksome labours" undergone and overcome—provides him with a sense of accomplishment and presumably prepares him for future struggles. Dido's reaction to this, however, is simply, "Aeneas, leave these dumps and let's away." Oliver believes that "dumps" here must mean "reminiscences," "moods of reverie," since the "context makes it unlikely that the other sense, 'doleful dumps', is intended."[39] It is possible that both meanings are intended; all this talk about irksome labor and undergoing "all kind of toil" has made Dido decidedly uncomfortable, and she cannot sympathize with anyone who would find anything positive in such experiences. To her, Aeneas's remarks are certainly doleful, and she wishes to hear nothing more of the kind.

Not that Dido lacks imagination. Like Aeneas, she indulges in fantasies that seem to temporarily loosen her hold on reality; she outdoes Aeneas, however, in her indulgence in fantasies of complete personal control. As noted earlier, she attempts to impose the identity of Sichaeus upon Aeneas the moment she first meets him. Just before the consummation of their love in the cave, she again reverts to this fantasy of her first husband:

> Sichaeus, not Aeneas, be thou call'd;
> The King of Carthage, not Anchises' son.
> Hold, take these jewels at thy lover's hand,
> These golden bracelets, and this wedding-ring,
> Wherewith my husband woo'd me yet a maid.
>
> (3.4.58–62)

But now it is Dido doing the wooing; the fantasy facilitates her appropriation of "male" control since she, not Aeneas, ultimately "becomes" Sichaeus. When Aeneas is brought back by Anna after his first attempt to depart, and has made his questionable excuses, Dido deludes herself into believing that his heart belongs solely to her, and willfully continues to fabricate the illusion of immortal love between them, even in the face of his plainly expressed doubts:

> Dido. O, how a crown becomes Aeneas's head!
> Stay here, Aeneas, and command as King.
> Aen. How vain am I to wear this diadem
> And bear this golden sceptre in my hand!
> A burgonet of steel and not a crown,
> A sword and not a sceptre fits Aeneas.
> Dido. O keep them still, and let me gaze my fill.
> Now looks Aeneas like immortal Jove:
>
> . . . .
>
> Heaven, envious of our joys, is waxen pale,
> And when we whisper, then the stars fall down,
> To be partakers of our honey talk.
>
> (4.4.38–54)

The fantasy is immediately reinforced, however, since Aeneas, swayed by the power of Dido's poetry, capitulates: "O Dido, patroness of all our lives, / When I leave thee, death be my punishment!" (55–56).

It may be objected that Dido's "indulgence" in fantasy is excused by the fact that she is the victim of the gods, since her passion is induced by Cupid's arrows. It is certainly her *destiny* to fall in love with Aeneas—"It lies not in our power to love or hate, / For will in us is overruled by fate"[40]—just as it is Aeneas's destiny to found Rome. Yet it is not her destiny to be destroyed by her loss, since she consciously chooses suicide. The despair arising over the failure of the romantic self-object is reflected and amplified in the brief subplot involving Dido, Anna, and Iarbas. When Anna offers herself to Iarbas in place of Dido, he rejects her cruelly: "I may nor will list to such loathsome change, / That intercepts the course of my desire" (4.2.47–48). His behavior indicates a certain depth of passion, since he cannot simply exchange one self-object for another. Yet all three characters in this love triangle exhibit the same uncontrolled willfulness, an inflexible insistence on fulfilling the "course of their desire," possessing what is denied them. Again, I do not believe the triple suicide on

the same funeral pyre at the end of the play should be taken
simply as comedy or burlesque. The obsessive love displayed by
Dido, Anna, and Iarbas indicates a potential for pathology in human emotional dependency that prevents our reception of the
final scene, in spite of its abruptness, as merely parodic or
amusing.

To Dido's credit she is not, even under the spell of Cupid's
arrows, completely deluded. "Ay," she muses, "but it may be he
will leave my love, / And seek a foreign land call'd Italy. . . . I
must prevent him; wishing will not serve" (97–98, 104). She has
Ascanius/Cupid taken to a country house and commands that
Aeneas's oars, tackling, and sails be brought to her. However, her
assertiveness is precarious, for in her lengthy address to this gear
(4.4.126–65) we watch her vacillate curiously, disturbingly, between the imaginative and the practical, the metaphoric and the
literal:

> Is this the wood that grew in Carthage plains,
> And would be toiling in the wat'ry billows
> To rob their mistress of her Trojan guest?
> O cursed tree, hadst thou but wit or sense
> To measure how I prize Aeneas's love,
> Thou wouldst have leapt from out the sailors' hands
> And told me that Aeneas meant to go!
> And yet I blame thee not, thou art but wood.
> The water which our poets term a nymph,
> Why did it suffer thee to touch her breast
> And shrunk not back, knowing my love was there?
> The water is an element, no nymph.
> Why should I blame Aeneas for his flight?
> O Dido, blame not him, but break his oars.
>
> (136–49)

She refuses to blame Aeneas for his faithlessness, transferring
her anger onto personified objects; yet at the same time, since
she cannot really deny to herself the fact of his infidelity, she
hates him for it:

> For tackling, let him take the chains of gold
> Which I bestow'd upon his followers;
> Instead of oars, let him use his hands,
> And swim to Italy. I'll keep these sure.
>
> (161–64)

This is an extremely significant moment in the play, since, in this struggle between metaphoric and literal interpretations, she foreshadows the later Marlovian exploration of Hermetic fantasies of rhetorical power and their eventual collapse: the metaphorical senses Dido entertains show the beginnings of a fantasy of potential magical control over the physical environment. This foreshadowing suggests that Marlowe in some ways identifies more closely with Dido than with the weakly masculine Aeneas. Certainly the playwright shows Dido struggling to maintain contact with reality in a way that introduces a very powerful pathos, rendering her appealing in spite of her narcissism.

By the end of the play, after Aeneas's second and final departure, Dido appears, pathetically and movingly, to succumb completely to fantasies:

> *Dido.* O Anna, fetch Arion's harp,
> That I may tice a dolphin to the shore
> And ride upon his back unto my love!
> Look, sister, look, lovely Aeneas's ships!
>
> . . . .
>
> Now is he come on shore safe, without hurt.
>
> . . . .
>
> See where he comes; welcome, welcome, my love!
> *Anna.* Ah, sister, leave these idle fantasies;
> Sweet sister cease; remember who you are!
>
> (5.1.248–63)

In response to Anna's admonition, Dido temporarily recovers herself. But almost immediately she decides that the only way she can assert her identity and maintain her self-worth is, paradoxically, to kill herself:

> Dido I am, unless I be deceiv'd,
> And must I rave thus for a runagate?
> Must I make ships for him to sail away?
> Nothing can bear me to him but a ship,
> And he hath all my fleet. What shall I do,
> But die in fury of this oversight?
> I, I must be the murderer of myself.
>
> (264–70)

Before she dies she prays to the gods that Carthage may be revenged upon the race that Aeneas will found; it is a way of projecting a fantasy of omnipotence even as she confirms her mortality. Dido thus finishes her life with the ultimate act of control, which is also, of course, the ultimate act of surrender.

It is, as suggested above, the intensity of this conflict that she experiences between the need to control and the desire to relinquish control, between self-assertion and self-surrender, that makes Dido, more than Aeneas, the prototype of the later Marlovian heroes such as Faustus and Edward. While Aeneas is faced with the choice between heroic duty and romantic love, in both cases his actions are so largely determined by external agents (the gods, Dido) that an internal conflict between assertion and surrender is not fully realized. A great deal of the dramatic tension of the play arises from Dido's conflicts: her attempts to assert herself as queen and ruler of Carthage and her desire to surrender to her passion for a man who, ironically, turns out to need commanding more than he commands. This conflict develops gradually. When first stung by Cupid's dart she is afraid of giving herself away:

> Love, love give Dido leave
> To be more modest than her thoughts admit,
> Lest I be made a wonder to the world.
>
> (3.1.93–95)

When Aeneas has examined the pictures of Dido's rejected suitors and exclaims, "O happy shall he be whom Dido loves!" (3.1.167), Dido vacillates between pride and coy submissiveness:

> Then never say that thou art miserable,
> Because it may be thou shalt be my love.
> Yet boast not of it, for I love thee not—
> And yet I hate thee not. [*Aside*] O, if I speak,
> I shall betray myself!
>
> (168–72)

She later proves that as a queen she can be quite forceful, even tyrannical, for when Anna asks whether the Carthaginians will complain if Aeneas marches, as Dido wishes, through the streets as "their sovereign lord," Dido replies:

> Those that dislike what Dido gives in charge
> Command my guard to slay for their offense.
> Small vulgar peasants storm at what I do?
> The ground is mine that gives them sustenance,
> The air wherein they breathe, the water, fire,

All that they have, their lands, their goods, their lives;
And I, the goddess of all these command
Aeneas ride as Carthaginian King.

(4.4.71–78)

Yet when Aeneas wonders out loud about the other kingdom destiny has promised him, Dido quickly replies, "Speak of no other land, this land is thine; / Dido is thine, henceforth I'll call thee lord." The almost absurd incongruity of this last line when compared with the above speech creates not so much a burlesque effect but rather pathos, as we view a simultaneous (and hopeless) need both to rule and submit. This desire for both personal assertiveness and self-surrender seems at last to be nicely resolved emblematically in Dido's evocation of the Icarus myth after Aeneas has sailed away:

> I'll frame me wings of wax like Icarus,
> And o'er his ships will soar unto the sun
> That they may melt and I fall in his arms.

(5.1.243–45)

But this, of course, is only another fantasy.

While Dido is torn between a need both to rule and submit, her sense of ruling does not take into account to any great degree her duties as a sovereign, for she is far more concerned with her personal needs than with her responsibilities as a queen. She tells Aeneas, "So thou wouldst prove as true as Paris did, / Would, as fair Troy was, Carthage might be sack'd, / And I be call'd a second Helena!" (5.1.146–48). She says to Anna, after Aeneas's second departure, "Now bring him back and thou shalt be a queen, / And I will live a private life with him" (5.1.197–98). Her attitude here, as Leech points out,[41] looks forward to Edward II's:

> Make several kingdoms of this monarchy,
> And share it equally amongst you all
> So I may have some nook or corner left,
> To frolic with my dearest Gaveston.

(1.4.70–73)

However, it is doubtful if Dido could really give up the power and privilege that go hand in hand with responsibility. She insists on having her own way, and in her egotism she cannot even entertain the existence of any will greater than her own, or one that would contradict hers:

> *Aen.* O Queen of Carthage, wert thou ugly-black
> Aeneas could not choose but hold thee dear;
> Yet must he not gainsay the Gods' behest.
> *Dido.* The Gods? What Gods be those that seek my death?
>
> (5.1.125–28)

She cannot conceive of any universal order that would require her to sacrifice her personal demands for a greater good.

The basic illusion under which Dido operates, then, is the paradoxical (and essentially infantile) dream of control without sacrifice, or power without responsibility. This fantasy of absolute control finds expression in the play's opening scene, where Jupiter promises Ganymede he will allow him to "Control proud fate, and cut the thread of time" (1.1.29); ironically, such omnipotence would be granted by Jupiter and exercised by the boy in a state of perpetual sensual indulgence. We question the validity of Jupiter's promises in light of Ganymede's retort "I am much better for your worthless love" (3) and the boy's claim that Juno gave him a rap on the head that "made the blood run down about mine ears" (8). The sudden, realistic evocation of human injury in these lines clashes strongly with Jupiter's images of godlike control, such as his driving back the horses of the night (26) to prolong their lovemaking. The narcissistic nature of this fantasy of power is suggested by the sadistic and infantile delight that Ganymede takes in Jupiter's promise to torture Juno—"Might I but see that pretty sport a-foot" (16). And Jupiter is finally called back from romantic indulgence to a sense of duty by, ironically, the Goddess of Love, who chides him: "Ay, this it it! You can sit toying there / And playing with that female wanton boy" (50–51). Yet, once more qualifying the comic irony, Jupiter's reply (82–108) concerning the fulfilment of Aeneas's destiny and the founding of Rome is delivered with all the dignity and grandeur we could expect from the ruler of the gods, and serves to refute Venus's provoking remark that Aeneas might as well die, "Since that religion hath no recompense" (81). Despite Venus's incredulity after this speech—"How may I credit these thy flattering terms"—Marlowe, unlike Virgil, actually increases Jupiter's concern and involvement by having the god directly order Aeolus to stop the storm, whereas in the *Aeneid* Neptune performs this function even before the Venus-Jupiter confrontation.

As with the Troy narrative, the prologue has given rise to various readings, since the exact nature or target of the satire is difficult to determine. Don Cameron Allen believes that *Dido* clearly reveals Marlowe's "characteristic attitude towards those who think that there is a divinity that shapes our ends. In his poetic philosophy men are surely better than their gods and have only one mortal weakness: they lend their ears and then their hearts to the advice and direction of the silly hulks they have themselves created."[42] It is undeniable that the gods in *Dido* are comically trivialized by appearing as human beings with human foibles, yet it is questionable that the only weakness of the humans in the play is that they obey divine direction. Marlowe took advantage of the anthropomorphic tradition in the myths of the Roman deities to present us in the prologue with an ironic mirror of humankind's dreams of unlimited, godlike powers and desires. The prologue oddly asserts a version of the reality principle—the assertion of manly destiny and responsibility—in the midst of its portrayal of narcissistic indulgence. If even *Jupiter* must eventually attend to his duties—"Come, Ganymede, we must about this gear"—in order to ensure the fulfilment of destiny, how much less likely is it that a mere mortal like Dido can willfully realize her own illusions in opposition to reality and fate. Ultimately it is humankind's *conceptions* of the gods (the projection through myth of the fantasy of absolute control) that Marlowe ridicules.

In all fairness to Dido, she is not the only character in the play who retreats from reality into a self-deluding fantasy world. The scene between the Nurse and Cupid/Ascanius (4.5) provides us with another ironic mirror of Dido's dilemma. Cupid's beauty has reawakened sexual desire in the old woman, and like Dido she vacillates between the realistic and the fantastic in attempting to control her response:

> Blush, blush, for shame, why shouldst thou think of love?
> A grave and not a lover fits thy age.
> A grave? Why? I may live a hundred years.
> Fourscore is but a girl's age; love is sweet.
> My veins are wither'd, and my sinews dry:
> Why do I think of love, now I should die?
>
> (29–34)

In the end she comes down on the side of delusion, her last words referring, presumably, to a wholly imaginary lover: "Well, if he come a-wooing, he shall speed: / O how unwise was I to say him nay!" (36–37).

This scene does not mirror only Dido's behavior; in the subsequent action we find Aeneas himself indulging in a purely escapist fantasy. Having earlier been commanded by Hermes "in a dream" (4.3.3)—a dream of future possibilities, if he maintains the heroic impulse—to resume his voyage to Italy, Aeneas succumbs to Dido's spell and begins to take part in the construction of a new city:

> Carthage shall vaunt her petty walls no more,
> For I will grace them with a fairer frame
> And clad her in a crystal livery
> Wherein the day may evermore delight;
> From golden India Ganges will I fetch
> Whose wealthy streams may wait upon her towers
> And triple-wise entrench her round about;
> The sun from Egypt shall rich odours bring
> Wherewith his burning beams, like labouring bees
> That load their thighs with Hybla's honey's spoils,
> Shall here unburden their exhaled sweets
> And plant [furnish] our pleasant suburbs with her fumes.
>   (5.1.4–15)

The intense lyricism, the surreal intensity, of the passage makes clear that Aeneas's mind is not bent on the practical aspects of urban planning or nation building; he has entered a dreamworld. The paradisial quality in his vision of Carthage finds expression elsewhere in the play: Venus lays the sleeping Ascanius in a grove "with sweet-smelling violets, / Blushing roses, purple hyacinth" (2.1.318–19), where he spends most of the play in "cooling shades / Free from the murmur of these running streams" (334–35); and the Nurse promises Cupid/Ascanius a country house with "an orchard that hath store of plums, / Brown almonds, services [pear-trees], ripe figs, and dates, / Dewberries, apples, yellow oranges" and a "garden where are bee-hives full of honey, / Musk-roses, and a thousand sort of flowers, / . . . in the midst [of which] doth run a silver stream" (4.5.4–9). The play is thus punctuated with references to idyllic scenes that contrast sharply with the images of war, suffering, and destruction. In a very Spenserian manner, this pastoral strand woven through the epic tapestry contributes to a sense of longing, a desire for release and escape, in the emotional texture of the play.

Aeneas's apparent weakness is therefore perhaps not so surprising or incongruous with respect to the overall tone of the play. Carthage holds much the same attraction for him as the Bower of Bliss for Verdant. He in fact receives the kind of advice from Achates that one might expect Guyon to give Verdant:

Banish that ticing dame from forth your mouth,
And follow your foreseeing stars in all;
This is no life for men-at-arms to live,
Where dalliance doth consume a soldier's strength,
And wanton motions of alluring eyes
Effeminate our minds inur'd to war.

(4.3.31–36)

Aeneas, however, seems to have great difficulty following this advice—"I fain would go, yet beauty calls me back" (46)—and when Dido convinces him to stay, he exclaims in her arms: "This is the harbour that Aeneas seeks, / Let's see what tempests can annoy me now" (4.4.59–60). Therefore the self-surrender he feared during his first attempt at departure has come true:

Her silver arms will roll me round about
And tears of pearl cry, "Stay, Aeneas, stay!"
Each word she says will then contain a crown,
And every speech be ended with a kiss.

(4.3.51–54)

Everywhere in *Dido* we find the idea of being surrounded, protected, enclosed, contained. This idea is expressed in various images of enclosure throughout the play. References to walls, for example, occur frequently. As William Godshalk suggests, "the image is taken from the *Aeneid*,"[43] where it also recurs frequently. When Virgil's Aeneas first sees Carthage under construction, he remarks, "How fortunate these are / Whose city walls are rising here and now!" (1.595–96); it is the desire to be through with the heroic struggle, to have achieved the final resting place *now*. In Marlowe, Ganymede says he was brought to Jove "wall'd-in with eagle's wings" (1.1.20) to spend a life of ease in the god's "bright arms" (22). Troy, of course, falls because Priam "Enforc'd a breach in that rampir'd wall" (2.1.174). Before the lovers' consummation in the cave, Aeneas promises, "Never to leave these new-upreared walls / Whiles Dido lives and rules in Juno's town" (3.4.48–49), but Hermes persuades him to go to Italy to build, finally, as Jupiter prophesies to Venus, "those fair walls I promis'd him of yore" (1.1.85). Godshalk argues that "'wall' becomes a significant image, conveying its traditional suggestions of safety, integrity, and unity,"[44] yet he misses the ironic implication of some of these images. As we have seen, Ganymede "wall'd-in with eagle's wings" is not as safe as he would like to be. And Aeneas's projected "crystal" walls around Carthage, because of their inherent fragility, suggest a sense of false security or integrity, a potential fragmentation.

The cave is another enclosure in the play with negative implications. Godshalk suggests "one might see Aeneas's entry into the cave with Dido as a symbol, not so much of sexual union, as of reabsorption into the maternal womb."[45] Marjorie Garber, in her essay "Closure and Enclosure in Marlowe," sees the cave as an emblem of Dido's attempts to encircle and enclose, but the lovers' exchange before they enter suggests "the irony of [Dido's] situation, the binder bound":

> *Dido.* Tell me, dear love, how found you out this cave?
> *Aen.* By chance, sweet Queen, as Mars and Venus met.
> *Dido.* Why, that was in a net, where we are loose;
> And yet I am not free—O would I were!
>
> (3.4.3–6)

As Garber explains, "In her innocence, Dido thinks her lack of freedom comes from the need to tell her love; in fact, the net of passion holds her, and cannot hold Aeneas."[46] The "binder," however, continues her attempts to enclose, and her fantasies of absolute control often involve images of enclosure:

> O that I had a charm to keep the winds
> Within the closure of a golden ball,
> Or that the Tyrrhene sea were in mine arms,
> That he might suffer shipwreck on my breast
> As oft as he attempts to hoist up sail!
>
> (4.4.99–103)

In her desperation she even goes so far as to imagine Aeneas both sailing for Italy and simultaneously remaining a prisoner in her room in the palace:

> I'll hang ye [the sails] in the chamber where I lie.
> Drive, if you can, my house to Italy:
> I'll set the casement open that the winds
> May enter in and once again conspire
> Against the life of me, poor Carthage Queen;
> But, though he go, he stays in Carthage still,
> And let rich Carthage fleet upon the seas,
> So I may have Aeneas in my arms.
>
> (4.4.128–35)

The irony of her fantasy underlines the hopelessness of her manipulation. The binder is, in the end, bound indeed, for Dido at last chooses what Garber terms "the ultimate enclosure of the funeral pyre."[47] Dido is thus finally contained in an emblem that literalizes her fiery passion, a state she has described earlier in response to Aeneas's question about whom she loves:

> The man that I do eye where'er I am,
> Whose amorous face, like Paean, sparkles fire,
> When as he butts his beams on Flora's bed.
> Prometheus hath put on Cupid's shape,
> And I must perish in his burning arms.
> Aeneas, O Aeneas, quench these flames.
>
> (3.4.17–22)

Dido's tragedy is that such flames of passion have been raised by a man incapable of quenching them, a man who does not in fact "burn" nearly as much as she imagines. Dido is deluded when she implies that Aeneas will be able to "balance [her] content" (3.4.35). Whether "content" suggests the "pleasure she might have in the relationship" or "what is contained in [her]; what [she] can offer,"[48] Dido certainly finds no balance in Aeneas. His *will* simply cannot, could not ever, equal hers.

It in fact cannot be denied that, artistically, Aeneas's characterization remains the most problematic and discomfiting aspect of the play. Particularly during the scene (4.4) after his first attempt at departure, Aeneas's vacillation borders on the ludicrous, and the play comes very close to burlesque. The comic undertones are here a forerunner of the characteristically Marlovian mélange of comedy and anxiety that is to be found, to a lesser extent, in *Tamburlaine*, and, more fully developed, in *Faustus* and *The Jew of Malta*. This particular aspect of Marlovian drama has always caused critical disagreement and confusion; Kuriyama provides one explanation in her citation of Ernst Kris's *Psychoanalytic Explorations of Art*, which contains "a discussion of comedy and particularly of double-edged effects, which [Kris] attributes to the uncontrolled intrusion of wishes or anxieties that the comic approach was employed to disguise or ward off."[49] The comic absurdity arising from Aeneas's passivity and Dido's desperate attempts to manipulate him helps Marlowe to distance himself from a sense of "manly" inadequacy; the parody (partially) displaces the anxiety. In the case of *Dido*, this distancing effect would be reinforced theatrically by the fact that the play was presumably written for, and definitely performed by, boy actors; "the inevitable preciosity of a production acted solely by boys would tend

to undermine the gravity of the play."[50] The conditions of performance in a sense facilitate this mode of displacement.

In the context of the relationships within the play, we can relate
Aeneas's tenuous manhood to a failure of self-objects, in particular the failure of the idealized father figure. Aeneas has lost his
father, and his divine parent is feminine. There are no masculine
figures to be idealized and imitated in the play; this failure of
masculine ideals seems in fact personified in the prologue
through the indulgent Jupiter, who rather than a convincing master of his minion Ganymede, seems himself almost an infantile
pederast, "toying" and "playing" with a "female wanton boy."
Marlowe's parody of the Roman pantheon, in light of the absence
of idealized male self-objects, speaks to psychological problems
for men in a Christian context. Like Jupiter, the Christian Father
cannot be idealized or imitated as a masculine role model; he is
certainly no hero in the world, as *Paradise Lost* makes painfully
clear. At best he can only serve as a mirroring self-object for the
grandiose self who believes in its own election; in this sense the
Heavenly Father really constitutes, in psychological terms, a
Mother (like Aeneas's Venus): "I am watching over you." God in
his penetrating, self-usurping aspect is Christ, the only male.
Thus, either way a profound desire for spiritual connection in
Christian terms can only mean effeminization. Marlowe links this
effeminization, if the Baines Note is to be credited, with sodomy:
"St John the Evangelist was bedfellow to Christ and leaned alwaies in his bosome, . . . he vsed him as the sinners of Sodoma."
The prologue to *Dido* in itself suggests this uncomfortable conflation of heightened spirituality and sexual predation; Brian Gibbons points out that "Ganymede traditionally represented the
baseness of physical desire [the name was a common term for
boy prostitute], but was also interpreted in neo-Platonic terms as
the *mens humana*, beloved by Jupiter: that is, the Supreme being:
and abducted to heaven by means of the eagle to a state of enrap-
tured contemplation, divorced from the body and free of corporeal things."[51] Admittedly, Marlowe appears to go out of his way
to ridicule any potential spiritual-allegorical meaning in the Ganymede figure; yet the ridicule can be related to Marlowe's own
anxiety concerning a persistent subconscious desire for both spiritual and sexual surrender.

In *Dido Queen of Carthage* Marlowe identifies with both Aeneas
and Dido according to psychological principles suggested by Paul
Kocher's conclusion to his discussion of *Tamburlaine:* "Tamburlaine is wrestling with God, from whom he cannot escape. He

must conquer God, or else succeed in feeling that he stands in a special relation of favor to Him. And so perhaps it was with Marlowe."[52] Aeneas, as the subject of anxious solicitation from the gods, is the one who stands in special relation to the divine power. Dido, with her disbelief that there can exist a greater will in the world than her own, is the one who wishes to challenge the gods' dominion. As has been argued, the double identification with the two protagonists is clearly unbalanced in ways significant to Marlowe's psychological conflicts. Even in terms of strictly aesthetic concerns, Marlowe leans towards Dido, who does not feel particularly attracted to the kind of man who would willingly undergo all sorts of toil to be well stored with a winter's tale. Artistically Marlowe has become enamored with Dido's fantasy of poetic control; in the plays that follow, he cannot resist a poetic exploration of the dream of omnipotence; his narcissistic tendencies fuel his creative muse. There is in fact other evidence for these tendencies in *Dido* besides a strong identification with the female protagonist. Jupiter, in his speech of prophecy, refers to "bright Ascanius" as "beauty's better work / Who with the Sun divides one radiant shape" (1.1.96–97). Ascanius, the god foretells:

> Shall build his throne amidst those starry towers
> That earth-born Atlas groaning underprops;
> No bounds but heaven shall bound his empery,
> Whose azur'd gates, enchased with his name,
> Shall make the morning haste her grey uprise
> To feed her eyes with his engraven fame.
>
> (98–103)

Ascanius's enclosure becomes the whole created universe conceived of as a work of art; it is a setting for the jewel of his glory or fame ("enchased," line 101, can mean to place a jewel in a setting, as well as to enclose, or engrave). Marlowe's preference for Ascanius as "beauty's better work" (a phrase not in Virgil) may indicate the playwright's own homoerotic tendencies, which will become more apparent in his later works. More importantly, the image is in a sense Marlowe's personal indulgence in the kind of fantasy the play exposes, for there is no recognition of the struggle or suffering Ascanius will undergo before becoming this great and mighty emperor. (As far as *Dido* goes, we know that Ascanius spends the major part of the action in an unconscious stupor in Venus's grove.) The image of Ascanius's final triumph, then, is very much another dream of obtaining power without effort or sacrifice. While Marlowe recognizes this dream *as* a fantasy or impossibility, it nevertheless maintains a strong hold over his imagination and the imagination of his later characters.

In *Dido Queen of Carthage* the male hero fails as a character partly because he is not willful enough to make a legitimate attempt at self-fashioning; the beginnings of his efforts at individuation are quickly subsumed in the narcissistic fantasies entertained both by him and the other characters, which overwhelm the narrative of the play. In the *Aeneid* narrative the hero eventually resumes the heroic struggle, goes off in the voyage of self-assertion, paradoxically *in compliance* with the commands of the gods, but Marlowe's mind is far more engaged by characters who assert themselves *in defiance* of destiny or traditional modes of conduct, and in this play his identification with Dido is too strong for Aeneas's desertion of her to function in any way as a validation of heroic masculinity. The playwright's next hero, almost it seems in compensation for Aeneas, is much more consistent (and unorthodox) in his campaign of self-assertion, and much more brutally successful in his resistance to beauty's powerful glance. Yet the dream of divine substantiation, and troubling sexual insecurities, continue to find various expression in the worlds of the later plays.

3

Tamburlaine the Great: Tenuous Godhood

As suggested at the end of the previous chapter, Tamburlaine is a compensatory figure for the weak and uncertain Aeneas. Since Aeneas's failure is in part due to an absence of satisfactory masculine idealized self-objects, Marlowe's response, under the influence of Hermetic writings, is to create a character who egoistically asserts this ideal from within himself. In terms of the striving toward adequate manhood, the movement from *Dido* to *Tamburlaine* reflects an "important rule" Kohut draws attention to: "When [potentially] higher forms of adaptation fail, then the grandiose self emerges."[1] The result is that while *Tamburlaine* represents an artistic advance over *Dido,* it is also in some ways a psychological regression. Tamburlaine becomes a kind of God, a self-creating being, who seems to enjoy absolute confidence and absolute rhetorical control, but his divinity is in fact a pathology that, to borrow Kohut's terms, takes the form of a relentless exhibitionistic perversion. This perversion involves a constant manipulation of self-objects by the protagonist so that they mirror his own grandiosity. Tamburlaine's self-assertions might therefore be termed, in a clinical sense, not healthy but essentially pathological. However, we are of course not dealing with a patient undergoing psychotherapy but one of the most important historical moments in the history of English theater, and I am left, like my critical contemporaries and predecessors, striving to explain why a play "executed . . . in bold, broad strokes . . . episodic in structure, occasionally stupefying in the monotonous pitch of its rhetoric, indelicate in its avowed appetites and immoderate in its gratification of them"[2] nevertheless remains a deeply impressive and obsessively fascinating work of art.

Like *Dido* but to an even greater extent, the two parts of *Tamburlaine* constitute an extremely controversial play,[3] what Catherine Belsey calls "a notoriously plural text."[4] Mulryne and Fender

73

remark that "critical dispute about the play, too familiar to summarize, centres round whether we 'blame' or 'sympathize with'
the hero."[5] This statement does not quite cover the entire controversy, for there is also the question of whether Marlowe intended
such a divided response and, if so, to what purpose. Mulryne
and Fender in fact offer a rather generalized answer to this question, since they argue that Marlowe deliberately "develops and
sustains an ambivalent attitude to Tamburlaine" in order to "produce in the audience a state of mind that is at once contradictory
and yet profoundly true of thinking and feeling about the play's
central topic, the fulfilment of will."[6] Other critics, though their
numbers have decreased in recent years, do not believe that Marlowe in *Tamburlaine* is in control of the ambiguities of his text.
C. L. Barber claims that the play "is deeply naive, a drama written
partly in defiance and partly in ignorance of the limits of art.
One way to describe *Tamburlaine* is to say that it is based on an
unacknowledged pact, the author's identification with his protagonist, for the enjoyment of unacknowledged magic."[7] Constance Kuriyama asserts that it is "fatal to approach this play with
the conviction that the author is a totally conscious creator";[8]
for her, *Tamburlaine* renders experience in terms "that all seem
ultimately related to a basic preoccupation with sexual identity,"
and she hypothesizes that "the authorial mental state" is "one of
intense conflict of a marked homosexual character."[9]

A good case for Marlowe as a highly conscious craftsman in
Tamburlaine has been made by considering the prologue to part 1:

> From jigging veins of rhyming mother-wits
> And such conceits as clownage keeps in pay,
> We'll lead you to the stately tent of War,
> Where you shall hear the Scythian Tamburlaine
> Threat'ning the world with high astounding terms
> And scourging kingdoms with his conquering sword.
> View but his picture in this tragic glass
> And then applaud his fortunes as you please.[10]

As Robert Kimbrough points out, this last line "should not be
taken as a typical Elizabethan plea for applause. Because it comes
at the beginning of the play and because of the way in which the
play develops, it is meant to suggest that within pageantry and
through amazing rhetoric, the play will present a study of a grand
figure in action, judgment of whom is left to the viewers."[11] The
fact that judgment is left, almost as a challenge, to the audience
suggests that Marlowe was well aware that there is more than

one way to view Tamburlaine, and that those viewers not wholly dominated by one particular response would react ambivalently to the hero. The question is, to what moral or artistic end has Marlowe sought to create such a response? Furthermore, do Marlowe's intentions concerning our response to the hero represent the entire meaning of the play, or are we still inclined, with Kuriyama, to look for "unconscious" meaning?

Although I have distanced myself from cultural materialist approaches, it may be useful to examine, as a prototype, one of the earlier materialist attempts to cope with the question of divided response. Catherine Belsey believes that the play does not answer questions such as whether we are to regard Tamburlaine as "a popular hero or an imperialist tyrant" but "poses them with a certain sharpness to an Elizabethan society preparing to embark on a series of colonialist adventures."[12] This view may well have been influenced by Stephen Greenblatt, who begins his chapter "Marlowe and the Will to Absolute Play" with an account of the gratuitous destruction of an African village by English explorers. Greenblatt concludes: "If we want to understand the historical matrix of Marlowe's achievement, the analogue to Tamburlaine's restlessness, aesthetic sensitivity, appetite, and violence, we might look not at the playwright's literary sources . . . but at the acquisitive energies of English merchants, entrepeneurs, and adventurers."[13] A. D. Wraight calls attention to an even more convincing historical analogue to Tamburlaine's exploits by pointing out the parallel between Tamburlaine's siege of Damascus and Raleigh's actions at the siege of Fort Del Ore in Ireland. Quoting from Eleanor Grace Clark,[14] Wraight summarizes the incident thus:

Hooker, in his continuation of Holinshed, describes the slaughter of 400 Spaniards and Italians who were assisting the Irish rebels, and who held out although repeatedly called to surrender until they

"began to fear, somewhat prophetically, that what they had built for a garrison would prove their monument, and they should be buried alive in the ruins of it. Therefore, finding no succours arrive, they beat a parley, and hung out the white flag, crying out, *Misericordia, misericordia*. But the deputy would not listen to any treaty with the confederates of traitors and rebels."

Ralegh, with Macworth, was placed by Lord Grey, then Lord Deputy of Ireland, in charge of the brutal massacre that followed, in which not even the women were spared.[15]

While these historical analogues are of great interest and may very well have influenced, even inspired Marlowe in his creation of Tamburlaine, it is questionable whether the playwright's primary moral purpose was, as Belsey suggests, to promote contemplation among the more thoughtful Elizabethans about the social and ethical implications of colonialism. If Marlowe's challenge to the audience were of that nature, surely the text would offer more evidence of an authorial concern with political and social policy with respect to colonial expansion. The play in fact seems barely concerned with social or political reality at all. The responsibility of rule, the relationship between king and commons, foreign policy—these are questions hardly even raised by the play, let alone seriously explored. As Richard A. Martin argues, the world of *Tamburlaine* lies closer to romance than to realistic fiction. In romance "the imagination masters reality, and earthly glory becomes the medium of a limitless fulfillment of desire." In *Tamburlaine* the "language transforms the material world into art . . . and generates in the spectator a willing enthusiasm for the quest for an earthly crown."[16] Although historical analogues provide important contributing factors in a formal sense, and while the play may indirectly comment on the brutality of action displayed by Elizabethan public figures such as Raleigh, the central or essential artistic inspiration of the work lies in the "Piconian moment." *Tamburlaine* seems Marlowe's test case for the idea of man as a sublime poet who "does not limit himself to writing words of ink on perishable paper" but "writes real things in the grand and living book of the universe." The most fascinating effect of the *Tamburlaine* plays is that they set our minds to work on the question of what exactly constitutes "real things" in the play—and, ultimately, in real life as well.

One of the critical commonplaces about *Tamburlaine*—that the play draws a parallel between rhetorical skill and personal power, between the word and the sword—has been reexamined by critics such as Martin, Judith Weil,[17] and Johannes Birringer.[18] These critics all see the play as an exploration of the power of the imagination, although they offer different theories concerning the extent to which the play exposes, or intends to expose, the failure or even the foolishness of human imagining. Since it is Tamburlaine's imagination that dominates in the play, we are in a sense thrown back to the question of whether we sympathize with or blame the hero. With respect to this question, it is my belief (and here I am in general agreement with Weil) that the play introduces a steady stream of ironies, some of which may register with the audience retroactively, which gradually override our sympathies with and encourage our detachment from the hero. Whereas Martin argues that the power of imagination to master reality is not called into question until part 2, it is actually questioned (though fairly subtly at first) early in part 1, and both parts of *Tamburlaine* together must be regarded as a tragedy of "the consequences of human imagining."[19] However, the human imagining in question is, in the Marlovian context, specifically a narcissistic fantasy of omnipotence, and the sense of tragedy is oddly qualified from the start by a sense of parody and comic deflation.[20]

Returning to the prologue once more, we find in fact that the potential for irony is introduced with the play's opening words. For one thing, the prologue promises that

> From jigging veins of rhyming mother-wits
> And such conceits as clownage keeps in pay,
> We'll lead you to the stately tent of War. . . .

Yet, as Birringer points out,[21] the play that has "announced itself in the heroic mode" immediately presents us with the clownage it has promised to eschew. The figure of the effete and rhetorically inept Mycetes easily becomes the butt (literally) of Cosroe's jokes:

> *Mycetes.* Well, here I swear by this my part royal seat—
> *Cosroe.* You may do well to kiss it then.
>
> (part 1 1.1.97–98)

He even speaks in rhymes that, if not exactly the "jigging veins" of a poulter's measure derided by the prologue, nevertheless serve to render his rhetoric fatuous:

> Return with speed, time passeth swift away,
> Our life is frail, and we may die today.
>
> (67–68)

The effeminate, inadequate Mycetes is the object "of the play's most merciless ridicule," which is largely directed at his apparently homosexual nature—he is "discernibly enamored of Meander."[22] This is the first clue that part of the artistic energy of the play is invested in a denial or displacement of homosexual feelings. Kuriyama states that "Mycetes' masquerade as a man and a king deceives no one,"[23] although it may have some relation to postmodern concepts of "camp," which Jonathan Dollimore defines as "the quintessential expression of an alienated, superficial inauthenticity."[24]

But the play's opening lines introduce a greater irony, inherent in the equation of rhetoric and personal might:

> . . . you shall hear the Scythian Tamburlaine
> Threat'ning the world with high astounding terms
> And scourging kingdoms with his conquering sword.

Notice that these lines do not introduce a second verb to correspond to the second participial phrase; we shall "hear" Tamburlaine threatening the world with high astounding terms, but we shall not "see" him scourging kingdoms. We shall only hear, or hear about, him doing that as well. In other words, the prologue subtly suggests that Tamburlaine will be all talk and no action, which in fact is very much what happens throughout both parts. Marlowe is very careful to deny us the kind of combat scenes that Shakespeare provides between Hal and Hotspur, Macduff and Macbeth, or Edmund and Edgar. It is of course partly dramatic convention and practical considerations that place much of the epic action offstage, but we are denied even the kind of *report* of specific valor in battle (though we get much general eulogizing) that, for example, the Captain supplies to Duncan concerning Macbeth's prowess at the beginning of Shakespeare's play. Tamburlaine's first potential battle, toward which the play has built up a great deal of suspense, is postponed in a manner that, in spite of the hero's subsequent rhetorical triumph, seems inescapably bathetic:

> *Tamburlaine.* Then shall we fight courageously with them,
> Or look you I should play the orator?
> *Techelles.* No: cowards and faint-hearted runaways
> Look for orations when the foe is near.
> Our swords shall play the orators for us.
> *Usumcasane.* Come, let us meet them at the mountain top,
> And with a sudden and an hot alarm
> Drive all their horses headlong down the hill.
> *Techelles.* Come, let us march.
> *Tamburlaine.* Stay, Techelles, ask a parley first.
>
> (part 1 1.2.128–37)

The first battle scene in *Tamburlaine* involves nothing more than the farcical exchange between Tamburlaine and Mycetes concerning who gets to keep the crown (1.4). When Zenocrate's betrothed, the King of Arabia, enters mortally wounded near the end of part 1, he does not, as one might expect in a heroic/romantic context, ascribe his defeat to the mighty Tamburlaine, but to the "infamous tyrant's soldiers" (5.1.405). The only time we see Tamburlaine in military action in either part is the battle with Bajazeth in part 1; after we have observed Zenocrate and Zabina "tirad[ing] like fishwives,"[25] Bajazeth briefly flies across the stage pursued by Tamburlaine. Such action, like the king-drawn chariot in part 2, would inevitably border on the comic or ludicrous; it is unlikely that a director could manage the scene in such a way as to avoid inducing laughter from the audience.

There is also, in part 1, a structure of parallel scenes that begins to make the whole idea of rhetorical prowess ridiculous. Bajazeth, like Tamburlaine, speaks in a mighty line (see 3.1.1–40) but his rhetorical excesses are rapidly exposed by the sycophantic affirmations he receives from his followers:

> *Argier.* They say he is a king of Persia—
> But if he dare attempt to stir your siege
> 'Twere requisite he should be ten times more,
> For all flesh quakes at your magnificence.
> *Bajazeth.* True, Argier, and tremble at my looks.
> *Morocco.* The spring is hindered by your smothering host,
> For neither rain can fall upon the earth
> Nor sun reflex his virtuous beams thereon,
> The ground is mantled with such multitudes.
> *Bajazeth.* All this is true as holy Mahomet,
> And all the trees are blasted with our breaths.
>
> (3.1.45–55)

The heroic defiance of the Soldan is even more seriously undercut in his exchange with the messenger at the beginning of 4.1; after he attempts to rouse the Egyptians and the messenger speaks fearfully of the "frowning looks of Tamburlaine" (13), the Soldan replies:

> Villain, I tell thee, were that Tamburlaine
> As monstrous as Gorgon, prince of hell,
> The Soldan would not start a foot from him.
> But speak, what power hath he?
>
> (17–20)

The strong suggestion of doubt in the final query immediately, and rather comically, deflates the Soldan's courageous stance. On one level these examples certainly reflect well on Tamburlaine by demonstrating his verbal superiority. However, at the same time they have the unsettling effect of demonstrating that vaunts and boasts are, after all, only just that, so much hot air, and gradually encourage us to question our admiration for Tamburlaine's rhetorical power.

Moreover, there is an inherent incongruity between the Hermetic/Neoplatonic inspiration behind the rhetorical power glorified in the play and Tamburlaine's military ambitions. Dollimore points this out in his comparison of Tamburlaine and Pico: "the objective of Tamburlaine's aspiration is very different from Pico's; the secular power in which Tamburlaine revels is part of what Pico wants to transcend in the name of a more ultimate and legitimate power. Tamburlaine defies origin, Pico aspires to it."[26] When we consider Howe's suggestion that Tamburlaine is a kind of "metaphoric figure" representing the Renaissance magus, we cannot help feeling that Marlowe has chosen a rather strange vehicle, an inherently ironic one. Nevertheless, Howe's exploration of Giordano Bruno's writings does offer some convincing parallels between Tamburlaine and Bruno's particular style of Hermeticism. Bruno's godlike magus

> depends not on the grandeur of his birth, but on his own intellectual and spiritual power—qualities which have been seen in common as well as in noble families. Indeed, in *Cause, Principle and Unity,* Eliotropio says, "We usually find the rarer and choicer wits turning up where the commonfolk are very ignorant and bumble-headed, and where in general people are less urbane and courteous." Shortly after, he makes a specific example: a Scythian, like Tamburlaine. Harry Levin's observation that Marlowe's hero is the common man who controls his fate is very much to the point here. Indeed, Bruno himself came from Nola, a rustic village then, several miles outside of Naples.[27]

Bruno's ideas find a clear parallel in Marlowe's source material, as summarized by J. S. Cunningham:

> To read George Whetstone's version of Mexia in *The English Myrror,* not long after its publication in 1586, was to encounter a prodigious military figure, hailed as the equal of "the illustrous Captaines *Romaines,* and *Grecians*"—among whom the freshest in Marlowe's mind [owing to his translation of the first book of the *Pharsalia*] was perhaps Lucan's Caesar, the "diabolical 'superman'" to whom Tamburlaine alludes in part 1. Not the lame Timur, one of the line of Tartar Khans,

but "a pure appearance out of nothing," barely impeded by his obscure birth: "*Tamberlaine* being a poore labourer, or in the best degree a meane souldiour, descended from the *Partians:* notwithstanding the povertye of his parents: even from his infancy he had a reaching & imaginative minde, the strength and comelinesse of his body, aunswered the hautines of his hart."[28]

The narrative of a supreme figure "barely impeded by his obscure birth" would naturally appeal to the ambitious Marlowe and no doubt a large proportion of the theater audience in the class hierarchy of Renaissance England. Moreover, Tamburlaine's material and worldly ambitions—"the sweet fruition of an earthly crown"—may also find "spiritual" justification (though the relationship seems more problematic to me than Howe argues) in Bruno, who denies a Platonic dichotomy between sensible and intelligible: "we should hence speak rather of matter containing forms and implicating them than think of it as void and excluding them. And matter which unfolds what it holds folded-up should be called a thing divine."[29] Bruno's philosophy may even partly explain Tamburlaine's cruelty: the magus "has thoughts of nothing but things divine and shows himself insensible and impassible to those things which ordinary men feel the most and by which they are most tormented."[30]

But then why exactly the recurrent parodic element, especially if Tamburlaine is a vehicle for the Hermetic ideas that intrigued and inspired Marlowe? A disturbing speculation based on recent scholarship can be offered here to explain Marlowe's "divided mind" in *Tamburlaine*. Charles Nicholl has explored Marlowe's connection to the "Wizard Earl," the ninth earl of Northumberland, whose "chief bent was for science, mathematics and philosophy, which in the popular verdict meant 'magick.'"[31] In the earl's retinue were Thomas Hariot and Walter Warner, who according to Kyd were close associates of Marlowe's, and the playwright presumably shared many of the interests of the Northumberland coterie; one of these interests was clearly Bruno's writings, since the "Earl himself was an assiduous collector of Bruno texts."[32] As Nicholl points out: "Though his occultist interests later earned him suspicion, in the mid-1580s the Earl of Northumberland was the object of a rather different kind of suspicion. He was a young nobleman with a profoundly Catholic pedigree . . . [and] became a target, a figurehead, of Catholic aspirations."[33] Nicholl argues that Marlowe may have worked as a "government tale-bearer within the Northumberland retinue

. . . using literary *entrée* into a nobleman's household for ulterior ends. . . . The poet's patron becomes, in some measure, his target as a spy."[34] This argument does not I think prove that Marlowe was completely feigning his interest in occult and Hermetic philosophies, but it does suggest that his attitude was profoundly ambivalent. His interest is partially, and disturbingly, a voyeuristic one, a kind of game. A figure like Bruno, for example, can lay claims to heroic self-sufficiency and godlike control of the universe, but "Marlowe's involvement in 'magick' . . . has this double edge, this dimension of government service which is also a dimension of betrayal."[35] Unlike the manly and self-sufficient magus, Marlowe must act as a spy and a *servant*, of Walsingham and later of Cecil, in order to rise socially. There thus arises a tendency to parody philosophies that nevertheless fascinate him on a poetic or artistic level.

What then is our final response to Tamburlaine's magical military prowess? We cannot say it becomes laughable, because thousands of people die, if not at Tamburlaine's hands, then at the hands of his soldiers. It is impossible to deny the remarkably sadistic quality of the *Tamburlaine* plays, and also C. L. Barber's claim that "Marlowe has gone out of his way to *include* moral condemnation [of Tamburlaine's cruelty] and then quite literally—and sadistically—to stifle it."[36] Yet such horror is strangely tempered by a sense of unreality in the play. This was in fact the response of J. C. Trewin to Tyrone Guthrie's 1951 production. Trewin in his reviews speculated about both Elizabethan and modern reaction, as George Geckle comments:

> [Elizabethan audiences] gloried . . . , as Trewin noted, in the savagery that the play displays; "This can sicken, if you allow yourself to be sickened by it. But I doubt whether many people who see *Tamburlaine* will let it eat into their minds. We have supped full with horrors in our own day, horrors compared with which these Marlovian barbarities are shapes in the mist. We must realize that the people of *Tamburlaine the Great* come to life very rarely. They are figures in a monstrous shadow-show against a background lurid with flame."[37]

Any kind of generalization regarding audience response—be it transhistorical, or across a single culture or even across a single audience—remains tenuous; and of course the particular production will make all the difference. Although everyone might not respond as Trewin did, even to the Guthrie production, the romantic elements of the text of *Tamburlaine* do increase the sense of unreality he identifies. When Tamburlaine cuts his arm as an example to his sons, he exclaims:

> View me, thy father, that hath conquered kings
> And with his host marched round about the earth
> Quite void of scars and clear from any wound,
> That by the wars lost not a dram of blood,
> And see him lance his flesh to teach you all.
>
> (part 2 3.2.110–14)

Amazing, we think to ourselves, Tamburlaine has come through all his battles without a scratch. How is this possible, we wonder? And if it were possible, what could this man know about the "fear of wounds," of the sufferings of war? What could he possibly know about the processes of experience that go on in the real world? What could he possibly teach his sons, who are (unlike their father) *human*? They do, in fact, seem to occupy a world more *real* than their father's world, which in part 2 begins to displace the Tamburlaine world. To borrow from Frye's theory of modes, the play seems at times a curious mixture of romance and low mimetic. The incongruency is particularly evident in part 2 when Olympia (whose name ironically suggests the immortal abode of the gods) achieves her heart's desire—the release of her "troubled soul" from the "prison" of her body (4.2.33–36)—by making Theridamas believe in something as patently unreal as a magical ointment. Tamburlaine's world is not truly "romantic"; it is not imagination mastering reality, but imagination masquerading as reality, acting as a substitute for it. It is (and we become more aware of this fact as the play progresses) a denial of reality in which Tamburlaine perversely attempts to become the all-controlling Word Itself, Christ incarnate:

> Come, boys, and with your fingers search my wound
> And in my blood wash all your hands at once,
> While I sit smiling to behold the sight.
>
> (part 2 3.2.126–28)

In one sense, this parody of the resurrected Christ and the atonement ironically serves to emphasize, through the hero's distorted vision, the *unreality* of suffering: Tamburlaine's sons must not fear wounds nor, by extension, must they scruple to inflict them on others. But this scene may also be viewed as the one small sacrifice that Tamburlaine ever makes, the one time he *suffers* for others. (Should the director have the actor *wince* when he cuts his arm? After all, Tamburlaine, as he himself states, has never felt a wound.) Curiously, this one moment of passivity is expressed not only in religious terms but also, secondarily (perhaps subconsciously on Marlowe's part), in sexual terms, for the fingers in the wound involve an image that suggestively places Tamburlaine in the female sexual role,[38] endowing him with the effeminacy that above all things he seems to fear.

The extent to which Marlowe was either intentionally exploring psychological experiences, working through them in his art, or on the other hand was being driven and controlled by personal conflicts, has long fascinated readers and scholars. An introduction for readers interested in these questions may be found in Norman Rabkin's short essay "Marlowe's Mind and the Heart of Darkness," where the author compares Judith Weil's emphasis in *Merlin's Prophet* on "Marlowe's intentionality, his control of himself as well as his audience" with Kuriyama's insistence that Marlowe is "the creature of his own psychology."[39] Many readers may feel more sympathy with Weil's approach (although it sometimes seems overingenious), since it acknowledges more readily what Rabkin calls Marlowe's "intellectual brilliance."[40] Weil's study also has the advantage that a great deal of evidence for careful and conscious artistic control can be garnered from the texts as they have come down to us (even in their mangled state), whereas Kuriyama must rely on the presence of Freudian sexual motifs (often convincing but sometimes questionable) and a biographical sketch that speculates, from extremely limited historical data, on the character of Marlowe's parents, particularly his mother. It is interesting to observe that Kuriyama and William Urry come up with diametrically opposed portraits of Marlowe's mother, Katherine. Kuriyama argues that the wills of Katherine's niece, Dorothy, and of her husband, John—"in their brevity and in their dominant theme of complete surrender to Katherine"—suggest "the coercive power of her personality." She thus "dominated the Marlowe household."[41] Urry, on the other hand, observing that Katherine may not have had her final wish "of being buried by her husband in the churchyard of St. George's," refers sentimentally to "John Marlowe's patient and long-suffering wife and widow, of whom so little is heard in the records which contain so much about her family."[42] Moreover, when one reads Kuriyama's concluding remarks—"the psychological and intellectual cul-de-sac that Marlowe flailed about in was probably inescapable, and his human insight might never have broadened or deepened significantly"[43]—one feels that, at the time of *Hammer or Anvil*, she had neither read Marlowe as sympathetically as he deserves nor yet appreciated the extent of his achievement, ironically in spite of her own deeply perceptive critical insights. However, by dealing directly with homosexuality and the concern with sexual identity, Kuriyama began to cover very necessary ground in our understanding of the playwright's work, and she employs, in my opinion, an honesty that is sometimes lacking in readings of Marlowe.

Objections of course have been raised to Kuriyama's study. Those interested in a psychoanalytic reading of Marlowe from a classically Freudian point of view, with an emphasis on unresolved Oedipal conflicts, should still consult *Hammer or Anvil* (it remains a landmark study), though they may keep in mind Summers's warning that the book's "naive and inaccurate concept of homosexuality (based on a discredited 1962 study of psychiatric patients) is fundamentally homophobic."[44] Peter S. Donaldson's psychological reading, "Conflict and Coherence: Narcissism and Tragic Structure in Marlowe," does more justice, I believe, to the central meaning of *Tamburlaine*. Donaldson suggests that while Tamburlaine's military conflicts "have the character of Oedipal victories," the hero's progress eventually leads to a revelation of "the precariousness of his self-cohesion and his radical dependence on the mirroring of others";[45] that is, he constantly requires the presence of others as self-objects that provide him with his sense of identity. Therefore "the effect of the play's interest in Tamburlaine's impressive appearance and its quasi-magical potency is to point, finally, to his underlying need for assurance of his own worth and coherence, a need that leads him either to avoid conflict or to be unable to be nourished by it in a way that would assuage his hunger for endless repetition of approving, mirroring reactions from other characters."[46] This reading explains the episodic structure of the play, which may also have some relation to Marlowe's evocation of a primitive sense of manhood that relies for its definition only on a sense of continually violent and amoral assertiveness, rather than on any sense of protecting, nurturing, or serving the "other." The episodic structure is reminiscent of the *Iliad*, which Marlowe's play alludes to several times.

While I regard Donaldson's essay as one of the most illuminating of the psychological studies of Marlowe, I believe certain modifications in his argument are necessary. At one point he remarks: "There is little sense of achievement in the military sphere, because Tamburlaine's opponents are knocked down too easily, almost automatically, and there is little sense of intimacy in the gaining of a wife, for, like Tamburlaine's male companions, Zenocrate is to Tamburlaine little more than an extension of himself, or 'portion of his glory.'"[47] There is no question that Tamburlaine reduces those around him to self-objects, extensions of himself, including (and especially) his wife, but surely the status of Tamburlaine's friends, particularly Theridamas, is different. Tamburlaine's relationship with these men is, contrary to Donaldson's suggestion, curiously intimate.

The difference between Tamburlaine's rapport with his followers and with his wife is evident in the scene in which the hero and Zenocrate first appear (part 1 1.2). Although Tamburlaine's heroic identity seems already dependent on the "mirroring chorus"[48] of the adoring Techelles and Usumcasane, the protagonist treats them clearly as equals and not subordinates:

> Nobly resolved, sweet friends and followers.
> These lords, perhaps, do scorn our estimates,
> And think we prattle with distempered spirits;
> But since they measure our deserts so mean
> That in conceit bear empires on our spears,
> Affecting thoughts coequal with the clouds,
> They shall be kept our forcèd followers
> Till with their eyes they view us emperors.

> (60–67)

Tamburlaine sees his friends as partners in his imaginative project ("That *in conceit* bear empires on *our* spears") and is willing to share center stage with them ("Till with their eyes they view *us* emperors"). The homosocial bonding may be explained simply in terms of cultural and historical considerations; as Bruce Smith points out:

> For 99 percent of its history as a species, *homo sapiens* has been directly involved in hunting for sustenance; for 100 percent of its history, *homo sapiens* has been forming itself into social groups, marking off territory, and defending that group-space from other members of the species. Superior physical strength equips males for these two basic activities, and carrying them out together, with other males, is more effective than carrying them out alone.[49]

Yet when we recall the peculiar nature of the imaginative project that Tamburlaine pursues, his behavior toward his men becomes in a sense the invitation to share actively in a fantasy. (It is interesting to note, as Smith suggests in his study, that much of the homoerotic literature of the Renaissance offered the solitary reader a kind of imaginative holiday, whose pleasures must be abandoned upon return to the strictures of Elizabethan society, the "real" world; Tamburlaine's rhetoric implies a desire to share the fantasy with other men.) Unlike Tamburlaine's comrades, Zenocrate is simply an ornament to him; she must "grace his bed" (37), although he disrobes for her only to reveal "complete armour" and cutlass—not very inviting sexually. And while she is extremely valuable to him as a mirroring self-object—"Thy person is more worth to Tamburlaine / Than the possession of the Persian crown" (90–91)—she is still very much a possession, booty that he has seized.

The greatest contrast in this scene, however, is between the wooing of Zenocrate and the much more intense and personal wooing of Theridamas. As C. L. Barber points out, Tamburlaine addresses Zenocrate with love poetry that is "literally frigid":[50]

> With milk-white harts upon an ivory sled
> Thou shalt be drawn amidst the frozen pools
> And scale the icy mountains' lofty tops.
>
> (98–100)

The sexual threat of Zenocrate is thus put on hold, on ice. When, in his imagination, Tamburlaine conceives of Zenocrate's beauty melting the ice, he delays the dreaded consummation, the surrendering of himself, by the offering of "martial prizes, with five hundred men," who sound like sexual surrogates, or a multimale bolster to Tamburlaine's threatened masculinity. This love speech is concluded by the adolescent, embarrassed aside between Techelles and Tamburlaine: "What now? in love? / Techelles, women must be flattered" (106–7). How different is the "love speech" to Theridamas, in which Tamburlaine has no trouble imagining himself united with his new friend:

> Both we will walk upon the lofty clifts,
> And Christian merchants that with Russian stems
> Plough up huge furrows in the Caspian Sea
> Shall vail to us as lords of all the lake.
> Both we will reign as consuls of the earth,
> And mighty kings shall be our senators.
> Jove sometimes maskèd in a shepherd's weed,
> And by those steps that he hath scaled the heavens
> May we become immortal like the gods.
> Join with me now in this my mean estate

> (I call it mean, because, being yet obscure,
> The nations far removed admire me not),
> And when my name and honour shall be spread
> As far as Boreas claps his brazen wings
> Or fair Boötes sends his cheerful light,
> Then shalt thou be competitor [partner] with me
> And sit with Tamburlaine in all his majesty.

> (192–208)

It may be objected that the difference in intensity between the two speeches arises from the fact that Zenocrate has been easily seized, while Theridamas, who is in command of a thousand horsemen, needs to be seduced into political and military compliance (hence the wedges of gold set out before him). However, a more personal reading is encouraged by the evident awe both Tamburlaine and Theridamas express at each other's appearance. It is possible to read the Tamburlaine-Theridamas rapport as the typically homosocial one that Bruce Smith discusses under the "myth" he terms "Combatants and Comrades": [The] story about how a pair of arch enemies became fast friends reconciles two conflicting traits that anthropologists have observed among human males in cultures all over the world: the tendency of . . . males to be aggressive toward other males and, at the same time, to form strong bonds with them."[51] After examining this phenomenon in Shakespeare's plays, Smith concludes: "Two conflicting imperatives govern the actions of all these paired heroes: 'fight this man' and 'love this man.' That conflict of impulses helps explain why the violent and the erotic so often coincide in Shakespeare's plays about soldiering."[52] In the case of the encounter between Tamburlaine and Theridamas, the aggression dissipates surprisingly rapidly, and the poetry is far more weighted with the erotic than the violent. Tamburlaine's speech of seduction ends with a description that sounds very much like a royal marriage, formalized by the concluding rhyming couplet and Alexandrine. Theridamas replies in terms not far removed from sexual surrender—"Won with thy words and conquered with thy looks, / I yield myself"—and continues in terms that sound like a marriage vow: "To be partaker of thy good or ill / As long as life maintains Theridamas" (227–30). Tamburlaine then replies in a speech that reinforces the idea of a "marriage" with Theridamas:

> Theridamas my friend, take here my hand,
> Which is as much as if I swore by heaven

And called the gods to witness of my vow:
Thus shall my heart be still combined with thine
Until our bodies turn to elements
And both our souls aspire celestial thrones.

(231–36)

What is truly remarkable, besides the fervor of the emotion, is the aspiration toward a celestial throne, in direct contradiction to the coveted "earthly crown" at the conclusion of the more famous "Nature that framed us" speech (2.7.18–29). What do we make of this? Must we say that the above speech is out of character, since it reveals an atypical aspiration of the hero? Tamburlaine certainly speaks elsewhere of becoming "immortal like the gods," but usually he does so in the sense of achieving the condition through heroic self-assertion. His speech to Theridamas is the only time, in part 1 at least, that he speaks both of giving himself to another and of the dissolution of his body.

I suggest that Tamburlaine and Theridamas are expressing homosexual longings that Marlowe felt but had not yet fully accepted, and that were therefore conveyed in quasi-religious terms that nevertheless do not quite mask the sexual nature of the desires ("sit with me," "take my hand," "my heart combined with thine / *Until* our bodies turn to elements" [my emphasis]). Tamburlaine can conceive of surrendering himself only in the context of masculine intimacy, since the Neoplatonic frame for this surrender allows Marlowe to evade the possibility of sexual involvement. Dollimore's discussion in *Sexual Dissidence* of a "perverse dynamic," in relation to Freud's theory of perversion, is relevant here:

> Perversion, in the form of the perverse dynamic, destroys the binary structure of which it is initially an effect. Freud brilliantly identifies these processes in psychic terms. . . . I am thinking especially of his concepts of repression, disavowal, negation, and splitting. One of the most astute accounts is in his article "On Repression" (1915):
>
>> the objects to which men give most preference, their ideals, proceed from the same perceptions and experiences as the objects they most abhor, and . . . they were originally only distinguished from one another through slight modifications. . . . Indeed . . . it is possible for the original instinctual representative to be split in two, one part undergoing repression, while the remainder, precisely on account of this intimate connection, undergoes idealization.[53]

The most positive sexual feelings expressed (though indirectly) in the play carry strong homoerotic overtones. The degree of affection Tamburlaine shows for his friends is unlike anything he shows for his wife until she is on her deathbed (when, significantly, she is no longer a sexual threat). Although Tamburlaine's male friends function for the most part as mirroring self-objects for his grandiose self, they function liminally as potential idealized masculine self-objects with which he wishes to merge. We recognize Tamburlaine's speech to Theridamas as one of the rhetorical high points of the play, and I therefore do not want to imply that the Neoplatonic sentiments become merely a neurotic façade for an inability to deal with physical realities. Marlowe's emotional identification with his hero is particularly strong here, since the speech is in effect a call for affection and companionship (and thus a much grander precursor of Barabas's pitiful "What, all alone?" outside the walls of Malta). It is possible to link the assertiveness here—"I hold the Fates bound fast in iron chains"— to Marlowe's intimation of the defiant and thus potentially "heroic" nature of these desires. Significantly, the heroic energy is here directed against the limiting power of Fate and Fortune, not destructively and cruelly against other human beings.

It is, in fact, whenever Tamburlaine is forced into a heterosexual role, where heterosexual performance is required or expected, that the unconscious fears and stresses on the author take on rather ugly manifestations in the play, many of which Kuriyama has explored. Tamburlaine's marriage to Zenocrate, whom he has preserved as a virgin all through part 1, is prefaced by the Siege of Damascus and the murder of the Four Virgins, who appear to plead for mercy:

> *Tamburlaine.* Virgins, in vain ye labour to prevent
> That which mine honour swears shall be performed.
> Behold my sword, what see you at the point?
> *Virgins.* Nothing but fear and fatal steel, my lord.
> *Tamburlaine.* Your fearful minds are thick and misty, then,
> For there sits Death, there sits imperious Death,
> Keeping his circuit by the slicing edge.
> But I am pleased you shall not see him there:
> He now is seated on my horsemen's spears.
>
> (5.1.106–14)

The sword and the spear here carry obvious phallic suggestions; Tamburlaine reacts to the upcoming threat of sexual surrender with the other virgin, Zenocrate, by expressing his fear as aggression and transferring it onto the Virgins of Damascus. Significantly, however, the actual act is again passed on to surrogates, his "horsemen." A similar case of displaced sexual aggression against women occurs in Tamburlaine's treatment of the concubines in part 2:

> Hold ye, tall soldiers, take ye queens apiece—
> I mean such queens as were king's concubines—
> Take them, divide them and their jewels too,
> And let them equally serve all your turns.
>
> (4.3.70–73)

Indeed, if, as Kuriyama argues, Tamburlaine's conquests are all attempts to prove his masculinity, it is interesting how often the hero displaces the phallic aggression onto his soldiers:

> Now in the place where fair Semiramis,
> Courted by kings and peers of Asia,
> Hath trod the measures, do my soldiers march;
> And in the streets, where brave Assyrian dames
> Have rid in pomp like rich Saturnia,
> With furious words and frowning visages
> My horsemen brandish their unruly blades.
>
> (part 2 5.1.73–79)

There is a suggestion in the play, related to Greenblatt's claim that the family is "something to be neglected, despised, or violated,"[54] that this displaced heterosexual aggression has its roots in a feeling of alienation from heterosexual—in Renaissance terms—"natural" pleasure. Before the Virgins of Damascus are ruthlessly executed, the First Virgin gives a tremendously moving description of the sufferings of the citizens:

> Most happy king and emperor of the earth,
> . . . .
> In whose sweet person is comprised the sum
> Of nature's skill and heavenly majesty:
> Pity our plights, O pity poor Damascus!
> Pity old age, within whose silver hairs
> Honour and reverence evermore have reigned;
> Pity the marriage bed, where many a lord
> In prime and glory of his loving joy
> Embraceth now with tears of ruth and blood
> The jealous body of his fearful wife,
> Whose cheeks and hearts, so punished with conceit
> To think thy puissant never-stayèd arm
> Will part their bodies, and prevent their souls

From heavens of comfort yet their age might bear,
Now wax all pale and withered to the death.

(5.1.74–91)

The Virgin presents images of natural bliss and an acceptance of generational difference and natural process, now disturbed by a relentless opposer of nature, who seeks to destroy what, on a latent level, he knows he can never enjoy. His displaced phallic aggression will indeed "wither" to death their phallic/heterosexual pleasure.

In more general terms Tamburlaine's resistance to sexual surrender reveals the fragility of his own self-image, so that the irony of his repeated, and increasingly brutal, acts of self-assertion becomes progressively more evident. Donaldson points out how Tamburlaine's sexual reluctance and his physical cruelty are ironically linked at the end of part 1. With the corpses of Bajazeth, Zabina, and the King of Arabia lying onstage, Tamburlaine calls attention to these "sights of power" as

> objects fit for Tamburlaine,
> Wherein as in a mirror may be seen
> His honour, that consists in shedding blood.

(5.1.476–78)

The Sultan seems perfectly agreeable—nullifying Tamburlaine's Oedipal victory—and replies:

> Mighty hath God and Mahomet made thy hand,
> Renownèd Tamburlaine, to whom all kings
> Of force must yield their crowns and emperies;
> And I am pleased with this my overthrow
> If, as beseems a person of thy state,
> Thou hast with honour used Zenocrate.

(480–85)

The repetition of the word "honour," Donaldson argues, "makes it plain that Tamburlaine's chastity, his sparing of Zenocrate's hymeneal blood, is related to his savagery, not an alternative to it—both are attempts to increase his own honor, conceived in self-reflexive terms."[55] Tamburlaine never really gives himself to Zenocrate; she

> is not the prize of a conflict in which fully formed selves have engaged with the risk of injury, nor is it clear that her husband to be has any

firm conviction that she possesses a self of her own: she is, like her father and the corpses which are still littering the stage even as he places the crown on her head, just another mirror of a self that must desperately find its reflection everywhere rather than face its own emptiness.[56]

Perhaps the most famous revelation of Tamburlaine's failure to "engage with the risk of injury" is his apostrophe to beauty. This speech contains several ironies, the most obvious of which springs up through the simple pronoun "my" in "What is beauty, saith my sufferings, then?" Tamburlaine has just consigned the Virgins to an excruciating death at the point of his horsemen's spears, and proceeded to contemplate, rather placidly, the agony Zenocrate will feel at viewing the slaughter of her countrymen, and then he narcissistically speaks of *his* suffering. The beauty of Zenocrate's sorrow, he seems to reason, tempts him to desist in the destruction of Damascus and "lays a siege unto [his] soul." He wonders:

> What is beauty, saith my sufferings, then?
> If all the pens that ever poets held
> Had fed the feeling of their masters' thoughts
> And every sweetness that inspired their hearts,
> Their minds and muses on admirèd themes;
> If all the heavenly quintessence they still
> From their immortal flowers of poesy,
> Wherein as in a mirror we perceive
> The highest reaches of a human wit—
> If these had made one poem's period
> And all combined in beauty's worthiness,
> Yet should there hover in their restless heads
> One thought, one grace, one wonder at the least
> Which into words no virtue can digest.
>
> (5.1.160–73)

This passage, the finest moment in the work of a writer who produced some extremely fine poetry, presents us with two major ironies. First, it achieves what it states is impossible; it *contains* what it claims is uncontainable, a description of the ineffable, indescribable power of beauty. Kimberley Benston suggests this in his essay "Beauty's Just Applause: Dramatic Form and the Tamburlanian Sublime": "The remarkable order and control of this verse almost belies its own subject and is, therefore, exactly suited to the expression of an ascesis leading to inexpressibility."[57] The second irony, which must be considered in light of the overall movement of Tamburlaine's soliloquy and is perhaps most evident from our more modern perspective, is that the speech does *not* contain what we would expect: consciousness of the loved one who supposedly inspired these sentiments. This may in fact be related to the Neoplatonic and Petrarchan conceptions of love prominent in the earlier Renaissance. According to Mary Beth Rose's summary,

> Sexual desire, even when conceived as leading to a consciousness of the divine, was never considered beneficial or good in itself. Loved women were better left exalted, remote, and untouched. It is therefore not surprising to discover that where idealization of women occurred, misogyny was rarely far behind. With significant exceptions, English Petrarchism and its corollary, anti-Petrarchism, tend to articulate that consciousness which exalts and idealizes the image of Woman while simultaneously regarding actual women with neglect and contempt.[58]

It is clear Zenocrate falls out of sight, out of mind, long before Tamburlaine reaches the end of his musings, so what begins as a kind of love poem motivated by concern for her ends, ironically, with her total exclusion; even, in fact, with an affirmation that he will continue to resist her—or at least resist what she represents to him ("thoughts effeminate and faint"), since by that point she no longer seems to exist. While "the humanizing effect of Beauty presupposes a recognition of what Kant calls a 'ground external to ourselves,' a sense of the Other," the final passage of Tamburlaine's soliloquy, as Benston argues, is "nothing less than a grand act of sublime revision and restitution. What it revises— by recasting the soliloquy's essential terms of Beauty and virtue— is the relation between Eros and imagination; what it restitutes is the primacy of agonistic eloquence."[59] Tamburlaine claims the power of "conceiving and subduing, both," yet the beauty he conceives he does not create but only mirrors, and if he were a true lover, he would not subdue it but surrender to it. Rose argues that during the Renaissance the polarizing consciousness of ideal- ization/neglect was being displaced by "a more complex, problem- atic moral and emotional reality"[60] whose conflicts were resolved symbolically in the marriages celebrated at the end of Elizabethan romantic comedies: "If the audience is meant to be reminded of any paradox about the loving surrender of individual identity to society, it is the Christian one of losing in order to gain, dying in order to live."[61] There is certainly no sense of loving surrender in the marriage with which *Tamburlaine* part 1 ends, though, as we have seen, there is a suggestion of it in the metaphorical marriage between Tamburlaine and Theridamas. In the speech inspired by his wife's suffering, Tamburlaine manages to appropriate beauty and encase it in an exquisite apostrophe, yet he fails to appreciate beauty's true worthiness: that it inspires love. In the soliloquy the possibility of both romantic and divine love are annihilated, and his poetic response is therefore not even "ideally" Petrarchan. It is true that something that Tamburlaine calls love—"Of fame, of valour, and of victory" (181)—is still present in his thoughts, but he fails to recognize the true love of an "other" that encourages the lover to surrender himself, to "engage with the risk of injury." For him Eros can only be sublimated into heroic action—of a self-serving kind, in no cause higher than his own aggrandizement. Thus he does not use imagination to come to terms with love as a process or experience, but effectively to exclude it. Psychologically, Tamburlaine's use of the "narrative" of his soliloquy is a defensive rather than a compensatory maneuver.

Tamburlaine's exclusion or sublimation of Eros with the power of "agonistic eloquence" finds an interesting contrast in the behavior of his son, Calyphas. Calyphas, unlike his father, is rhetorically weak, and speaks with such halting rhythms and clumsily repetitive verbal constructions that he seems barely capable of blank verse:

> The bullets fly at random where they list,
> And should I go and kill a thousand men
> I were as soon rewarded with a shot,
> And sooner far than he that never fights.
> And should I go and do nor harm nor good
> I might have harm, which all the good I have,
> Joined with my father's crown, would never cure.
> I'll to cards: Perdicas!
>
> (part 2 4.1.52–59)

While Calyphas is certainly no poet, he seems in the context refreshingly human, and though self-indulgent and cowardly he at least expresses a healthy sexual appetite, one major step toward a natural, sane acceptance of Eros:

Calyphas. They say I am a coward, Perdicas, and I fear as little their *taratantaras*, their swords, or their cannons, as I do a naked lady in a net of gold, and for fear I should be afraid, would put it off and come to bed with me.
Perdicas. Such a fear, my lord, would never make ye retire.
Calyphas. I would my father would let me be put in the front of such a battle once, to try my valour!

It is just such a battle that Tamburlaine wants to avoid, and one wonders if Tamburlaine murders his son simply because Caly-phas's military cowardice forms an unwelcome mirror of his fa-ther's glory ("Image of sloth and picture of a slave" [91]) or if, as well, Calyphas reminds Tamburlaine on some level of his own heterosexual inadequacy. Tamburlaine orders the "effeminate brat" buried by concubines so that "not a common soldier shall defile / His manly fingers with so faint a boy" (162–64), a comment carrying homosexual overtones (the phallic "manly fingers") that oddly seem to rebound more on Tamburlaine and his soldiers than on Calyphas. Immediately Tamburlaine commands: "Then bring those Turkish harlots to my tent, / And I'll dispose them as it likes me best" (165–66). How, we may ask (considering his usual sexual reluctance), will he deal with these concubines, who, in the context of his own rhetoric, amount to necrophile sexual partners of his own dead son?

Rhetoric, which Tamburlaine has used so successfully to both express his heroic self-assertiveness and to stave off the demands of reality and natural process, in the end acts as a kind of trap, exposing his own inadequacies in ever more disagreeable ways. The suggestion of necrophilia recurs, more obviously and sig-nificantly, at the end of the play, where the dying Tamburlaine addresses Zenocrate's embalmed corpse with the words:

> Now eyes, enjoy your latest benefit,
> And when my soul hath virtue of your sight,
> Pierce through the coffin and the sheet of gold
> And glut your longings with a heaven of joy.
> (part 2 5.3.224–27)

Donaldson comments: "Part I ended with a mirror in which Tam-burlaine's honor was reflected, and the content of that image was the lifeless bodies of his victims; here the image is of merger, not mirroring, and we are meant to know that the heaven of joy Tamburlaine proposes to himself amounts to fusion with a corpse."[62] Not only, then, is Tamburlaine's "honor" ironically mir-rored by dead bodies, but his final vision of heaven is yet another dead body. What greater, more painful irony could there be than this failure of imagination? Can the mind of this man in the end reach no farther than a coffin? While this merging with Zeno-crate's corpse is the closest Tamburlaine comes to expressing sex-ual desire for his wife, the penetration is to be accomplished by the soul's eyes, therefore saving him one last time from imagining real physical intimacy. If we remember that the most significant image of enclosure in each of Marlowe's plays—Dido's funeral pyre, Barabas's cauldron, Faustus's Hell, Edward's dungeon—occurs at or near the end, then it is difficult to overemphasize the importance of Zenocrate's coffin in terms of the overall meaning of the play. Though Tamburlaine refers to his vision as a heaven of joy, the piercing of the coffin and the glutting of his longings with the contents therein makes this enclosure as much of a personal hell as the four enclosures mentioned above. In spite of Tamburlaine's vision of Paradise as Zenocrate lay dying, his imagination at the last seems tragically unable to transcend the physical world.

Tamburlaine's desire to escape into this enclosure is intensely ironic for other reasons. His rhetoric has always been notable for the frequency of cosmic imagery—"And with our sun-bright armour as we march / We'll chase the stars from heaven and dim their eyes" (part 1 2.3.22–23)—leaving the impression that all the world was not enough room for him to move around in, as he himself claims: "For earth and all this airy region / Cannot contain the state of Tamburlaine" (part 2 4.1.119–20). (In this respect he differs so much from the more pusillanimous Aeneas, who, seeking enclosure, complains, "But hapless I . . . have not any coverture but heaven" [*Dido* 1.1.227–30].) And Tamburlaine, with his penchant for sacking cities, has always seemed intent on breaking down, annihilating enclosures, rather than escaping into them. Finally, he has used the practice of enclosing *others* as a demonstration of his power; capturing Zenocrate, putting Bajazeth in a cage, and harnessing the kings to his chariot.

The last example, perhaps the most notorious piece of stage spectacle in Elizabethan drama, has received much critical attention. As Marjorie Garber points out, the spectacle literalizes Tamburlaine's self-chosen role as the scourge of God.[63] Mulryne and Fender argue that Tamburlaine's tendency to literalize metaphor weakens our sympathetic identification with the hero by imposing a comic distance that encourages our detachment: "Tamburlaine's word—in both senses of 'word' [his literal words and his promises]—becomes a kind of cage too, and the price he pays for making good his hyperbole is the kind of ridiculousness that comes of trying to turn metaphor into fact. Equally powerful as our wonder at his ability to make good his threats is our sense of the ridiculousness of hyperbole enacted."[64] Tamburlaine's desire to be reunited with Zenocrate's corpse may be seen as an extreme example of this tendency to "literalize"—to reduce all

experience to a material state that can be handled and controlled—yet at that point such behavior no longer appears ridiculous or comic but becomes horrifying. Such, the play suggests,
is the ultimate result of the refusal to recognize the ontological
gap between language and being. The great irony—and this pattern recurs in the later plays—is that while the hero attempts to
escape into an imaginative realm, the material world actually
seems to become more intrusive, more powerful. Tamburlaine
tries to avoid dealing with the physicality of experience, but the
"body" in the end takes its revenge in the form of Zenocrate's
corpse and the hero's obsession with it.

The revenge of the physical body is suggested in other ways
in the play. Mark Thornton Burnett argues that "'classical' and
'grotesque' notions of the body are thematized" in the play, with
the "grotesque" notions gradually winning out.[65] In part 1, Tamburlaine carefully preserves Zenocrate's virginity because it is a
source of magical power: "in the medieval and Renaissance periods . . . [chastity] was supposedly able to mediate between the
human and the divine, and . . . was equated with the power to
transcend the corporeal."[66] Yet in the interval between part 1 and
part 2 Tamburlaine has certainly become a father:

> Copulating with Zenocrate . . . involves the discharge of his semen
> or "spirit" and the loss of his power and purity, it marks the beginning
> of his dissolution and the approach to death, and it undermines his
> individualistic conception of himself as unique, single. Coarsened, it
> seems, by propagating, Tamburlaine has been diluted and adulter-
> ated by incontinence. The three sons he fathers signal the "grotesque"
> re-emerging and Tamburlaine becoming multiple, heterogeneous.
> Wracked by this change in his bodily circumstances, Tamburlaine can-
> not accept having reproduced and, in his eyes, his sons are therefore
> "bastards" (II.1.3.32).[67]

Not only has the Neoplatonic flight from the body failed; Tamburlaine's psychological refusal of the role of parent can again be
linked to narcissistic pathology. Kohut writes: "Optimal parents
. . . are people who, despite their stimulation by and competition
with the rising generation, are also sufficiently in touch with the
pulse of life, *accept themselves sufficiently as transient participants in
the ongoing stream of life,* to be able to experience the growth of
the next generation with unforced nondefensive joy" (my emphasis).[68] Tamburlaine's failure to achieve his own self-cohesion and
accept physical process means that he cannot adequately assist
his children in these tasks. His children are, like his wife, only

reflections of his grandiosity, self-objects that he manipulates and on which he depends. Thus Calyphas as "Image of sloth and picture of a slave" must be annihilated, and, as there is no possible growth into Oedipal conflict, the previously vital Calyphas is strangely reduced to complete silence throughout the scene of his murder.

Donaldson argues that Tamburlaine's new role as father "is really no radical change in perspective since . . . Tamburlaine has trouble distinguishing himself from his sons, just as he had trouble untangling his self-conception in Part I from the kings he overcame." Thus there arises in part 2 a "different kind of attention to the special role of women—and especially dying mothers—as mirrors of the self."[69] Tamburlaine's extreme grief at Zenocrate's death is not so much caused by the loss of a loved one as by the loss of a mirroring self-object; "he has made of Zenocrate a figure of cosmic grandeur [which] adds to the potential for inner annihilation when she dies."[70] Thus in his lamentation, Tamburlaine emphasizes the loss of Zenocrate's power of sight in cosmic terms:

> Zenocrate, that gave him [the sun] light and life,
> Whose eyes shot fire from their ivory bowers
> And tempered every soul with lively heat,
> Now by the malice of the angry skies,
> Whose jealousy admits no second mate,
> Draws in the comfort of her latest breath
> All dazzled with the hellish mists of death.
>
> (part 2 2.4.8–14)

Without Zenocrate to mirror his noble pursuits, he despairs; the loss of her sight is tantamount to his own death, to the end of creation. Even the masculine ideal that he seems to have created from within himself has apparently partly been derived from Zenocrate, who is here equated with the masculine sun. Yet here, as so often in the play, our identification of Tamburlaine's psychopathology is discouraged by the astounding success of his rhetoric, which has the power to move us deeply even while we sense he mourns more for himself than his wife:

> Black is the beauty of the brightest day;
> The golden ball of heaven's eternal fire
> That danced with glory on the silver waves
> Now wants the fuel that inflamed his beams.
>
> (part 2 2.4.1–4)

In a sense, then, Tamburlaine, like Aeneas, suffers in his separation from the maternal mirroring self-object. However, the perversity of Tamburlaine's imaginative manipulations may be contrasted with the tentatively constructive imagination of Aeneas. While Aeneas turns artifacts into real people (Priam's statue), Tamburlaine turns real people into artifacts, either as sideshows (Bajazeth), elements in an emblem (the harnessed kings), or, most extreme of all, a literal piece of art (Zenocrate's embalmed and gold-covered corpse). While Aeneas's imagination encourages his acceptance of the heroic project destiny has chosen for him, Tamburlaine's encourages him to believe that his project is self-chosen, always under his complete control, so that he in effect becomes "God," the scriptwriter and director of his life. There is one moment, however, where the hero's imaginative response vaguely resembles Aeneas's. In part 1, 1.2, Tamburlaine concludes Theridamas's acceptance into his inner circle of friends with the remark:

> These are my friends, in whom I more rejoice
> Than doth the king of Persia in his crown;
> And by the love of Pylades and Orestes,
> Whose statues we adore in Scythia,
> Thyself and them shall never part from me
> Before I crown you kings in Asia.

> (240–45)

Here Tamburlaine allows himself to be influenced and inspired by the work of other artists (the sculptors who created the statues and the poets who have retold the myth) to give of himself, to experience an outpouring of affection toward his friends. It is a minor attempt at a transmuting internalization. He for once allows himself to be affected, rather than being the one who always affects and effects. It is another example of Tamburlaine directing his most natural, human feelings toward his close male friends.

Eventually Tamburlaine fails as his own scriptwriter and director; not only his rhetoric but the action of the play ultimately betray his fantasy of absolute control and expose his increasing constriction. The episode of the king-drawn chariot demonstrates that the stage itself can act as an ironic enclosure, according to the theatrical analysis carried out by Birringer:

> At the beginning of his long speech, we find an implicit stage-direction in the text; answering Techelles' proposal to start with the

attack on Babylon, Tamburlaine shouts; "We will, Techelles—forward then, ye jades!" (IV.iii.97). The chariot cannot be swung round and moved off since Tamburlaine here begins his long triumphant speech (36 lines) for which he will need at least two or three minutes. The staging, therefore, becomes problematic because the chariot ought to keep moving according to the text-direction. Most likely, the performance will provide us with a most significant "speaking picture" at this point: the chariot will move in a *circle* . . . The circling movement of Tamburlaine's earth-bound chariot conveys a sense of the maddening futility that is the reverse side of the triumph and glory of his exulting pride.[71]

The "maddening futility" of Tamburlaine's heroic project becomes more evident in part 2. Weil is certainly correct to suggest that the "tension between [Tamburlaine's] conceits and the intransigent matter of experience grows stronger"[72] after the death of Zenocrate. For one thing, the most obvious failure of rhetorical power occurs immediately after her death, when Tamburlaine rails and Theridamas must gently admonish him: "Ah, good my lord, be patient, she is dead, / And all this raging cannot make her live" (2.4.119–20). Moreover, at his next appearance, Tamburlaine briefly falls into what for him is a surprisingly realistic mode, lecturing his sons on the "rudiments of war" (3.2.53–92) before resuming his quasi-divine stance in the doubting Thomas parody. For a moment we are convinced that here is a man who does actually have to make use of the practical strategies of war; his series of triumphs, for once, does not appear as simply an epic poem he is writing about himself. Still, part 2 only magnifies chinks in Tamburlaine's imaginative armour that have been present from the start. There is, for example, an interesting moment early in part 1, just after Tamburlaine's wooing of Theridamas. The Persian lord, having listened in awe to Tamburlaine's dazzling rhetoric, exclaims, "Not Hermes, prolocutor to the gods, / Could use persuasions more pathetical," to which the hero replies, "Nor are Apollo's oracles more true / Than thou shalt find my vaunts substantial" (1.2.209–12). Yet the utterances of Apollo's oracle were notoriously ambiguous, and the allusion invites us, even at this very early stage of the play, to question the substantiality of Tamburlaine's heroic project.

This undermining of Tamburlaine's theatrical presence is admittedly much subtler than ones that occur later, and the reader may thus suspect that Marlowe's method resembles the technique that Stanley Fish claims for Milton in *Paradise Lost:* to lure the spectator into a sympathetic identification with the hero, only to gradually expose the foolishness of this response. But why exactly is the audience tempted to identify with Tamburlaine, other than that, as mentioned earlier, a low-born superman would appeal to the lower classes in Tudor England? Offering a more subtle historical reason, Simon Shepherd makes an interesting suggestion concerning an Elizabethan audience's identification with Marlowe's protagonist. Shepherd argues that "with the uncertainty about succession and Elizabeth's policy of pacifying where possible, the ideology of Protestant aggression produced the need for heroes."[73] These would be "new men," somehow closer to or more in touch with the people than the absolute monarch. Yet the

> final irony of *Tamburlaine*'s reflection on the Elizabethan need for heroes . . . is that the new cruelty is eventually not an opposition to but a completion of the old order. Tamburlaine receives the Soldan's permission to marry Zenocrate, the new man weds the established family and makes a financial deal with its father. The man who overthrows Turks himself has a "Turkish" cruelty, and both the heroism and the cruelty can be accommodated to the old order of the Soldan.[74]

It is rather like the end of *Animal Farm*, where one can no longer tell the difference between the pigs and the men. Shepherd's reading interestingly suggests that the avoidance of Oedipal conflict in the play may actually have a historical and political rationale within the Elizabethan context.

Mulryne and Fender offer a more universal, transhistorical explanation in their claim, quoted at the outset, that the playwright sought to "produce in the audience a state of mind that is at once contradictory and yet profoundly true of thinking and feeling about the play's central topic, the fulfilment of will." However, deliberately creating an ambivalent response does not itself constitute a "surprised-by-sin" approach, and Mulryne and Fender do not believe that we ever resolve our ambivalence in outright condemnation of the hero; it is in fact their argument that Marlowe's work "provides models of an absurd universe," and they quote a statement from Camus to illustrate the kind of worldview they feel Marlowe was endeavoring to communicate: "There is in the human situation (and this is a commonplace of all literatures) a basic absurdity as well as an implacable nobility. The two coincide, as is natural."[75] However, Mulryne and Fender wrongly insist that this "coincidence in *Tamburlaine* is maintained throughout"; the hero's "nobility" hardly remains "implacable." If *Tamburlaine* is about the fulfillment of will, it is not as morally neutral as Mulryne and Fender imply.

Not that I wish to argue that *Tamburlaine* is a morally straightforward text, or to refute the critical consensus that finds something "absurd" in Battenhouse's claim that the play is "one of the most grandly moral spectacles in the whole realm of English drama."[76] As Greenblatt points out, "*Tamburlaine* repeatedly teases its audience with the *form* of the cautionary tale, only to violate the convention."[77] Part of what Marlowe challenges in *Tamburlaine* is the conventional morality of his day, which postulated a neat moral universe in which divine power operated to punish tyrants and overreachers and protect the innocent. Kuriyama suggests that the "four major concepts of godhead . . . in *Tamburlaine* [gods as rivals, gods as protectors, gods as examples to be emulated, gods as avengers and punishers of the wicked], all of them more or less in conflict," are evidence of "irrationality," unconscious motivation on Marlowe's part.[78] But it is also possible that Marlowe consciously satirizes, as he did in *Dido*, humankind's *conceptions* of the roles of God or the gods in earthly experience. The gods are seen in whatever role is needed to justify an individual's action, or placate his terror, or provide hope for his salvation or the destruction of his enemy; as such needs change according to circumstance, so does the image of God entertained by the individual. It should not be particularly disturbing or remarkable that Tamburlaine can at one point conceive of himself as under Jove's special protection (part 1 1.2.177–80), while later he denigrates that same deity by claiming that "Jove, viewing me in arms, looks pale and wan, / Fearing my power should pull him from his throne" (part 1 5.1.453–54). Such examples reflect Tamburlaine's remarkable egotism and suggest that he never seriously and deeply subordinates himself psychologically to his concepts of the deity. (He certainly has no *fear* of the gods, unlike Aeneas or Faustus.) The play suggests that often in human experience God is an act of imagination; if the divine being seems inconsistent or variable, such disparity arises, to paraphrase Weil, from the tension between the divine conceit and the intransigent matter of experience. Yet just as in *Dido*, where lurking behind the seemingly parodic version of the Olympian gods there is a Destiny or Fate that is never called into question, so behind the human concepts of Godhead in *Tamburlaine* there lurks a God, an Absolute Will (call it what you will) whose existence the play eventually confirms.

Admittedly, the actuality of this divine presence has always been a contentious issue in Marlowe criticism. It will be helpful to begin with Steane's statement that "God is the great unseen actor" of the play, since "on both occasions when supernatural power is challenged [Tamburlaine daring Mahomet out of his heaven and Orcanes invoking Christ's aid against the Christians who have broken faith] the challenge is met."[79] I believe Steane is essentially correct; although these challenges are not free from complicating ambiguities of their own, the effect of these two episodes in performance would certainly go far in convincing the audience of a divine force in operation behind the human action onstage. While it is sometimes objected that Christ's supposed assistance to Orcanes is completely undercut by Gazellus's cynical comment after the fact, "'Tis but the fortune of the wars, my lord, / Whose power is often proved a miracle" (part 2 2.3.31–32), nevertheless a "slender" power ("Too little to defend our guiltless lives" [2.2.60]) has been suddenly surprised and has emerged victorious. The bare fact of the odds encourages the audience to accept the "miracle" over Gazellus's cynicism. Moreover, it is very difficult for us *not* to identify with, or approve of, the grateful Orcanes when he replies to Gazellus, "Yet in my thoughts shall Christ be honourèd, / Not doing Mahomet an injury" (2.3.33–34); he is given the last word in the exchange, and his generosity of mind is rare in the play and undeniably attractive.

Tamburlaine's challenge to Mahomet raises perhaps a more difficult problem of interpretation. Ian Gaskell points out that if "the audience sees Tamburlaine's seizure as divine retribution then not only must they now imaginatively accept the power of the god [Mahomet] whose holy writ has been enthusiastically burned . . . ; they must also logically deny the power of the God Tamburlaine asserts in his stead."[80] The first half of the objection is perhaps best answered by recognizing that Marlowe's deity is not the partisan Christian one; as Steane argues, the "universal spirit" that Marlowe imagines "has power and dignity which extend beyond local allegiances, nomenclatures, rites and myths, and his essential attribute is energy."[81] Yet if this is so, why, as suggested by the second half of Gaskell's objection, is Tamburlaine punished for recognizing such a deity?

> There is a God full of revenging wrath,
> From whom the thunder and the lightning breaks,
> Whose scourge I am, and him will I obey.
> So Casane, fling them in the fire.
>   [*They burn the books.*]
> Now, Mahomet, if thou have any power,
> Come down thyself and work a miracle.

. . . .

Well, soldiers, Mahomet remains in hell;
He cannot hear the voice of Tamburlaine.
Seek out another godhead to adore,
The God that sits in heaven, if any god,
For he is god alone, and none but he.

(5.2.182–201)

After all, Tamburlaine's concept of Godhead is not dissimilar, as Steane points out, to the one expressed by Orcanes in his prayer to Christ:

. . . he that sits on high and never sleeps
Nor in one place is circumscriptible,
But everywhere fills every continent
With strange infusion of his sacred vigour.

(2.2.49–52)

At one point in his argument Steane suggests that Tamburlaine is punished because of the doubt expressed in the phrase "if any god,"[82] but surely the effect of the play in performance would show the retribution as a result of Tamburlaine's *challenge* rather than his doubt.

The main difference between Orcanes and Tamburlaine is, I suggest, that Orcanes recognizes the special manifestation of God in the Son, while Tamburlaine does not. I have argued in the introduction that Marlowe's interest in Arian doctrine suggests a desire to eradicate the need for a Mediator. He wanted to imagine a God who would not impose limitations, a divine spirit immanent throughout creation and not restricted to one incarnation or manifestation—that is, a God such as Orcanes describes. For this reason he would have found Bruno's philosophy "congenial." Yet, in addition to the qualifications I have already suggested concerning Marlowe's occult sympathies, his desire for the eradication of a Mediator, because of the burden of personal responsibility it introduced, would raise concomitant doubt and fear.[83] Such doubt or fear manifests itself artistically as the retribution resulting from Tamburlaine's challenge to Mahomet. The primacy of the Son is reaffirmed, as is the subordinate nature of the human individual. Tamburlaine is not Christ, the all-controlling Word, after all.

To this argument it may be objected that in Islam, which lacks the doctrine of the Trinity, Mahomet is not God's Son but only his inspired prophet. It is difficult to ascertain what exactly Marlowe's, and other Elizabethans', conception of Islam would have been. Samuel C. Chew, in *The Crescent and the Rose: Islam and England during the Renaissance,* discusses the welter of misconceptions about Islam that were propagated during the period. Chew does quote one writer who failed to realize the "unitarian" aspect of the Moslem religion.[84] With respect to *Tamburlaine* specifically, I think a close analogy between Mahomet and Christ can be established. Mahomet's supreme miracle was the revelation of the Koran, the divine word. Thus in a sense for Mahomet, as for Christ, the ontological gap between language and being is bridged through direct contact with the Godhead. Tamburlaine fails, in the end, to achieve this kind of "rhetorical" mastery, for his physical being is endangered by his violation of the scripture of a truly inspired prophet. Moreover, as Kocher remarks,[85] Tamburlaine's challenge to Mahomet, "Come down thyself and work a miracle," is very likely an allusion to the challenge to Christ on the cross (Matt. 27:40).

Another point raised by Chew is too interesting to pass over without comment. The scholar informs us:

> Towards the close of the sixteenth century rumours were afloat about a certain scandalous treatise entitled *De Tribus Impostoribus Mundi.* The "three impostors" who had deceived the world were, it was said, Moses, Jesus Christ, and Mahomet. The blasphemous charge against the Saviour and the association of Him with the Arabian impostor roused general indignation.[86]

Marlowe dismissed Moses, the divinely inspired author of the Pentateuch, as "but a Jugler"; Christ, the Word made flesh, "deserved better to dy then Barrabas"; and Mahomet, the revealer of the Koran, was notorious in the Elizabethan age as himself a "Jugler," a perpetrator of cheap tricks.[87] Yet still Marlowe allows Mahomet (in lieu of Christ-Moses-God?) to have his revenge, as if the playwright could not help ultimately respecting or fearing the authority figures he wished to eradicate.

While Tamburlaine the character never seriously and deeply subordinates himself psychologically to his concepts of the deity, Marlowe himself cannot quite escape the fear of retribution, even while his iconoclastic impulses are expressed vicariously through his hero. In one sense the playwright may be laughing at his own fear. According to Greenblatt, Marlowe is after all a big tease: "The slaughter of thousands, the murder of his own son, the torture of his royal captives are all without apparent consequence; then Tamburlaine falls ill, and when? When he burns the Koran!

The one action which Elizabethan churchmen themselves might have applauded seems to bring down vengeance."[88] It is perhaps, on one level, a joke—a very Marlovian one, directed at "Elizabethan churchmen," whom Marlowe, according to Baines, did not hold in high esteem. But Marlowe, as I have already argued, was apt to laugh at what disturbed him most. The fact that he did not succeed in thoroughly exorcising his fear in *Tamburlaine* is strongly suggested by the existence of *Doctor Faustus*, a more intensely wrought conflation of comedy and anxiety.

The fear is of course much more contained in *Tamburlaine*, where there is perhaps after all an "existential" element, for it is interesting to realize that the illness that strikes Tamburlaine is not, in actual fact, what destroys him. The disease, as the Physician makes clear, is serious but need not be fatal. In a diagnosis that shatters completely the already severely tarnished image of Tamburlaine as pure poetic force, the doctor remarks:

> I viewed your urine, and the hypostasis,
> Thick and obscure, doth make your danger great;
> Your veins are full of accidental heat
> Whereby the moisture of your blood is dried:
> The humidum and calor, which some hold
> Is not a parcel of the elements
> But of a substance more divine and pure,
> Is almost clean extinguishèd and spent,
> Which, being the cause of life, imports your death.
> Besides, my lord, *this day is critical*,
> Dangerous to those whose crisis is as yours:
> Your artiers, which alongst the veins convey
> The lively spirits which the heart engenders,
> Are parched and void of spirit, that the soul,
> Wanting those organons by which it moves,
> Cannot endure, by argument of art.
> *Yet if your majesty may escape this day,*
> *No doubt but you shall soon recover all.*
>
> (5.3.82–99, my emphasis)

The speech is a perfect deflation of the fantasy of absolute control; the phallic assertion has collapsed into a mundane consideration of urinary sediments and other bodily fluids. The Physician is in effect telling Tamburlaine to be *flaccid*, to rest. Tamburlaine is flesh and blood, *of* a substance more divine and pure, bound by other laws than his own will; he is a *creature*. Though the hero appears to accept the doctor's advice, immediately an alarm is heard, and he must go to face Callapine's army, an effort that exhausts him and destroys his chance of recovery. He is thus in effect killed by the demands of his own endlessly repeating heroic project rather than by the illness per se. God, it seems, has only warned him, has demonstrated to him that he is subject to natural processes that he cannot control or transcend. But it is, at least, a warning; Gaskell attempts to argue that Tamburlaine's death is "portrayed as a natural consequence of the human condition,"[89] but this is a more accurate description of the demise of the historical Timur the Lame. Marlowe's hero does not die of old age, and the disease he suffers arises from *unnatural* assertion.[90]

As if his heroic project is too much to bear, Tamburlaine has at moments contemplated release, such as in the speech to Theridamas discussed earlier, and at the conclusion of the chariot scene: "So will I ride . . . / Until my soul, dissevered from this flesh, / Shall mount the milk-white way and meet him [Jove] there" (part 2 4.3.130–32). Yet such surrender for him seems mainly a function of the afterlife; while alive he can never stop defending a self so precarious that it must constantly reestablish its identity by destroying or controlling others. Like Macbeth, Tamburlaine, once he has begun, cannot stop; he has "murdered sleep" for, having defined himself solely through assertiveness, he can never risk temporary surrender.

It is therefore Tamburlaine's lack of integrity that in the end establishes the play's strongest moral comment. His obsession with honor appears in the end to be essential lovelessness and a fear of disintegration. Perfect fear has, in fact, cast out love and masqueraded under the guise of honor and heroism. "Let not thy love exceed thine honour, son," Tamburlaine warns Amyras (5.3.199), yet the real tragedy of the play is that unlike Amyras, Tamburlaine has never learned to love, has never learned that self-surrender sometimes takes more courage, constitutes a greater act of heroism, than self-assertion. Moreover, Tamburlaine's failure to nurture his sons with love results paradoxically in their being less assertive than is necessary, for Amyras's startling gesture of self-sacrifice as he ascends the "royal chariot of estate" does not augur well for the future of the empire:

> Heavens witness me, with what a broken heart
> And damnèd spirit I ascend this seat—
> And send my soul, before my father die,
> His anguish and his burning agony!

(5.3.206–9)

Tamburlaine has given so little to his sons that they now feel incapable of functioning without him as their necessary self-object. The tragedy is not only that Tamburlaine dies but that he leaves those closest to him unable to live. Having been so concerned with the exercise of his own will, he has never taught others to exercise theirs.

Tamburlaine's imaginative response to experience has encouraged only savage assertion and control, not acceptance. Though he seems courageously to accept the "necessity" of his own death at the end, he does so only by monomaniacally projecting his suffering onto one last mirror of his greatness, his visions of his sons and companions grieving after his death:

> Farewell my boys, my dearest friends farewell,
> My body feels, my soul doth weep to see
> Your sweet desires deprived my company.
>
> (5.3.245–47)

In spite of the undying egotism, there is in the final speech a hint of the terror of self-destruction and dissolution in the allusions to Phaeton and Hippolytus. As Donaldson argues, these allusions superficially suggest competition with his sons and generational conflict but ultimately suggest that Tamburlaine is "haunted at the end by a confusion of self with others . . . [He] never enjoyed the fruits of the conflicts he has engaged in because he never really believed in the cohesiveness of the self that entered into those conflicts."[91] The terror of dissolution only hinted at here, and so much more fully developed in *Doctor Faustus*, may have a source in Bruno's Hermeticism. As mentioned earlier, Bruno denied a Platonic dichotomy; Hilary Gatti writes that "although Bruno's universe is formed of two principles, soul or form and matter, he sees them as complementary and inseparable. The individuality of the soul becomes at most expressable [sic] in the image. . . . It was these ideas that allowed Bruno to dismiss visions of death, both Platonic and Christian, which contemplated in an after life the judgement of the individual soul. To such a vision Bruno opposes a Lucretian joy at the idea of a dissolving of individual formation into the infinite whole."[92] But while this vision of dissolution is a "Lucretian joy" it is a narcissistic (and perhaps a Christian) terror. The world of *Doctor Faustus* brings us more fully into this terror, into a very different kind of theatrical and artistic experience.

The theatrical experience of *Tamburlaine,* on the other hand, involves not the terror of *Faustus* but rather a dark fascination. The tragic glass tempts its audience at first to accept and even applaud the effort of will behind the act of self-fashioning, since every human individual must heroically struggle to establish and maintain an identity—"heroically" because the task is so difficult and seemingly never ending. Tamburlaine, by striving to be his own idealized self-object, becomes in a sense *ours,* and the play's fascination for us consists in its temporarily encouraging in us a kind of voyeuristic pathology. It is difficult to resist this kind of wish fulfillment that distances its own cruelty and sadistic pleasure through a subtle and oddly engaging parodic humor. At the same time, the ironies of the play cause us to reflect upon the dramatic action and to gradually realize that heroic self-fashioning is *only* an act of imagination (and perfect heroes ultimately illusory, as Shepherd's argument suggests); that human consciousness is not God, and that as we fashion ourselves we must take into account the presence of other selves and the exigencies of a universe that demands acceptance and surrender as often as it demands assertion and struggle. This process of audience response in fact resembles what Kohut believes should happen with the idealized self-object: the self gradually, not prematurely or massively, recognizes that the ideal is not ideal.[93] *Tamburlaine* succeeds as a play partly because it encourages, through its dialectic of fantasy and realism, a development, a kind of maturation in spectator or reader that is ironically heightened by our own painful realization that no character within the play experiences this process. That is, the play teaches us a kind of empathy, and evokes in us a range of feeling, that the text and characters themselves seem to lack. *Tamburlaine* is undeniably a bleak play because the hero dies with a total absence of anagnorisis: he recognizes neither the enormous suffering he has caused nor that Amyras is completely unequipped to take over the reins of his father's heroic project. If Marlowe created Tamburlaine in compensation for the weak Aeneas, he has come full circle, for Tamburlaine's sons display the same tenuous self-image and nervous dependency as the earlier hero did. They are still in great need of a true father. Though Marlowe may not share Augustine's faith in a God of succor and relief, he does seem to intimate the saint's belief in the fragility of the human personality, since Tamburlaine can maintain his identity, his sense of masculine power, only by the wholesale destruction of almost everyone and everything around him. In *Doctor Faustus* the heroic struggle for self-definition resumes, but the later hero becomes more crippled by his psychological dependency (which he manages much less adeptly than does Tamburlaine), and the dream of "a substance more divine and pure" that haunts the poetry of *Tamburlaine* becomes a nightmare.

4

Doctor Faustus: The Exorcism of God

IF *TAMBURLAINE* IS A NOTORIOUSLY PLURAL TEXT, THEN THE MUCH shorter *Doctor Faustus* is even more remarkable for density and complexity of meaning, and has been equally controversial. Considering its obvious concern with magic, it might be expected that *Doctor Faustus* even more than *Tamburlaine* would involve Marlowe's engagement with Hermetic thought. However, as James Robinson Howe briefly points out, Faustus's magic is black, not Hermetic natural magic.[1] The significance of this distinction is more fully explored by William Blackburn in his informative essay "'Heavenly Words': Marlowe's Faustus as a Renaissance Magician." Blackburn, examining the *Oration on the Dignity of Man*, points out that while Pico believed that man could be maker and molder of himself partly through magic, he warned that there are two kinds: *goetia* (witchcraft) and *magia*: "The former, [Pico] says, 'depends entirely on the work and authority of demons, a thing to be abhorred . . . and a monstrous thing. The other, when it is rightly pursued, is nothing else than the utter perfection of natural philosophy.'"[2] But while "Pico's *magia* sounds innocuous enough . . . it involves far more than a knowledge of the astrological or 'occult' properties of plants and stones. Pico . . . argues that, while *goetia* 'makes man the bound slave of wicked powers,' *magia* can 'make him their ruler and their lord.'"[3] According to Blackburn, Faustus "utterly and abysmally confuse[s] the two traditions of magic which Pico so carefully distinguishes."[4] Blackburn examines Faustus's incantation and finds it "utter nonsense": "In it Faustus calls upon both the Trinity and the gods of Acheron; in it the name of Jehovah is both abjured and invoked as a source of power. Faustus, while presuming to command the fallen angels . . . has also 'prayed and sacrificed to them' . . . as a witch or sorcerer would do."[5] Faustus's mistake, in strictly Hermetic terms, is not that he deals with spirits or devils but that he foolishly subordinates himself to them.

Yet the "utter nonsense" of Faustus's incantation is meaningful on a deeper psychological level. *Doctor Faustus*, like *Tamburlaine*, is obviously about human aspiration to unlimited power, but it introduces more acutely the problem of self-subordination. Like Tamburlaine's, Faustus's identity is extremely unstable, yet he exercises less control over the "other" or "others"—that is, the potential self-objects—against which he has defined himself; thus, while the desire to assert himself is still very strong, he is less successful in doing so, and experiences a more intense —a more hellish—personal conflict. Faustus's damnation, his descent into hell, may be seen as a theatrical metaphor expressing his inability to resolve the conflict between self-assertion and self-surrender, although I am not suggesting that this "metaphor" involves a kind of artistic detachment that leaves the play devoid of religious or eschatological terror. In the final analysis the play is less an objective critique of Reformation theological systems and beliefs such as predestination[6] than a personal (and desperate) effort by Marlowe to attempt to free himself psychologically, by directly facing and thus exorcising his own desire for religious surrender and self-subordination. As a result, almost by psychological accident, the play begins to uncover Marlowe's repressed sexual desires.

While Faustus appears to exercise less control than Tamburlaine over the "others" against which he defines himself, defining the mirror of his identity is a difficult task because the point is that Faustus himself (as his incantation suggests) cannot decide who or what it is. The confusion becomes most striking at the end of the play. The hero in his final soliloquy exclaims:

> Ah, my Christ!
> Ah, rend not my heart for naming of my Christ!
> Yet will I call on him. O, spare me, Lucifer!
>
> (5.2.79–81)[7]

The continuity of thought or intent in line 149, and thus the conflation of Christ and Lucifer, is more strongly implied by the punctuation of the earlier texts:

> Yet wil I call on him, oh spare me *Lucifer!*
>
> (A 1466)
>
> Yet will I call on him: O spare me *Lucifer.*
>
> (B 2051)[8]

The hero is already "tumbl[ing] in confusion" as the Bad Angel predicts in the B-text (5.2.137), and has in fact been doing so since the beginning of the play. From what does he wish Lucifer to spare him? The most conservative reply to this question is considered by Max Bluestone: "Following Boas as sanctioned by Greg, most critics assume that the dark powers here fulfill their threat to torture Faustus for calling on Christ or forgetting his vow."[9] Yet according to the dramaturgy of the play, the dark powers always appear *in person;* but Faustus during the final soliloquy stands alone, or, according to the B-text, the devils stand on the upper stage or balcony observing Faustus. Thus it is unlikely that the devils exercise, either here or at the slightly earlier moment when Faustus claims that Mephistopheles and Lucifer hold his hands, a direct physical effect on the hero. Their hold is psychological rather than physical. What Faustus wants to be spared from in his final soliloquy is, I suggest, having to surrender to Christ, since that would mean a loss of self, of his own identity, a loss he cannot face. Of course by extension Faustus would also be spared having to surrender to Lucifer, for the same reason. It is the fear of disintegration that torments Faustus at the last but that has also tormented him to a lesser degree all along. Yet at the same time he cannot help praying to Christ-Lucifer since he needs him/them as a source of (displaced) identity and power. He is reduced to a state where he wishes first that his body may disintegrate to allow his soul to fly—intact—into heaven; wishes next to become a soulless beast that cannot consciously experience the pain of disintegration since at death the animal soul simply "dissolves" (108–11); finally, does indeed wish for what he has feared all along, complete dissolution, though a perfectly painless variety of a Brunian kind:[10] "O soul, be changed into little water-drops, / And fall into the ocean, ne'er be found" (118–19). Despite this final emphasis on the terror of physical pain, much of the anguish in the final soliloquy arises from Faustus's simultaneous aversion to and desire for self-subordination. Lucifer and Christ for Faustus represent the same thing, the "other" from which he has acquired power (the one through his creation, the other through a special pact) and to whom he must eventually surrender himself. They become conflated in his final nightmare vision because he can live neither with nor without them. They both, in this sense, tear him to pieces (literally, in the B-text)[11].

Faustus is tortured by metaphysical "others" that he fails, in mature human terms, to internalize; that is, they do not serve as viable self-objects. Kuriyama argues that "one of the primary

obstacles to Faustus's repentance, insofar as we can identify them
at all, is his intense fear and mistrust of God, a trait for which
the play neither blames him nor offers any explanation. This fear
and mistrust . . . has to be distinguished from despair, since it
exists independently of an overwhelming sense of guilt."[12] It is
questionable whether the fear can be distinguished from despair,
but the absence of guilt does suggest that Faustus's dilemma
might be understood in pre-Oedipal rather than Oedipal terms,
since guilt is a more typical feature of Oedipal conflicts. Kohut
in fact distinguishes between what he terms "Guilty Man" and
"Tragic Man":

> The (sexual and destructive) id and the (inhibiting-prohibiting) super-
> ego are constituents of the mental apparatus of Guilty Man. Nuclear
> ambitions and ideals are the poles of the self; between them stretches
> the tension arc that forms the center of the pursuits of Tragic Man.
> The conflictual aspects of the Oedipus complex are the genetic focus
> of the development of Guilty Man and of the genesis of the psycho-
> neuroses; the nonconflictual aspects of the Oedipus complex are a
> step in the development of Tragic Man and in the genesis of the
> disorders of the self. The conceptualizations of mental-apparatus psy-
> chology are adequate in explaining structural neurosis and guilt-de-
> pression—in short, the psychic disturbances and conflicts of Guilty
> Man. The psychology of the self is needed to explain the pathology
> of the fragmented self (from schizoprenia to narcissistic personality
> disorder) and of the depleted self (empty depression, i.e., the world
> of unmirrored ambitions, the world devoid of ideals)—in short, the
> psychic disturbances and struggles of Tragic Man.[13]

It should be pointed out here that Kohut's clear distinctions between Guilty Man and Tragic Man have been criticized by other
psychoanalysts. Robert S. Wallerstein, for example, has questioned the usefulness of the distinction "between deficit and conflict . . . the very centerpiece of the claim of self psychology to
being a different psychology, alongside of, complementary to, but
not (or not yet anyway) to be integrated with so-called 'classical'
psychoanalytic metapsychology (which is avowedly centered on
conflict)." Wallerstein notes the use by self psychologists of conceptions such as the "tension arc," and "faulty interactions" with
self-objects, and points out that they "connote, in some fashion,
the concept of something out of kilter—in other words, conflicted."[14] Kohut's concept of a tension arc between ambitions (vis-
à-vis the mirroring self-object) and ideals (vis-à-vis the idealized
self-object) does parallel the conflict between self-assertion (ambi-

tion) and self-surrender (honoring/imitating the ideal) that I have identified in Marlowe, and I endorse Wallerstein's suggestion that the psychology of the self cannot be seen as completely free from a consideration of conflict. Nevertheless, it appears legitimate to claim that the conflicts of self psychology are more profoundly intrapsychic, solipsistic, than the interpersonal conflicts of the Oedipal transition.

I have to as well qualify some of Kohut's other claims, especially regarding the idealized self-object as he conceives it in potentially religious terms. Kohut writes: "For the religious person, the adult replica for the idealized object is the absolute God, particularly the God of the mystics. The great mystic writers of the Middle Ages, for example, described over and over again this experience of merging into something great, into something perfect, the God life, and feeling themselves to be absolutely nothing."[15] Kohut claims that both one's grandiosity with respect to the mirroring self-object and one's insignificance with respect to the idealized self-object may involve merger,[16] but the specific context—the stage in life of the individual, and the exact nature of the merger— must be considered carefully. Clearly in *Faustus* this potential merger with God is regarded with terror rather than joy. The reason is succinctly articulated by Donaldson at the end of his essay: "Where there is severe self pathology the inevitable dissolution of the self cannot be accepted because its full cohesion has never been achieved."[17] The desire for spiritual self-surrender in *Faustus*, because accompanied by narcissistic terror (specifically a terror of dismemberment and engulfment), constitutes a potentially regressive merger. Stephen Frosh's distinction between the ego ideal and the superego may be helpful here. As he points out, the

ego ideal was originally employed [by Freud] to describe a strategy for recovering the lost narcissism of early infancy; the super-ego is quite clearly an agency set up at the time of the stunning repressions that close the Oedipus complex—as a mode of identification with the aggressor. The former concept refers to a desire for absorption in the I-thou unboundedness of the first two-person relationship . . . whereas the latter is linked to the three-person definitiveness of culture and reality, the "ego-other-Law" mode. . . . The significance of this is to make it clear that the pursuit of oneness, of narcissistic nirvana, of the ego ideal, is the pursuit of the pre-Oedipal relationship, the time when there was not only no father, but no structure either, no *mediation* between the untrammelled desire of the infant and the illimitable response of the mother.[18]

Frosh's reference to mediation is intriguing. According to this scheme, the individual must submit to "mediation," not through the surrogate Mediator Christ, but through his or her own individuation and experience in the world, which necessarily involves a personal acceptance of difference, struggle, and loss. But we should also keep in mind Frosh's observation that "it is not the ego ideal in itself which is regressive; rather, it is the pursuit of the ego ideal without the mediation of reality represented by the Oedipus complex—without, that is, acceptance of separation. The ego ideal actually offers the possibility of creative striving which, being based on a search for the original mothering experience, can have a loving rather than a punitive aspect."[19] The potentially ambiguous nature of the desire for the ego ideal may explain the irresistible attraction as well as the danger of religious self-surrender that Marlowe's tragedy communicates, leaving the play itself profoundly ambiguous. No sensitive reader can fail to recognize Faustus's deep need to be loved and nurtured, coupled with his rigid inability to believe that God loves him. The intensity of the anxiety may be partly attributable to the Reformation context; as C. L. Barber has argued (citing Lily B. Campbell), Calvinistic Protestants "had to cope . . . with God's terrifying, inclusive justice . . . [and] they had to do without much of the intercession provided by the Roman church, its Holy Mother, its Saints, its Masses and other works of salvation."[20] Barber argues convincingly that a hunger for such "physical resource" or embodiments of Grace finds expression in *Faustus*, and may also be reflected in Baines's quotation of Marlowe's seemingly grudging assertion that "if there be any god or any good religion, then it is in the Papists' because the service of god is performed with more ceremonies, as elevation of the mass, organs, singing men, shaven crowns, etc."[21] The loss of cultural and institutional mediation of religious belief (and of the ego ideal) was probably, as Barber suggests, traumatic.

The eerily indifferent God in *Doctor Faustus* is not so much a vengeful Oedipal father or a potential idealized "mystical" self-object, but a dark version of a mirroring self-object that cannot substantiate the hero's grandiose illusions; he is a spiritual parent who cannot tolerate growth on the part of his children, because he recognizes only one perfect (male) child, Christ. The figure of God, as I pointed out in the conclusion to *Dido*, is psychologically problematic as an idealized masculine self-object because he is, in human terms, inimitable. While Marlowe's great tragedy does not reduce the concept of God to merely a failed self-object in human development, it does I think offer a warning concerning the overwhelming desire for spiritual self-surrender without or before the risk of individuation. That Marlovian drama seems more theologically concerned than the work of other Renaissance playwrights suggests a specific psychological dilemma; the plays hint at Marlowe's failure to achieve a loving merger with a masculine ideal in early life, through a sense of alienation and of longing for masculine support on the part of his adult male characters. This emotional longing would be exacerbated by the teasingly, frighteningly paradoxical nature of the Augustinian God (or neo-Augustinian versions)—"simultaneously distant and near, withholding and giving, judging and loving"[22]—who might otherwise perhaps serve, imaginatively, as a partly viable self-object substitute. Regardless of the exact etiology in Marlowe's psyche, Faustus's conflict clearly resembles the pattern, already noted, associated with narcissistic disorders: the failure to realistically modify the grandiose and idealizing inclinations leads to later vacillations of the ego between irrational overestimations of the self and feelings of inferiority.

While this general pattern of behavior has certainly been observed before, what needs emphasizing is that beneath this vacillation in *Faustus* is a desperate drive toward self-cohesion that, in a patriarchal Renaissance context, figures as a struggle toward manliness. The metaphysical, whether hellish or heavenly, is resisted as interfering in this project of asserting a manly, naturally accomplished sense of self in the world; on another level, the supernatural is desired as a release from the burden of such a project. Yet the desire for self-surrender is quickly translated into a fear of disintegration. The prominence of this fear explains the seemingly subversive but rigorously consistent conflation of heaven and hell in the play. Whenever the possibility of repentance is raised, it is answered by a resurgence of hellish forces, because inherent in the desire for self-surrender is the frightening failure of self-cohesion. For example, the moment in act 2 when Faustus calls out "Ah, Christ, my Saviour, / Seek to save distressèd Faustus's soul" (2.3.82–83), and instead is answered by the terrifying entrance of the Infernal Trinity of Lucifer, Beelzebub, and Mephistopheles, has caused great disagreement (like so much else in the play) between orthodox and heterodox readers. But according to the play's logic, Faustus gets what he asks for, since his calling out in frightened prayer means he has failed as a man, failed in his own self-possession, self-confidence, self-cohesion.

The dramatic dialectic of *Doctor Faustus* is not between good and evil, but between the "natural" and the "unnatural" or supernatural. Setting aside for a moment a consideration of his specific narcissistic pathology, we can say that Faustus suffers because he refuses to accept his human condition, the condition of a creature, his natural place in the hierarchy of created beings. In this sense the play is vigorously orthodox—moral in a commonplace fashion. When we are told by the Chorus that

> swoll'n with cunning of a self-conceit,
> His waxen wings did mount above his reach,
> And melting heavens conspired his overthrow
>
> (prologue)

the lines may not finally argue for a malevolent divine force plotting to overthrow Faustus[23] so much as they indicate the normal operation of the universe, "conspiring" or "breathing together" in a teleological harmony that, like a healthy body, corrects or checks disorderly elements in the system as naturally as "waxen" (unnatural) wings melt in the heat of the sun. Yet at the same time the play as a whole leads us to question whether Faustus's "chiefest bliss" (27) is really, as (orthodox) editors of the play usually suggest, his hope of divine salvation, since his obsession with his eschatological destiny seems as damaging as his foray into necromancy; they begin to look like two sides of the same coin. As Edward A. Snow in his essay "*Doctor Faustus* and the Ends of Desire" concludes, "heroic overreaching" and "Christian self-abnegation" are merely the inverted images of each other.[24] They are both unnatural and therefore ultimately destructive. In the context of Faustus's dilemma, Snow reasons,

> *summum bonum medicinae sanitas* [from Faustus's review of medical art in his opening soliloquy] begins to acquire gnomic resonance. Within the pre-Christian, pre-dualistic ontology that informs Aristotle's ethical vision, *sanitas* can be understood not merely as physical health but, more comprehensively, as regularity, soundness of being, discretion, good sense, etc.—as if (to translate the vision back into the terms of post-Christian experience) what we term psychic or spiritual "sanity" *were* in the final analysis a matter of "our bodies health" (and madness the fear of or for it, or disgust with it, or a fever in it), the state of being grounded and stabilized in the continuity of physical existence. The values implied would seem to be in equal opposition to both Christian and Faustian man—who, from this point of view, seem but two manifestations of a single phenomenon.[25]

There is thus a suggestion in the play that Faustus is not altogether wrong to bid "Divinity, adieu" (to leave it "to God"). He
has turned to it presumably to increase a sense of personal power,
to extend himself into the supernatural realm, the same reason
he turns finally to necromancy. However, divinity is a denial of
his human selfhood, his necessary life as a man. It is true that
Faustus omits from his biblical quotations the subsequent passages that offer the hope of divine salvation. For example, the
entire quotation of Romans 6:23 reads, "For the wages of sinne
is death: but the gifte of God *is* eternal life through Iesus Christ
our Lord."[26] Yet it is possible that Faustus omits the second part
not because he willfully deceives himself—or because Mephistopheles leads his eye as the B-text (5.2.99–101) implies—but
because they are for a man of his energy and ambition essentially
meaningless. "Yet art thou still but Faustus, and a man" (1.1.23)
implies not only his dissatisfaction with the human condition but
also highlights that condition. He is still a man, and must go on
with his manly life. How then, to fill the gap between now and
the gift of eternal life through Jesus Christ, except as Faustus, a
man? While it may be ultimately true that "*When all is done,* divinity is best" (1.1.37, my emphasis), clearly, for Faustus, all is not
yet done.

Mistakenly, Faustus is willing to overreach all natural endeavors, and forgo living a manly life. Until his fall into necromancy,
Faustus's progress, the Chorus implies, has been remarkable but
nonetheless natural, like the development of a healthy new strain
of fruit tree or flower. Born of "parents base of stock" (11), he in
"riper years" (13) goes to Wittenberg, where he "graces" (adorns)
the "fruitful plot of scholarism" (16). But then the disease sets in,
and he metamorphoses from a thing that gives and nourishes,
into one that seizes and devours: "swoll'n with cunning of a self-
conceit . . . And glutted more with learning's golden gifts, / He
surfeits upon cursèd necromancy" (20, 24–25). This process is
repeated for us in the opening soliloquy, as we observe Faustus
review and dismiss the various professions he claims to have mas-
tered. They are indeed "professions," practiced only "in show"
(and the pun occurs again in *The Jew of Malta*), because, while he
has the wit and talent to have acquired rudimentary knowledge
of them or even to have practiced them very skillfully, he has not
dedicated or given himself to any of them. He has, in spite of his
stated intention, sounded none of their depths. Faustus pursues
instead his desire for a "world of profit and delight, / Of power,
of honour, of omnipotence" (1.1.55–56), and the crescendo from

"power" to "omnipotence" signifies his movement from manly self-assertion to a foolish attempt to equal God. But a note of exhaustion is sounded: "Here Faustus, try [tire][27] thy brains, to get a deity" (65).

Through "all [his] labours" (71) Faustus's brains do actually succeed in begetting a dichotomized deity in the form of the Good and Bad Angels, whose entrance at this moment signals the beginning of the disturbing vacillation in the doctor's mind that will reach a nightmare pitch in his final soliloquy. The angels are the first symptoms of a severe mental crisis. The Good Angel introduces for the first time the frightening image of a wrathful God (74), and the repetition in the (albeit typically Protestant) admonition to "Read, read the Scriptures" (75) suggests an unquiet, restless searching, almost as if such reading is ultimately as unwholesome and unfruitful as reading the book of necromancy. (Cf. Simon Shepherd's argument: "The Good Angel encourages Faustus to read scriptures, but reading in the play is marked as a problem.")[28] There is certainly a curious and disturbing grammatical effect in the whole of line 75—"Read, read the Scriptures. That is blasphemy." It may be that the singular "is" prevents us from linking "blasphemy" with the scriptures, but I think the ambiguity is there; many editors in fact feel compelled to clarify for the reader that "that" refers back to the book of magic (mentioned three lines earlier) in order to dispel a lurking temptation to misread the line. One wonders if the actor playing the Good Angel would feel compelled to walk up to Faustus on stage and point histrionically to the book of magic (which, unless covered with sparkles and stars, might look a lot like the Bible anyway) in order to clarify the meaning in performance. Read in a subversive way, the line "Read, read the Scriptures, that is blasphemy" seems an almost perfect inversion of Faustus's earlier line, "And necromantic books are heavenly" (52). The irony of the latter line may thus be not that Faustus confuses black magic with a more positive spiritual power, but that he fails to realize that any kind of spiritual aspiration carries him away from a natural, sane, human mode of existence. It is significant as well that the word "spirit" in the play always refers to evil spirits or devils, as if the supernatural is inevitably something negative and destructive.

Doctor Faustus is certainly an extremely ironic play, but its ironies run to ever increasing depths that serve to undermine rather than reinforce the Christian morality of the play. For example, what Greenblatt terms Faustus's "extraordinary, and in the circumstances ludicrous"[29] remark "I think hell's a fable," receives

Mephistopheles' devastatingly ironic reply, "Aye, think so still, till experience change thy mind" (2.1.130–31). Faustus is deceived, and is quickly on his way to that "fable" in a handcart. Yet Greenblatt adds: "The chilling line may carry a further suggestion: 'Yes, continue to think that hell's a fable, until experience *transforms* your mind.'"[30] Hell is a function of the mind; Mephistopheles can bring Faustus there only by encouraging him in experiences that will radically alter his worldview. Hell, theologically or psychologically, either a place of torment or a state of mind, has its roots in a sickness of the self, a swelling of the self, to be "swollen with cunning of a self-conceit." Mephistopheles can only describe a spatial hell rather vaguely: "Under the heavens . . . Within the bowels of these elements [which may mean only somewhere (anywhere) in the created universe][31] / Where we are tortur'd and remain for ever [as created beings]" (2.1.121–23). But as a condition it becomes much more convincing:

> Hell hath no limits, nor is circumscribed
> In one self place, but where we are is hell
> And where hell is must we ever be.
>
> (2.1.124–26)

Mephistopheles' description of hell sounds remarkably like a parody of the famous description of the nature of God as "a circle of which the centre is everywhere and the circumference nowhere";[32] yet perhaps not so much a parody as a proof that the satanic and the divine dilemma are surprisingly similar. The expansion of the self into omnipotence/omnipresence results in the nightmare of having no viable "other" to give to or receive from, of being eternally alone, self-enclosed in a world where everything is a function only of one's own mind.

A similar complication of irony occurs slightly earlier when Faustus stabs his arm in order to write the "deed of gift" for Lucifer. "Why streams it not" (2.1.66), the doctor exclaims when the blood congeals, and while we may be tempted to succumb to the Faustian temptation always to look for supernatural signs and wonders, the most obvious explanation is that his blood has simply coagulated, the way it should naturally. Blood streaming out of the body is as unnatural (the physiological processes resist it) as Christ's blood streaming in the firmament in his final nightmare phantasmagoria—a sacramental parody that, following Barber's reading, reveals a yearning for the denied or repressed physical embodiment of desire. But then a wonder does occur:

> *Consummatum est.* This bill is ended,
> And Faustus hath bequeathed his soul to Lucifer.
> But what is this inscription on mine arm?
> *"Homo fuge!"* Whither should I fly?
> If unto God, he'll throw me down to hell.—
> My senses are deceiv'd, here's nothing writ.—
> O yes, I see it plain. Here in this place is writ
> *"Homo fuge!"* Yet shall not Faustus fly.
>
> (2.1.74–81)

The appearance of the miraculous *Homo fuge* seems to be evidence
of a beneficent power watching over him, telling him to get the
hell out of there (the pun is irresistible). Faustus's inability to
believe in God's mercy ("he'll throw me down to hell") ironically
nullifies the intent of the miracle. Yet Faustus's question "Whither
should I fly?" also alludes, as Weil and Birringer note,[33] to
Psalm 139:7–10:

> Whether shal I go from thy Spirit? or whether shal I flee from
>   thy presence?
> If I ascend into heauen, thou art there: if I lie down in hel, thou
>   art there.
> Let me take the wings of the morning, & dwell in the vttermost
>   parts of the sea:
> Yet thether shal thine hand lead me, & thy right hand holde me.

The allusion thus suggests the mystical presence of God in the
self. *God* could not tell him to fly, because God is already there.
And Faustus cannot escape, because no one can flee from himself.
Whither shall he fly, indeed, for if to (a conscious realization of)
God, that being will require him to surrender himself, which he
is not prepared to do. Birringer calls the appearance of *Homo fuge*
an explicit *Mene Tekel* (cf. the writing on the wall in Daniel 5:24–
30), yet the biblical writing was a promise of *doom* rather than a
kind of warning. The writing on Faustus's arm seems rather a
miraculous response of the body and the mind to preserve their
own health and sanity. In that sense Faustus could flee his necromantic practice and return to a more normal activity; his obsession with divine salvation only increases his personal conflict, his
hell: "If unto God, he'll throw me down to hell."

Faustus's "damnation" is a manifestation of a devastating psychological dilemma. While he has the will to be omnipotent, his
human consciousness must define itself against an "other" external to it, which is more powerful than he. Faustus must therefore

limit or contain a self that wishes to be uncontained, that wants to stretch "as far as doth the mind of man" (1.63). For the supernatural "other" he has of course the two choices. God can offer him omnipotence through Jesus Christ, through the annihilation of his own personality, for Faustus an unacceptable alternative. However, Lucifer, while in a sense demanding the same thing (he obtains Faustus's soul in the end) offers, or Faustus is under the illusion that he offers, more in the meantime: personal power. That Faustus seems to receive rather less, in the way of power, than he bargained for is a commonplace of criticism. The interesting point is that he must *bargain* for something that he should be able to establish on his own: personal power in the sense of normal self-assertion, a cohesion of self. Perhaps this is the true meaning of the B-text's line "A sound magician is a demigod" (1.1.61) which, rather than being evidence of censorship, strikes me as poetically superior to the A-text's rather lame tautology, "A sound magician is a mighty god" (1.1.64) (although Marlowe conceivably may have wanted to shock his audience with a precariously close phonetic equivalent to "A sound magician is Almighty God"). A sound, a *sane*, magician does not attempt to become omnipotent, to control the universe, but is rather satisfied with being *half* a god; he recognizes and respects the presence of the "other"; he does not try to evade it or deny it or sell his soul to it, and is thus not constantly tormented with the nightmare dread of having to face the final reckoning; he operates out of his own integrity because he accepts his limits. Faustus could, without soliciting supernatural aid, garner some of the honor and wealth he covets by pursuing one of the careers he has dismissed. However, like Dido he dreams of power without responsibility, control without sacrifice (a dream apparently embodied in the romance world of *Tamburlaine* until completely deflated by the attendant ironies). Yet for Faustus the shortcut to omnipotence can only be achieved (and then only as an illusion) by postponing, not evading, the ultimate sacrifice.

Like Dido and Tamburlaine, Faustus expresses his fantasies of absolute control through images of enclosure: "I'll have them [the conjured spirits] wall all Germany with brass / And make swift Rhine circle fair Wittenberg" (1.1.90–91). As Snow points out, "the formula by which [Faustus] characteristically aspires is not even 'I will' or 'I want' but 'I'll have . . . I'll have . . . I'll have,' so anxious is he to feel himself a containing self rather than merely the voice of a nameless emptiness or an impersonal rush to the void."[34] Necromancy itself is described by the Bad Angel metaphorically as a kind of treasure chest, which will place the entire created universe in Faustus's controlling hands: "Go forward, Faustus, in that famous art / Wherein all nature's treasury is contained" (1.1.76–77). Yet to achieve any of this, Faustus must ironically enclose *himself* within the conjurer's circle, to protect him from the power of the devils he is supposedly controlling. He thus becomes trapped by his own unnatural desires. In his narcissistic dilemma, Marlowe's Faustus demonstrates a remarkable conflict of assertive and passive impulses. The same man who can state commandingly, "How pliant is this Mephistopheles, / Full of obedience and humility!" (1.3.30–31) also relies subserviently on the devil's protection: "When Mephistopheles shall stand by me, / What power can hurt thee, Faustus? Thou art safe; / Cast no more doubts" (2.1.24–26). The same man who aspires to be "great emperor of the world" (1.3.106)—significantly *"by"* Mephistopheles, through the devil's power—later seems satisfied with being entertainer and servant to the emperor of Germany and the duke of Vanholt. He needs not only to control and command, but also to be subservient, almost (with respect to Mephistopheles) coddled.

This conflict between self-assertion and self-surrender is first apparent in Faustus's exclamation to Valdes and Cornelius: "'Tis magic, magic, that hath ravished me" (1.1.112). Faustus paradoxically sees his instrument of power, the thing he is to control, as taking over or controlling him. The erotic suggestion in "ravished" raises the question of the sexual nature of the doctor's desires, and several critics have remarked on the erotic energy that surfaces at various moments in the play. Constance Kuriyama argues that *Doctor Faustus* "amounts to a reluctant step on Marlowe's part toward confronting his own homosexuality, in its original form of 'feminine' weakness and submission, which Marlowe desperately strove to deny in *Tamburlaine*."[35] Another critic who has explored the sexual meaning of the play, Kay Stockholder, believes that while "homosexual elements are strong in the play . . . the strongest struggle depicted is toward the heterosexual."[36] Certainly any sexual interpretation of *Doctor Faustus* must be conducted with caution since the issue is complicated and the text, as Kuriyama points out, relatively "thin."[37] While interpretation of sexual imagery remains tentative, there is evidence to show that the play exhibits the same fear of sexual surrender that we have observed in *Tamburlaine*, and this fear is to an extent, as in the earlier play, a fear of heterosexual involvement. At the same time there is evidence of a growing realization that the homosexual longing recognized earlier only in a Neoplatonic sense will begin to demand physical expression as well. This realization involves a certain amount of repugnance, resistance, and fear on Marlowe's part, again carrying with it a sense of manly failure. It is worth noting here, as Alan Bray points out, that sodomy was linked in the popular imagination of the Renaissance with sorcery and heresy,[38] and sorcerers were unmanly men who, as Blackburn points out, failed to control and command demons but instead, like witches, prayed and sacrificed to them.[39] Such mythologizing may have, on a latent level, encouraged Marlowe's identification with the historical Faustus. Bray also makes clear that homosexuality in the Renaissance existed "outside the ordered world of Creation"; "it was not a sexuality in its own right, but existed as a potential for confusion and disorder in one undivided sexuality";[40] it was hence completely *unnatural*. Marlowe had to contend with this ideology that insisted on the unnaturalness of homosexual response. I wish to clarify here that I use the terms natural/ unnatural in this discussion as a reflection of culturally determined beliefs, and not because I endorse then as constituting an essential truth about human sexuality.

Faustus's relationship with the devils, especially Mephistopheles, carries homoerotic overtones. Levin remarks that "Faustus has in Mephostophilis an alter ego who is both a demon and a Damon. The man has an extraordinary affection for the spirit, the spirit a mysterious attraction to the man."[41] Kuriyama, though eventually consenting that "Levin's observation seems basically sound," initially objects that his "assertion lends itself admirably to scholarly punning, but unfortunately there is little or no direct evidence to support it. . . . The only demonstrable interest Mephostophilis has in Faustus is a passion for getting and keeping his soul, while Faustus regards Mephostophilis primarily as a servant."[42] While admitting the paucity of textual evidence, we must still recognize in Faustus's lines, "Had I as many souls as there be stars, / I'd give them all for Mephistopheles" (1.3.104–5), an emotional fervor incongruous with an ordinary master-servant relationship; likewise in Mephistopheles' remark, "O, what will not I do to obtain his soul!" (2.1.73), a similar fervor indicating more than just a mercenary interest (Mephistopheles, Devil of the Month, Highest Number of Souls Obtained).

Kuriyama does, however, rightly claim that the "shadowy nether world into which Faustus plunges . . . is characterized by persistent . . . innuendos of sexual ambiguity, first suggested by

Valdes in his reference to the 'serviceable' spirits' capacity for shape shifting":[43]

> As Indian Moors obey their Spanish lords,
> So shall the subjects of every element
> Be always serviceable to us three.
> Like lions shall they guard us when we please,
> Like Almaine rutters with their horsemen's staves
> Or Lapland giants, trotting by our sides;
> Sometimes like women, or unwedded maids,
> Shadowing more beauty in their airy brows
> Than in the white breasts of the Queen of Love.
>
> (1.1.123–31)

Like Mephistopheles, these "subjects" or spirits will be serviceable or pliant, but also perform a protective function by standing by with phallic staves (cf. "When Mephistopheles shall stand by me, / What power can hurt me?"), as if the magicians would experience both active and passive sexual roles. As with Mephistopheles, the "protective" function of the spirits seems to suggest a sexually aggressive one, and homosexual involvement is linked to the fantasy of simultaneous control and surrender. The emphasis on the beauty of the spirits' "airy brows" in preference to "the white breasts of the Queen of Love" also suggests a certain disinclination to heterosexual involvement on the part of Faustus's "dearest friends" (1.1.67), Valdes and Cornelius.

A suggestion of homosexual attraction finds expression in the play when Faustus asks Mephistopheles for a wife. Mephistopheles first attempts to dissuade Faustus, and, when the hero persists in his request, brings onstage a "Devil *dressed like a woman, with fireworks*":

> *Mephistopheles.* Tell, Faustus, how dost thou like thy wife?
> *Faustus.* A plague on her for a hot whore!
> *Mephistopheles.* Tut, Faustus, marriage is but a ceremonial toy. If thou lovest me, think no more of it.
>
> (2.1.152–55)

In the *Damnable Life* Mephistopheles' refusal to comply with Faustus's request is clearly due to the fact that marriage is a sacrament:

> Hast not thou (quoth *Mephostophiles*) sworne thy selfe an enemy to God and all creatures? To this I answere thee, thou canst not marry;

thou canst not serve two masters, God, and my Prince: for wedlock is a chiefe institution ordained of God, and that hast thou promised to defie, as we doe all, and that hast thou also done.[44]

While this explanation is sometimes offered by editors of the play, Marlowe pointedly leaves it out, suggesting instead that Mephistopheles somehow takes Faustus's request as a personal affront: "if thou lovest me, think no more of it." Mephistopheles also seems to play on Faustus's fears of heterosexual involvement. Stockholder suggests that the appearance of the "hot whore" is a literalization of Faustus's own sexual fears: "as he approaches his desire for forbidden sensuality he associates it with the familial and domestic in asking for a wife, but an approach to a fulfillment of his embattled desire appears to him in hideous and threatening images from which he again retreats."[45] It is true that Mephistopheles does willingly offer Faustus the "fairest courtesans," but he describes them in images that "are remote and aestheticized"[46] and that culminate with ideal beauty expressed in terms of the male form:

> I'll cull thee out the fairest courtesans
> And bring them ev'ry morning to thy bed.
> She whom thine eye shall like, thy heart shall have,
> Be she as chaste as was Penelope,
> As wise as Saba, or as beautiful
> As was bright Lucifer before his fall.

> (2.1.156–61)

We might also expect these courtesans would simply be more disguised spirits (for the same reasons Greg argues Helen of Troy being one)[47] and thus, with the general tendency to see the devils as masculine, Mephistopheles' apparent encouragement of heterosexual behavior is certainly lacking in conviction. But it is also interesting to observe that before his fall Lucifer was an almost feminized *object* of beauty, fitting for the climactic entry in a list of courtesans, and not the agent (or sexual predator) he has since become.

The resistance to heterosexual contact on the part of Faustus and the diabolical world is highlighted in other ways as well. The most remarkable instance is the B-text version (although Keefer retains a close version of it in his A-text edition) of the speech by Pride during the procession of the Seven Deadly Sins:

I am Pride. I disdain to have any parents. I am like to Ovid's flea: I can creep into every corner of a wench. Sometimes like a periwig I sit upon her brow; next, like a necklace I hang about her neck; then, like a fan of feathers I kiss her, and then, turning myself to a wrought smock, do what I list. But fie, what a smell is here! I'll not speak another word more for a king's ransom, unless the ground be perfumed and covered with a cloth of arras. (2.3.111–18)

One is tempted to read this speech as a reference to Faustus's own psychosexual development. His pride is compensatory for the lack of nurturing received as a child[48] ("I disdain to have any parents"). Consequently he has never matured enough to learn self-discipline ("I . . . do what I list") or achieved sufficient self-cohesion to be able to accept sexual surrender without fear, for the "image that suggests the fulfillment of a [heterosexual] sex act . . . brings with it disgust."[49] There is thus a failure, to borrow Snow's terms, to ground or stabilize oneself in physical existence, which instead must be denied or disguised ("perfumed and covered with a cloth of arras"). Pride's speech does in fact sound like a response to an exchange that occurs in Greene's *Friar Bacon and Friar Bungay*[50] between Prince Edward and his fool, Rafe:

> *Rafe.* . . . [Bacon] shall make thee [transform you into] either a silken purse, full of gold, or else a fine wrought smock.
> *Edw.* But how shall I have the maid?
> *Rafe.* Marry, sirrah, if thou beest a silken purse full of gold, then on Sundays she'll hang thee by her side, and you must not say a word. Now sir, when she comes into a great press of people, for fear of the cutpurse, on a sudden she'll swap thee into her plackerd [placket, slit at the top of a skirt or petticoat]; then, sirrah, being there, you may plead for yourself . . .
> *Edw.* But how if I be a wrought smock?
> *Rafe.* Then she'll put thee into her chest and lay thee into lavender, and upon some good day she'll put thee on, and at night when you go to bed, then being turned from a smock to a man, you may make up the match. (1.101–16)[51]

In this exchange Rafe serves to expose Edward's strong (if in the context of later developments morally questionable) attraction for Margaret; there is certainly no evidence of revulsion. The flea image in Pride's speech occurs earlier when Robin remarks: "No, no, sir. If you turn me into anything, let it be in the likeness of a little, pretty, frisking flea, that I may be here and there and everywhere. O, I'll tickle the pretty wenches' plackets! I'll be amongst them, i'faith!" (1.4.64–67). Similarly strong heterosexual impulses, with no sense of revulsion, are expressed later when Robin exclaims:

> O, this is admirable! Here I ha' stol'n one of Doctor Faustus' conjuring books, and, i'faith, I mean to search some circles for my own use. Now will I make all the maidens in our parish dance at my pleasure stark naked before me, and so by that means I shall see more than ere I felt or saw yet. (2.2.1–6)

It seems that away from the "shadowy, nether world" of Faustus and the devils, life goes on, if not very admirably or heroically, rather sanely and predictably. This predictability, this refusal to give in to the torturing sexual ambiguities of the supernatural world, results in a memorable moment of comic deflation as the matter-of-fact meets the diabolical. After his first encounter with the devils, Robin exclaims: "What, are they gone? A vengeance on them! They have vile long nails. There was a he devil and a she devil. I'll tell you how you shall know them: all he devils has horns, and all she devils has clefts and cloven feet" (1.4.54–57). Robin thus insists on compartmentalizing and delineating the unknown according to the standards or terms of reference he believes to be normal and natural.

Faustus, on the other hand, never escapes the sexual ambiguity of the supernatural world. After the Old Man's admonition and Mephostophilis' threat to tear him to pieces if he repents, Faustus asks the devil:

> One thing, good servant, let me crave of thee
> To glut the longing of my heart's desire:
> That I may have unto my paramour
> That heavenly Helen which I saw of late,
> Whose sweet embracings may extinguish clean
> Those thoughts that do dissuade me from my vow,
> And keep mine oath I made to Lucifer.
>
> (5.1.82–88)

Faustus's request places Helen in the role of sexual surrogate between him and Lucifer; intercourse with Helen is Faustus's way of committing himself—body and soul—to the lord of hell. Presumably Faustus knows (though apparently he chooses to repress the awareness) that he will be copulating with a "spirit" or devil. The doctor's explanation to the Emperor concerning the nature of these conjured apparitions is very clear:

> it is not in my ability to present before your eyes the true substantial bodies of those two deceased princes, which long since are consumed to dust.

But such spirits as can lively resemble Alexander and his paramour, shall appear before your Grace in that manner that they best lived in, in their most flourishing estate—which I doubt not shall sufficiently content your Imperiall Majesty. (4.1.46–57)

Thus when Helen reappears and Faustus exclaims, "Was this the face that launched a thousand ships / And burnt the topless towers of Ilium" (5.1.91–92), he should realize that the utterance is ironically not a rhetorical question praising Helen's beauty but a question of fact whose answer is definitely no. The sexual ambiguity and confusion reach their height at the climax of the speech:

> Brighter art thou than flaming Jupiter
> When he appeared to hapless Semele,
> More lovely than the monarch of the sky
> In wanton Arethusa's azured arms;
> And none but thou shalt be my paramour.
>
> (5.1.106–10)

As critics have observed, it is Helen, not Faustus, who is equated with the masculine gods; Faustus's sexual role therefore parallels that of Semele and Arethusa. In the case of the hapless Semele being burned up in Jupiter's arms, the image foreshadows Faustus's destruction by a seemingly wrathful God and a consuming Lucifer, who become conflated in his final nightmare vision: "My God, my God, look not so fierce on me! / Enter [Lucifer, Mephistopheles, and other] Devils" (5.2.120 and S.D.). The meaning of the Arethusa allusion is more elusive. Whether the "monarch of the sky" means Apollo as god of the sun or Jupiter as god of the sky, there is no myth concerning a liaison between either of these gods and the nymph Arethusa. Particularly surprising is the adjective "wanton," for the mythical Arethusa is notable for her attempts to flee her lover Alpheus and for her prayers to Artemis to preserve her chastity. Marlowe's Arethusa, in contrast, seems almost sexually aggressive (the god is in her arms, not vice versa).[52] The final images in Faustus's speech thus suggest simultaneous fear of sexual surrender (Faustus-Semele) as well as a desire for such release (Faustus-Arethusa).

Faustus is indeed ravished by his own magic. The culmination of his nightmare soliloquy at midnight seems in fact his final rape. Snow compares this last speech to the earlier one of solicitation (the blasphemous "Come, Mephistopheles, / And bring glad tidings from great Lucifer"),[53] and remarks that the "same erotic energy charges both utterances. . . . the later one is the genuine

consummation of the earlier one as well as its ironical inversion."[54] The climax of the speech does seem to communicate a
strong orgasmic quality:

> My God, my God, look not so fierce on me!
> Adders and serpents, let me breathe a while!
> Ugly hell, gape not. Come not, Lucifer!
> I'll burn my books. Ah, Mephistopheles!
>
> (5.2.120–23)

Wilbur Sanders remarks that "the irreducible love-hate that Faustus bears toward both God and Lucifer becomes that cry of erotic
self-surrender *and* horrified revulsion as he yields to the embrace
of his demon lover."[55] What needs to be more closely observed is
that the relegation of Faustus to the passive feminine position
vis-à-vis both God and the devils underlines again the threat to
manliness inherent in the supernatural generally. The "glad tidings" speech may parody the announcement of Christ's conception and birth, but even without the ironic inversion the parallel
underlines that the true reception of Christ in the soul is a "feminine" act of self-surrender. Lyndal Roper observes that Luther
"abuses Catholic clergy as hellish prostitutes and brides of the
Devil. In wonderfully energetic invective he sets them against the
true Brides of Christ as whores who do not obey, 'an apostate,
erring, married whore, a house-whore, a bed-whore, a key-
whore,' metaphors which convey how their sexual promiscuity
undermines household order."[56] However, ironically implicit in
Luther's invective is the assertion that the Protestant soul is a
"good whore," an obedient wife of Christ.

Faustus's involvement with the devils suggests his own failure
to believe in his natural self—in a (Renaissance) sexual sense, to
establish a stable, manly (heterosexual) identity. Ironically, Faustus could well profit from the advice he offers Mephistopheles:

> What, is great Mephistopheles so passionate
> For being deprivèd of the joys of heaven?
> Learn thou of Faustus manly fortitude,
> And scorn those joys thou never shalt possess.
>
> (1.3.85–88)

The dream of heaven interferes with the individual's attempts to
assert "manliness" or human cohesiveness, with its recognition
of sexual difference. This dissatisfaction with difference or distinc-

tiveness, the inability to rely on one's own integrity, is essentially the source of Mephistopheles' torment:

> Think'st thou that I, who saw the face of God
> And tasted the eternal joys of heaven,
> Am not tormented with ten thousand hells
> In being deprived of everlasting bliss?
> O Faustus, leave these frivolous demands,
> Which strike a terror to my fainting soul!
>
> (1.3.79–84)

God and Lucifer thus figure in homoerotic terms since the desire for these deities stems from the individual male's failure to assert his "manliness," to function as a source rather than a receptor of power, to accept the heroic burden of being a man in the world.

I have argued that Faustus's involvement with necromancy symbolizes his failure to believe in himself in terms of his sexual identity; as well it can be seen in more general terms as representing his entire failure of imaginative response to human experience. The false power of the play—magic—may thus be seen as a symbol of imagination,[57] and *Doctor Faustus* as much as *Tamburlaine* becomes a tragedy about the failure of human imagining. This failure arises in part from an excessive confidence in words, as if the poetic imagination gives one direct access to worldly power. As mentioned in the introduction, William Blackburn links Faustus's fantasy of verbal control to Pico's combination of Hermetic magic with practical cabalism, which involves "tapping the magical power of Hebrew, a language of supreme efficacy in magic because, according to scriptures, God created the world by speaking."[58] Blackburn suggests that Faustus's "ignorance of magic is a central metaphor in the play because . . . it is really an ignorance of the proper way to use language."[59] One of the central ironies of the play is that "Faustus has difficulty in distinguishing between things and his verbal descriptions of those things."[60] Thus Faustus can boast: "Are not thy bills hung up as monuments, / Whereby whole cities have escap'd the plague / And thousand desp'rate maladies been eased?" (1.1.20–22). Yet what "Faustus *says* is that his prescriptions ('bills') have in themselves the power to ward off disease, and so these lines obliquely assert the magician's confidence in his language—a confidence which is essential to his self-deception."[61]

We thus have a situation similar to *Tamburlaine*, where the word can be taken for the object or the deed, and one can control and create as easily as speaking. But of course Faustus, as Blackburn remarks, is deceived. The illusion of power gradually evaporates, and the general shrinking or constriction occurs:[62] Faustus goes from the *primum mobile* to the court of the pope, to the court of the German emperor, to the house of the duke of Vanholt, to his study, and finally to "hell"—which is in essence his own tortured mind. Yet I must part company with Blackburn when he remarks: "Preferring the vain books of Lucifer to the Bible is one instance of [Faustus's] preference for falsehood; it is also characteristic of his attempt to substitute a world of words for the real world."[63] The play draws a parallel, rather than a contrast, between divine and necromantic "scripture" by attacking the belief that words themselves—a magical utterance, a prayer, a pure act of poetic imagination—are so powerful that they can act as a substitute for natural human development.

The exploration of imagination is not limited to the power of words only, but is extended to the effect of artistic or dramatic presentations in general. As an instance of artistic production aiding ideological control, Simon Shepherd quotes one of Nashe's arguments for utility in theatrical pleasure: "it is very expedient they ['corrupt excrements' such as soldiers in peacetime] have some light toys to busy their heads withal cast before them as bones to gnaw upon, which may keep them from having leisure to intermeddle with higher matters."[64] Shepherd believes Marlowe's play explores the ideological use of shows as "controlling distractions":[65] for example, the dance of devils with which Mephistopheles cheers up Faustus when he entertains doubts about signing away his soul, and the pageant of the Seven Deadly Sins that the Infernal Trinity bring before Faustus after he has called on Christ. This pageant "is arranged by devils to distract Faustus and limit the questions he asks. The familiarity of the contents of the show, the old Morality-style performance, makes it less interesting in itself than the part it plays in the narrative," thus "foreground[ing Faustus's] response."[66] Shepherd thus emphasizes the audience's need to recognize the potential power of production—"The point of danger is not in the morality that is shown but in the power that does the showing."[67] However, Marlowe's emphasis may not be so much on the political uses of artistic presentations as on the individual's failure to control his or her own responses. The danger really arises from Faustus's willingness to let the pleasures of imagination ultimately blind him to his true circumstances and the consequences of his actions, as if art were a surrogate for experience and not in various ways a mirror of the real world. In his process of manly self-fashioning, Faustus does indeed have to control the appetites and passions exhibited (and trivialized) in this pageant. The original catalyst for the pageant was his calling on Christ, which was in essence an admission of a failure of manliness, discipline, and self-control. He in effect becomes no better than the "corrupt excrements" that need to be controlled and distracted by the theater.

The play nevertheless remains haunting in its exploration of the uses and abuses of imagination, for it is not always easy to make a clear moral distinction between the two. An interesting juxtaposition of creative and indulgent uses of imagination involves the two conjurations of Helen. The first occurs on the heels of Wagner's comment about the "belly-cheer" (5.1.6) of Faustus and the students, which certainly implies overindulgence. Nevertheless, what follows seems remarkably restrained, ordered, and calm:

Enter Faustus *with two or three* Scholars [*and* Mephistopheles].

First Scholar. Master Doctor Faustus, since our conference about fair ladies—which was the beautifull'st in all the world—we have determined with ourselves that Helen of Greece was the admirablest lady
   that ever lived. Therefore, Master Doctor, if you will do us that favour
   as to let us see *that peerless dame of Greece, whom all the world admires
   for majesty,* we should think ourselves much beholding unto you.

   Faustus. Gentlemen,
   For that I know your friendship is unfeigned,
   And Faustus' custom is not to deny
   The just requests of those that wish him well,
   You shall behold *that peerless dame of Greece* . . .
      . . . .

   Music sounds. [Mephistopheles *returns,*] *and* Helen *passeth over the
   stage.*
   Second Scholar. Too simple is my wit to tell her praise,
   Whom all the world admires for majesty.
   Third Scholar. No marvel though the angry Greeks pursued
   With ten years' war the rape of such a queen,
   Whose heavenly beauty passeth all compare.
   First Scholar. Since we have seen the pride of nature's works
   And only paragon of excellence,
   Let us depart; and for this glorious deed
   Happy and blest be Faustus evermore.
                                   (5.1.9–34, my emphasis)

To explain the repetition of phrases (indicated by italics), Jump in the original Revels edition suggested that "Perhaps this prose speech was inserted after the completion of the verse speeches which follow it."[68] Considering the uncertain nature of the text, this may well be the case; however, it is tempting to see the repetition as deliberate, so that both the artistic promise or intention and the audience response directly mirror or fulfill the initial request for an artistic experience. I am aware that there is a strong critical tendency to view both appearances of Helen as essentially negative moments. Max Bluestone, for example, comments:

> Helen "passeth over the stage" in her two appearances, and if Allardyce Nicoll is correct ["Passing over the Stage," *Shakespeare Survey* 12 (1959): 47–55], she passes from the theater yard up to the platform and back down to the yard. Hell, in short, begins to encroach upon the theater itself, for if Helen is a succuba, as Greg suggests, she begins and ends her progress in hell.[69]

Yet, according to B-text stage directions, during the first appearance of Helen, Mephistopheles as a kind of muse figure, a metaphor of Faustus's artistic control, brings up the perfect image (from the "hell" of the artist's unconscious) for the delight of Faustus's audience. The negative reminder in the Third Scholar's remark, "No marvel though the angry Greeks pursu'd / With ten years' war the rape of such a queen," seems *contained* by the image itself and by their appreciation of its beauty: " . . . such a queen, / Whose heavenly beauty passeth all compare." Thus art can distance the audience from life's suffering in a positive way. It is, however, possible to argue that the scene involves a voyeuristic evasion in which the Scholars use Faustus's art to shield them from the world's harsh realities. As Faustus's kind, innocuous, and rather sexless friends, the Scholars may be seen as his pre-Oedipal companions who can only quietly wonder at the sexual conflicts of Troy. Nevertheless, they seem in no way harmed by this particular act of necromancy; nor does their enjoyment of it seem sinful or wrong. It has been the simplest of artistic acts— the satisfaction of an aesthetic longing—and in this light the first Scholar's final words are not as ironic as they may first appear:

> Since we have seen the pride of nature's works
> And only paragon of excellence,
> Let us depart, and for this glorious deed
> Happy and blest be Faustus evermore.
>
> (33–36)

They have, in a sense, seen the pride of nature's work—a perfect mirror of it, at any rate. The deed is thus glorious. And if, quite clearly, Faustus will not be happy forevermore, it is not because he has offended God but because he proves unable to maintain control over his own imaginative resources; he has become "blest" or injured within his own mind.

During the second appearance of Helen (again according to the B-text stage directions), Mephistopheles no longer appears as controlling muse. Faustus becomes completely enthralled—ravished—by his own creation. The image for him is no longer simply a mirror of nature but the "real thing" with which he becomes actively involved—so completely, in fact, that certain orthodox interpreters (Greg, for one) have taken this as the point of no return with respect to the doctor's hope of salvation. There is certainly a sense that Faustus crosses a line at this point, but the crisis (at least in the A-text) seems precipitated rather than prevented by the intervention of the Old Man, who enters immediately after the Scholars have praised Faustus's first conjuration of Helen. The Old Man's initial speech constitutes one of the most radical differences between the A-text and the B-text. In the A-text the Old Man states:

> Ah, Doctor Faustus, that I might prevail
> To guide thy steps unto the way of life,
> By which sweet path thou mayst attain the goal
> That shall conduct thee to celestial rest!
> Break heart, drop blood, and mingle it with tears—
> Tears falling from repentant heaviness
> Of thy most vile and loathsome filthiness,
> The stench whereof corrupts the inward soul
> With such flagitious crimes of heinous sins
> As no commiseration may expel
> But mercy, Faustus, of thy Saviour sweet,
> Whose blood alone must wash away thy guilt.
>
> (5.1.36–47)

Faustus's response to this scathing admonition is, perhaps not surprisingly, to want to "despair and die." For this desire Mephistopheles stands obligingly by with a dagger, almost as if the Old Man and the devil are in fact working together for Faustus's destruction. The terms the Old Man uses—"vile and loathsome filthiness," "the stench whereof corrupts"—seem particularly harsh after the hospitality and pleasure Faustus has just offered the Scholars. Moreover, the peculiar grammatical postponement of the final goal of the heavenly path—"To guide thy steps unto the way of life [ah, there we are], / By which sweet path [oh no, we have further to go] thou mayst attain the goal [ah, now we're there], / That shall conduct thee [wrong again, we still have to keep going] to celestial rest!"—creates an even stronger sense of restless searching than the Good Angel's admonition to "Read, read the scriptures."

In contrast, the speech from the B-text seems warm and caring:

> O gentle Faustus, leave this damnèd art,
> This magic, that will charm thy soul to hell
> And quite bereave thee of salvation!
> Though thou hast now offended like a man,
> Do not persever in it like a devil.
> Yet, yet thou hast an amiable soul,
> If sin by custom grow not into nature.
> Then, Faustus, will repentance come too late;
> Then thou art banish'd from the sight of heaven.
> No mortal can express the pains of hell.
> It may be this my exhortation
> Seems harsh and all unpleasant. Let it not,
> For, gentle son, I speak it not in wrath
> Or envy of thee, but in tender love
> And pity of thy future misery;
> And so have hope that this my kind rebuke,
> Checking thy body, may amend thy soul.
>
> (5.1.35–51)

The speech should give pause to anyone who wishes simply to ignore the B-text, for poetically it is masterful and subtle, eminently worthy of Marlowe, and seems almost a revision of the harshness of the A-text Old Man. Keefer, citing the *Confessions*, finds this speech "strongly Augustinian in tone,"[70] since Augustine warns of the perverse act of will leading to desire, then to custom, and finally to necessity. While it is perhaps unsettling that such a warning comes after nearly all of the four and twenty years have been used up, and the "fatal time draws to a final end" (B-text 4.4.24), what is most striking in the speech is the love expressed to the man who throughout the play can never believe that God could love him: "For gentle son, I speak it not in wrath / Or envy of thee, but in tender love." Gentle son, tender love: the B-text Old Man, however briefly, approaches the idealized self-object, the divine father, that the emotional world of the play is so desperately searching for.

Nevertheless, whichever initial speech is chosen, Marlowe has included a devastating biblical irony in the Old Man's second speech, which occurs in both A and B:

> Ah, stay, good Faustus, stay thy desperate steps!
> I see an angel hovers o'er thy head,
> And with a vial full of precious grace
> Offers to pour the same into thy soul.
> Then call for mercy and avoid despair.
>
> (53–57)

As Bevington and Rasmussen point out, "images of vials in [Revelations] are instruments of divine vengeance, as at xvi.1: 'And I heard a great voice out of the temple, saying to the seven angels, "Go your ways, and pour out the vials of the wrath of God upon the earth."'"[71] As usual in the play, spiritual salvation and damnation are conflated. Faustus reacts by taking refuge in his own disturbed imagination. His acceptance of Helen as a lover reveals that he is no longer capable of distinguishing illusion from reality, or that he no longer believes reality worth coming to terms with. This desperate escape into imagination has in fact been adumbrated earlier in the play. When he has considered repenting in act 2 (that is, has failed as an independent man), he has heard "fearful echoes" in his ears speaking of damnation; he admits he is tempted

> . . . to dispatch myself;
> And long ere this I should have slain myself
> Had not sweet pleasure conquered deep despair.
> Have not I made blind Homer sing to me
> Of Alexander's love and Oenone's death?
> And hath not he that built the walls of Thebes
> With ravishing sound of his melodious harp
> Made music with my Mephistopheles?
>
> (2.3.23–30)

Here again the sufferings of life, and of sexual maturity, alluded to—heartbreak, betrayal, the Trojan war—are distanced by the beauty of art, which fulfills the fantasy of establishing a strong and protected haven for the self (the walls of Thebes) through no effort other than the deployment of artistic imagining.

Yet Faustus pays a horrible price for his retreat from reality. With respect to the increasing constriction mentioned earlier, it is interesting to note that Faustus regresses from Icarian flights of imagination to becoming himself a kind of restricted artifact, a character trapped in an old-fashioned morality. This is perhaps the point of the final appearance of the Good and Bad Angels in the B-text, in which the throne of heaven descends and the hell-mouth is discovered; here the behavior of the Good Angel is as vindicative and unattractive as the Bad Angel's. In spite of the overt moralizing and the crude stage spectacle here, the poetry, with its emphasis on gluttony, is quite consistent with the "oral-narcissistic dilemma"[72] of Marlowe's play, and thus the scene is conceivably Marlovian. The description of hell is in fact intensely frightening, and would have been even more so to a contemporary audience.

But how can a Faustus victimized, trapped, and tortured by the eschatological terrors of his culture and his age be regarded as a great tragic hero? Is it because we, seeking diversion from our own mundane lives, seeking pleasure in danger, have no qualms in identifying with a man who no longer believes reality worth coming to terms with? Marlowe implies in the prologue that, as in *Tamburlaine*, some kind of divided response is possible, for the Chorus remarks:

> Only this, gentlemen: we must perform
> The form of Faustus's fortunes, good or bad.
> To patient judgements we appeal our plaud. . . .
>
> (7–9)

But how can Faustus's fortunes, or at least the form of them, be construed as possibly good? Barber believes that Marlowe "dramatizes blasphemy as a heroic endeavour," and that, in this new situation, "blasphemy can be 'good or bad.'"[73] Faustus may attempt to extend the range of human endeavor and accomplishment, but what kind of anagnorisis, or recognition, does Faustus gain through his suffering? Snow argues that Faustus is "burdened with his conceit of self as the Duchess with her child (the last soliloquy his final labour)" and that he has "to engender upon himself, through consciousness, what the Robins and Wagners and Emperors and Horsecoursers of the world are prereflectively rooted in [a sound identity]: and thus fated (or chosen) to confront the ontological void in which ordinary experience is so imperturbably suspended."[74]

However, it has been traditionally argued that the horseplay of the clowns serves as a comic parody of Faustus's own degeneracy—that is, a mirror of Faustus's own situation, minus the heroism—and I think it is true that, in spite of his failure at self-fashioning, Faustus always compares favorably, somehow, with the play's other characters. Is it simply because he is gifted, so that the play is the tragedy of a genius unable to fit in with his less remarkable, more sane, fellow men and women? It is perhaps the tragedy of the artist, the tragedy (as so many suggest) of Marlowe himself. "Too simple is my wit to tell her praise," says the second Scholar after Helen passes over the stage; he has enjoyed the vision, thank-you-very-much, but it takes a greater mind, a more sensitized one, a more tortured one, to *produce* it—to actually succeed in telling her praise: "Was this the face that launched a thousand ships?" Or perhaps it is the tragedy of the homosexual (again the tragedy of Marlowe himself) whose strongest desires do not lead naturally to the psychologically reinforcing bond of marriage and the duties of child rearing (with the concomitant challenges and rewards), but instead to a life where every romantic attraction is necessarily a self-excluding act of social and moral defiance, an existence that culminates in a final nightmare of attraction and repulsion, desire and despair.

Yet neither of these suggestions explains why there is such a strong sense of Everyman about Faustus, how the character is drawn with enough specificity to communicate extraordinary aspiration but with enough vagueness to leave us feeling the spirit of the man is somehow universal. We perhaps identify most strongly with Faustus in the prose scene with the Scholars near the end of the play:

> Ah, gentlemen, hear me with patience, and tremble not at my speeches. Though my heart pants and quivers to remember that I have been a student here these thirty years, O, would I had never seen Wittenberg, never read book! And what wonders I have done, all Germany can witness, yea, all the world, for which Faustus hath lost both Germany and the world, yea, heaven itself—heaven, the seat of God, the throne of the blessed, the kingdom of joy—and must remain in hell for ever! Hell, ah, hell for ever! Sweet friends, what shall become of Faustus, being in hell for ever? (5.2.17–27)

Did Marlowe in his writing ever come closer to the heart of a man? (Especially, I think, in the way Faustus still clings to a sense of personal pride—"and what wonders I have done all Germany can witness, yea, all the world"—in the midst of his sorrow and despair.) There is in this scene, in spite of Faustus's concern for his future state, a strong nostalgic sense, a retrospective longing for lost innocence. Faustus's relation with the Scholars seems, in its exceptional tenderness, almost a regressive attempt to regain the merely latent sexuality that we observed between Tamburlaine and his men early in that hero's career. It is the desire to escape the demands of adulthood, to get back to when sexual difference (or sameness) made no difference, to recapture the world of childhood friends, to regain Eden before the fall; this perhaps explains the reference to Eden and the serpent ("The serpent that tempted Eve may be saved, but not Faustus" [16]). It is a desire we may condemn as puerile, but surely one we all understand. Faustus's terror of hell at this point seems to be less a fear of torment than a dread of being *alone,* of being permanently removed from all sources of true love or affection, separated from his "sweet friends." Yet Faustus demonstrates true love and affection himself in his concern for his friends: "Gentlemen, away, lest you perish with me! . . . Talk not of me, but save yourselves and depart" (49–52). His concern for them is thus perhaps not regressive at all, but actually transcends the sexual mercinariness of human desire by becoming truly selfless. On the other hand, Faustus in his eagerness almost seems to want to *get rid of* the Scholars. Like Juliet, he realizes that his dismal scene he needs must act alone, but perhaps as well he cannot bear to have the Scholars, in their innocence, observe the final consummation of his passions. Shame or fear, as much as altruism, seem to motivate him at this moment.

Nevertheless, the nightmare consummation signifies more than Faustus's personal failure to resolve inner conflicts; the scene moves us to the extent that we emotionally participate in the play's disavowal of religious faith. The Scholars' glib assurances about God's mercy are seriously undercut when the third pipes up bravely, "God will strengthen me. I will stay with Faustus," and the first immediately corrects him: "Tempt not God, sweet friend; but let us into the next room and there pray for him" (53–57). No one is willing to bet on what God is really up to in the world of this play, and Faustus must be forgiven if the first part of his reply is tinged with irony: "Ay, pray for me, pray for me! And what noise soever ye hear, come not unto me, for nothing can rescue me" (58–59). While the play does not, I believe, portray God as an actively malevolent force conspiring against the hero or predetermining his damnation, *Doctor Faustus* remains a strong indictment against the deity, by emphasizing his inability to aid his creatures. The story is, as Waldock says of the Genesis story of the Fall, a bad one for God, but perhaps only in the sense that *all* stories are bad ones for God, because all narratives describe the experience of the human personality crawling through the catastrophic void between creation and reconciliation. What makes *Faustus* unique as bad press theologically is that it communicates strongly, from a human perspective, the absurdity of grace, which, as it must come unsolicited, seems to come least to those who need it most. As Snow suggests, the Robins and Wagners and Dukes and Duchesses of the world enjoy a kind of natural grace[75] that constantly eludes Faustus. To him that hath shall be given; but conversely, the more you get into trouble, the more you get into trouble. For Faustus the act of prayer seems to constitute, or signify, the desperation that leads to personal destruction. In the end there is no external power who can step in to resolve internal conflicts.

It is, I believe, the play's radical humanism that establishes it most clearly as subversive in its historical context. Even the striking conflation of heavenly and hellish powers that I have pointed out does have literary precedence in book 1 of Spenser's *Faerie Queene*, which relentlessly and painfully explores the paradoxes of Protestant theology —that the salvation of the human self is the destruction of the human self, that from a human perspective it is difficult to tell the difference between God's burning wrath and the operation of evil, as if God and the devil (Redcrosse's dragon) were ultimately the same, and metaphysical good and evil impossible to tell apart. Spenser's influence on Marlowe is in fact much more substantial than has yet been examined. But Marlowe is far more willing to interrogate the worldview that Spenser so brilliantly and thoroughly analyzes from a more conservative perspective. The notorious plagiarism in *Tamburlaine* of Spenser's description of Arthur (*Tamburlaine* part 2 4.4.119–24; *The Faerie Queene* 1.7.32) seems a deliberate parody of the "graceful" manifestation of Arthur's military power. Marlowe is quick to perceive the irony of physical or material assertiveness under the guise of religious or ideological "salvation." Acts of power in Marlowe seem always to preclude true human tenderness and love, and Marlowe lacks Spenser's ultimate vision of a harmonious relation of the orders of nature and grace, in part because his most natural physical responses were inescapably "unnatural" in his historical context.

Snow makes much of Faustus's comment "till I am past this fair and pleasant green" (4.1.107) but fails to stress its greatest significance in the play: how *little* Marlowe makes of it. After *Dido* the pastoral vision vanishes almost completely from Marlovian drama, except for this fleeting reference by Faustus and a cruel parody of "Come live with me and be my love" in *The Jew of Malta*. It is as if the dream of Eden, the world of lost innocence, slipped out of Marlowe's consciousness so completely it could never again be seriously considered. And while Snow remarks that both the Christian and Faustian soul seem to be "denied the grace of all that is embodied in a dish of ripe grapes,"[76] I believe he underestimates how the Christian significance in the image of the grapes continued to haunt Marlowe's imagination. A discussion of this significance will conclude the present chapter.

Margaret O'Brien has argued that the reference in the concluding Chorus[77]—"Cut is the branch that might have grown full straight, / And burned is Apollo's laurel bough / That sometime grew within this learned man"—brings to mind (and to this we may add the grapes at Vanholt and the fruit imagery of the prologue) John 15:1–6:

> I am the true vine, and my Father is an housbandman.
> Euerie branche that beareth not frute in me, he taketh away: & euerie one that beareth frute, he purgeth it, that it may bring forthe more frute. . . .
> Abide in me. . . .
> If a man abide not in me, he is cast forthe as a branche, and withereth: and men gather them, and cast *them* into the fyre, and they burne.

While I agree that Marlowe intended this allusion, O'Brien misses a humanist irony, for while Faustus as a man "might have grown full straight," grapevines, dependent on whatever support they entwine, *never* grow straight; spiritual dependency vitiates manliness and human (phallic) creativity (Apollo's laurel). There is a further significance to the grape image in the play with respect to Christian iconography. In his analysis of Herbert's "Bunch of Grapes," Joseph Summers explains that the cluster of Eshcol signified a foretaste of the Promised Land to the Wandering Children of Israel, the full blessings of God. However, to the Israelites

> the bunch of grapes substantiated the report that it was "a land that eateth vp the inhabitants thereof, and all the people that we saw in it, are men of great stature. And there we saw the giants . . . and wee were in our own sight as grashoppers, and so wee were in their sight" (Num. xiii.32–33). From fear they turned to the rebellion which caused God to decree the wandering of forty years.[78]

Thus while the bunch of grapes "is a type of Christ and the Christian's communion" (cf. the wine of the Eucharist), the grapes of Eshcol also signify that "God's blessings [while man is still] under the Law could become . . . [the] occasion for the renewal of sin and the curse."[79] The image of the grapes thus becomes a token of suffering and fear—specifically a fear of being eaten up, like Christ's body in communion—for those who seek premature religious surrender, who attempt to enter the "Promised Land" before they have lived out their necessary lives in the realm of human experience.[80]

The imagery of grapes and burning branches thus suggests Marlowe's intimation that what Faustus struggles so hopelessly to achieve—a coherent sense of self, a sound identity—is always at risk of being undermined by the Creator who set the whole process in motion, who is waiting for humankind's true surrender to Christ. It is, in addition to related conflicts concerning sexual response, this religious suspicion of the illusory nature of the human self that makes self-fashioning such a tentative activity for Marlowe's heroes. The soundness of natural life in the end turns out to be the "real" illusion, and, for those unlucky enough to be stripped of this illusion prematurely—including the sensitive, "patient judgements" in the audience of *Doctor Faustus* and the sensitive soul of the poet himself—experience becomes a "dreadful night" (B-text 5.3.2) in which one is forced to look with unaccustomed eyes into the horrible fire at the heart of creation.

5

The Jew of Malta: The Failure of Carnal Identity

As M. M. MAHOOD STATED OVER FORTY YEARS AGO, *THE JEW OF Malta* "depicts a world which has cut itself off entirely from the transcendent,"[1] yet the play contains a great density of biblical allusions. We can account for this discrepancy by accepting G. K. Hunter's assessment that *The Jew of Malta* is, "apart from *Faustus,* the greatest ironic structure in Marlowe's work."[2] However, as in *Faustus,* biblical parody in *The Jew of Malta* fails to reinforce orthodox Christian morality: the play does not expose the folly of attempting to establish a "carnal" rather than a "spiritual" identity so much as it explores the tragic failure to establish a very necessary "carnal" identity. Like *Tamburlaine* and *Faustus, The Jew of Malta* presents a case of distorted self-assertion. Barabas's symbolic role as Antichrist does not pit him against a true Christian or Christ-like counterpart (an ideal that few characters in the play come close to embodying) but rather against those characters, most importantly Ferneze, who successfully operate within the limits of their natural and social selves. Barabas fails to establish a stable human identity for two reasons: in true Marlovian fashion he displays marked narcissistic behavior and therefore cannot accept the responsibility that is a concomitant of increased personal power, and, as an outsider, he is not supported in his self-fashioning by society's traditional values and beliefs. *The Jew of Malta* is, in fact, the first of Marlowe's plays to explore in detail the problems of self-fashioning in a social context.

The meaning of the play is largely dependent on the text's web of biblical allusions, which has been explored most recently by Sara Munson Deats in her article "Biblical Parody in Marlowe's *The Jew of Malta:* A Re-Examination." More than previous commentators, Deats recognizes the problematic nature of many of these allusions, yet insists, sometimes it seems in opposition to the implications of her own examples, on ultimately orthodox interpretations; that is, she argues for Marlowe's use of biblical parody "as a pointer to . . . typological norms" so that the play dramatizes "the choice between spiritual and carnal allegiance."[3] The difficulty arising from this approach becomes particularly evident in Deats's discussion of Ferneze's biblical paraphrases in his reply to Barabas:

> No, Jew, we take particularly thine
> To save the ruin of a multitude:
> And better one want for a common good
> Than many perish for a private man.
>
> (1.2.97–100)[4]

As Deats points out, "the sentiments voiced by Ferneze had long been proverbial,"[5] and so the Governor's position here would appear rational and acceptable; however, the lines also echo Caiaphas's statement in John 11:50: "it is expedient for vs, that one man dye for the people, and that the whole nacion perish not."[6] This surprising reversal, whereby Barabas assumes the role of Christ and the Christian Ferneze that of the Jewish High Priest, adds what Deats terms "ironic density" to the scene; the critic concludes that "by evoking both proverb and Scripture, Marlowe creates a puzzling and probably deliberate ambiguity."[7] Puzzling indeed, yet it is difficult to see how the ambiguity here points toward "implied standards"[8] that are biblical or godly in nature.

Although we may assume that Marlowe means to endow Ferneze with the kind of hypocrisy Christians generally associate with Caiaphas, there remains the question of how conscious Ferneze is of this hypocrisy (a matter to which I will return), as well as whether Marlowe would actually regard Caiaphas from the traditional Christian viewpoint. We remember that the playwright is quoted by Baines as saying that "if the Jewes among whome [Christ] was borne did Crucify him theie best knew him and whence he Came." Caiaphas and the other Jewish priests are traditionally condemned for seeking what was "expedient" for *them*, since Christ threatened the existing religious power structure and specifically the priests' ability to feather their own nests. A less traditional reading might venture to suggest that Caiaphas meant, "it is expedient for us—the Jewish people—that the whole nation perish not." With the fear of an uprising and the nation's subsequent destruction at the hands of the Roman forces, the High Priest's concern was perhaps—less selfishly than practically—for the welfare of his people and his state, for which he was willing to sacrifice a single life. Ferneze is in a similar position. While Deats suggests that the Turkish tribute has been neglected for ten years "*perhaps* for reasons of 'policy'"[9] (my emphasis), all the text tells us for certain is that a mighty Turkish fleet stands poised to invade Malta, and Calymath demands quick payment of the tribute. The political rationale is therefore understandable when Ferneze concludes that, for the preservation of their society, it is certainly better that "one want for a common good / Than many perish for a private man." The placement of Barabas in a radical Christ role of extreme individualism thus suggests conflation of Antichrist and Christ together as figures who oppose the common good. As in *Faustus*, the "metaphysical" opposes the viability of the "natural" man, who is now analyzed more thoroughly as a social and cultural being.

From Hunter's discussion in "The Theology of Marlowe's *The Jew of Malta* " we learn that "the name Barabbas . . . means *filius patris*; but this should be interpreted," the critic hastens to add, "in the light of John viii, 44, where Christ says to the Jews, 'Ye are of your father the Devil', and so Barabbas is to be interpreted as *Antichristi typus*."[10] However, in subtle but significant ways Barabas as "antitype" parallels rather than inverts the types he reflects. For example, Hunter discusses the several allusions to the Book of Job in the text of the play, points out that Job was seen as a type of Christ in the Old Testament, and concludes:

> Indeed the whole course of Barabas' career can be seen as a parody of Job's; both men begin in great prosperity, and then, for what appears to be no good reason, lose their possessions; both are restored to prosperity before the end of the action; both are accused of justifying themselves in the face of their adversity. But there the parallel ends; the frame of mind in which these events are lived through is precisely the opposite. Barabas' self-justification and self-will proceeds from a monstrous egotism, which is the basis of his character. . . . Job's justification, however one takes the difficult point, must be seen to spring from an anguished awareness that God is unanswerably just.[11]

On the most obvious level no one will deny that Barabas functions as an "Anti-Job," for Job is traditionally the figure of patience while Barabas actively seeks revenge. Yet Hunter's uneasy qualification, "however one takes the difficult point," must make us pause before accepting that the purpose of the allusions to Job is to invite us simply to condemn or dismiss Barabas for his failure to exercise "Christian" patience. I do not here intend an in-depth analysis of the Book of Job (and I wish to add, somewhat irreverently, that I am not sure it would be worth the effort). However, if I suggest that certain readers find the Book of Job one of the most vexing examples of theological obfuscation in existence—it seems to increase the sense of injustice it purportedly attempts to dispel—then it is conceivable that Marlowe, especially in light of the Baines Note, also may have reacted to it in this way. The Book of Job seems a prime example of that kind of religion whose only purpose is to keep men in awe. "Where wast thou when I layed the fundacions of the earth? declare, if thou hast understanding" and so on says God (38:4–39:35), continually hammering home to Job the fact of his own insignificance, finally reducing him to a state of abject submission and self-abhorrence; and God does this, ironically, after twice adjuring Job to "gird up his loins" and act like a man! (38:3, 40:2)

But it is not only our vague sense of injustice at the whole Job fable that dulls the moral edge of Barabas's anti-Job parody. One of Barabas's actions that critics understandably find most heinous is his replacement through murder of his daughter Abigail with his "adopted son" Ithamore. Kuriyama remarks that "One of Barabas's most marked egotistical . . . traits is his tendency to treat people as possessions and objects, rather like pieces of furniture that he can move about, employ, or discard at will."[12] What she observes in fact is the chronic manipulation of self-objects typical of narcissistic disorders. Yet this replacement of children as objects is exactly what happens in the Book of Job. God allows Satan to annihilate Job's original seven sons and three daughters, and then replaces them with seven more sons and three more daughters. Children are commodities that can be exchanged like Job's oxen and sheep, and neither Job nor God seems to have any scruples about this state of affairs. The fable, like Marlowe's play, thus violates our natural human feelings of familial loyalty and affection. The fact that we are meant to read certain parts of the Bible as allegory does not, I believe, alleviate our revulsion. Waldock's brief discussion of the *Pilgrim's Progress* is relevant here:

Bunyan, theoretically, would not have us abandon our customary human values—his allegory, like every allegory, owes its very point to an acceptance of those human values—yet he comes very near in [the opening] passage to affronting some of the chief of them. Christian running across the plain, his fingers in his ears to shut out the cries of his wife and children, desperately bent on his own salvation, is not the kind of person for whom in normal circumstances we should have a strong regard.[13]

The Bible's frequent contradiction or denial of what seem natural or normal emotional responses (one thinks of Christ's warning in Matthew 11:37 that "he that loveth son or daughter more than me is not worthy of me") problematizes biblical examples in *The Jew of Malta* and elsewhere in literature as easily acceptable guides for human behavior. An insistence or an assumption that we are always willing to accept these examples as worthy of imitation leads orthodox critics of Marlowe into questionable assertions. Deats, for example, claims that Jacomo's response, "Why stricken him that would have struck at me," when asked by Barabas (who has of course framed him) what he has done (4.1.174–75), recalls to us the Friar's failure to live up to Jesus' command: "But I say vnto you, Resist not euil: but whosoeuer shall smite thee on thy right cheke, turne to him the other also" (Matt. 5:39). "Probably few in Marlowe's audience," Deats piously concludes, "would have overlooked this violation of Christian ethics."[14] Yet it is extremely doubtful that Christ's admonition would spring to anyone's mind as the moral message at this point of the play, or that Marlowe ever intended that it should. Jacomo is destroyed through his own foolishness, not by his failure to live up to the ideals of Christian behavior. Turning the other cheek would certainly not help anyone survive for long in Maltese society. Rather than confirming such ideals, the biblical parody in *The Jew of Malta* makes evident the inadequacy, even the absurdity, of Christian ethics in the dog-eat-dog world that the characters inhabit.

Barabas of course is not at all concerned with Christian ethics, and my suggestion that in subtle ways his role as Antichrist or Anti-Job becomes conflated with the types he is supposedly inverting is not meant to imply that it is part of the Jew's heroic project consciously to reject the carnal ways of humankind. Barabas wants very much to establish and maintain his own sense of identity in the world. He very definitely makes the "Jewish choice," as it is described in the Herbert poem "Self-condemnation" which Hunter quotes in his article:[15]

> Thou who condemnest Jewish hate,
> For choosing Barrabas a murderer
>   Before the Lord of glorie;
> Look back upon thine own estate
>   . . . .
>   That choice may be thy storie.

He that doth love, and love amisse,
This worlds delights before true Christian joy,
    Hath made a Jewish choice:

    .   .   .   .

He that hath made a sorrie wedding
Between his soul and gold, and hath preferr'd
    False gain before the true,
Hath done what he condemns in reading:
For he hath sold for money his deare Lord,
    And is a Judas-Jew.

Thus we prevent the last great day,
And judge ourselves. That light, which sin & passion
    Did before dimme and choke,
When once those snuffes are ta'en away,
Shines bright and clear, ev'n unto condemnation.
    Without excuse or cloke.

I have requoted this poem not only because it establishes very plainly what constitutes the "Jewish choice"—a decision to make the most of this world—but also because the final stanza introduces a significance that Hunter does not consider but that is very important to my reading of Marlowe's play. "Thus we prevent the last great day" begins the final stanza, and, though the word "prevent" carries the archaic meaning of "anticipate" (our carnal allegiance thus anticipates the Last Judgment, as C. A. Patrides suggests),[16] there is a humanistic pun on the word "prevent" in the more modern sense of "to cut off beforehand, debar, preclude" (*OED*). We "prevent" the last great day, the annihilation of our human selves, out of a desire for self-preservation, in order to avoid premature self-surrender to a transcendental presence that denies our humanity. Once those "snuffs" of sin and passion (the ingredients of an ultimately illusory but very necessary sense of human identity in the world) are taken away, the light of Christ shines "bright and clear, ev'n unto condemnation," that is, even unto a complete loss of human integrity. Marlowe's obsession with this idea (recall *Faustus* and the unstable self terrified of its eventual surrender) accounts for the high frequency of biblical allusions in *The Jew of Malta*, particularly those concerned with the two covenants, the old versus the new man, the flesh versus the spirit.

Deats draws attention, for example, to the largely ignored allusions that associate Barabas with Abraham.[17] In a thematic extension of these allusions in 3.4, the scene of Abigail's disinheritance and Ithamore's adoption, we find a parallel to

> the expulsion by Abraham of the bondwoman Hagar and her son Ishmael; like Abigail, Abraham's first-born was deprived of his legacy and banished beyond the gates of his father. One tradition identified Ishmael and Isaac as the ancestors of the Arab and Hebrew races respectively; here, therefore, Barabas follows the pattern of ironic inversion established earlier in the play, reversing Abraham's actions by rejecting his freeborn Hebrew child Abigail in favor of his Turkish bondman Ithamore. Another Christian tradition, claiming for its adherents the promise of Isaac, frequently allegorized the Isaac-Ishmael rivalry as prefiguring the replacement of the old covenant of law, represented by the bondswoman Hagar, by the new covenant of grace, represented by the free wife Sarah. In this schema, Ishmael symbolizes not the Arab people but the heirs of the promise according to the flesh, the Jews, whereas Isaac symbolizes the heirs according to the spirit, the Christians, with father Abraham an emblem for God the father [cf. Paul's explanation of this "allegory" in Galatians 4:23–28].[18]

The two traditions together create an interesting ambiguity whereby the Jewish figure in one represents the chosen while in the other it becomes the discarded member. Marlowe probably appreciated this ambiguity, exposing as it does the tendency of every culture or religion to create its own self-justifying myth at the expense of some denigrated other. In both traditions, the inversions suggested by Deats would appear to hold true, for in the context of the Pauline reading Abigail as converted Christian is rejected in favor of "the infidel devotee of the flesh Ithamore."[19] Barabas's role as Abraham, symbolic of God the father, may explain his line at 1.1.138, "And all I have is hers [Abigail's]," which echoes Luke 15:31: "Sonne, thou art euer with me, and all that I haue, is thine." It is interesting, however, that Barabas's willingness to sacrifice his child parallels rather than inverts the biblical Abraham, who would have sacrificed Isaac, an incident clearly alluded to in the play when Barabas remarks: "I mean my daughter—but e'er he shall have her, / I'll sacrifice her on a pile of wood" (2.3.52–53, a biblical allusion that itself parallels the reference to Agamemnon and Iphigen at 1.1.137). Again we are reminded of the questionable nature of biblical ethics, for although God eventually "prevents" the sacrifice of Isaac, the test itself can only seem perverse to human sensibilities. Moreover, we cannot forget that the incident "prevents," in biblical typology, God's willing sacrifice of his own son.

Act 3, scene 4 contains another ironic parallel related to the Abraham allusions. The "mess of rice-porridge" (lines 64–65)—called "pottage" at line 89—recalls, as Bawcutt points outs, "the 'mess of potage' for which Esau sold his birthright, Genesis xxv."[20] Abigail loses Barabas's blessing (31) in this scene and ends up eating the porridge; thus the text suggests what Deats terms an "outrageous" parallel involving Barabas-Isaac, Abigail-Esau, and Ithamore-Jacob. Since the "allegorizing Christians moralized Esau's selling of his birthright for a 'mess of pottage' . . . as a paradigm for the profane man's rejection of a spiritual blessing for carnal gratification," we again get an ironic inversion whereby "Abigail's renunciation of her father's materialistic creed in favor of a spiritual vocation receives as its reward not a blessing" but death, while Ithamore is granted the birthright.[21] The inversion may not seem so complete if one is willing to admit that the treachery displayed by Barabas and Ithamore is not entirely at odds with the rather unscrupulous behavior, from the standpoint of *human* ethics, of the biblical Rebekah and Jacob. The anonymous author of *Jacob and Esau* is certainly at pains to present their actions in an acceptable light. This point aside, the biblical allusions in 3.4 indicate that Barabas is extremely determined to set aside the spiritual alternative open to humankind. Such an alternative, if symbolized by the unlucky Abigail, is not presented in a very positive or hopeful light in the play. If Barabas is so ruthless in his campaign of self-assertion, the crucial question is why does he fail to establish a viable carnal identity necessary for survival in the Machiavellian world of Malta?

One critic who discusses the character of Barabas in terms of abnormal psychology is Kuriyama, who believes that "the particular psychological conflict dramatized in *The Jew of Malta,* and Barabas's specific role in that conflict . . . are intimately bound up with Marlowe's."[22] She argues that "Barabas is exactly the kind of hero we might expect Marlowe to turn to once he had abandoned hope of achieving any kind of phallic mastery, and had ceased trying to reconcile his personal goals and ideals with those dictated by his society."[23] Thus psychological conflicts in the play are expressed not so much by physical confrontation, as they had been in *Tamburlaine,* but rather by "more subtle and 'civilized,' and at the same time, psychogenetically more primitive, modes of defining and regulating power relationships."[24] Her reading therefore comes closer to the pre-Oedipal matrix I have been ex-

ploring in the earlier plays. Kuriyama sees Barabas's hoarding as
a regressively anal or pregenital substitute for phallic confronta-
tions. The resulting emasculation of Barabas is expressed in the
play through images that suggest "a classic childish confusion
of anal and female procreative functions."[25] Whether or not the
majority of readers would recognize such confusion as "classic,"
Barabas's maternal behavior is clearly expressed on several occasions. Having recovered his bags of gold in act 2, Barabas joyfully
identifies himself with the mother lark:

> . . . wake the morning lark,
> That I may hover with her in the air,
> Singing o'er these [his bags], as she does o'er her young.
>
> (2.1.61–63)

Later in the play Ithamore tells Bellamira and Pilia-Borza that
Barabas "hides and buries [his wealth] up as partridges do their
eggs" (4.2.63–64). Moreover, Hunter has demonstrated that the
phrase "infinite riches in a little room" in Barabas's opening soliloquy blasphemously parodies a formula traditionally used to
describe the womb of the pregnant Virgin Mary;[26] as a consequence of the appropriation of this image, the Jew's counting-
house becomes itself a kind of womb, with the presiding Barabas
a pregnant mother-figure. Barabas internalizes the distanced or
indifferent "maternal" mirroring self-object of the earlier plays,
and thus functions—or rather, malfunctions in interesting
ways—without the need for an idealized self-object.

   With what Kuriyama calls Barabas's quasi-feminine character
in mind, I will make the claim that, through Marlowe's increasing
anxiety over his own thoughts "effeminate and faint,"[27] Barabas's
role as the Jewish alien in Malta becomes a kind of metaphor in
the play for the homosexual in society. As I argued in the introduction, it is likely, since homosexuality was not recognized as a
distinct personality type in the Renaissance, that the temptation
to surrender sexually to another man would have been perceived
not just as a failure of manly assertion, but also as the fear of
becoming "like a woman." Wilbur Sanders in *The Dramatist and
the Received Idea* mentions "the medieval libel of the *foetor judaicus*
(a vile smelling bodily secretion due to alleged menstruation in
Jewish males, which good Christians found intolerable and which
could only be obliterated by the waters of baptism)" and suggests
that Marlowe "maliciously re-applies it"[28] when Barabas tells Lodowick he must walk around to purge himself after talking with

Gentiles (2.3.44–48). Freud's argument that "anti-Semitism has connections with male castration fears born out of the idea of circumcision"[29] is also relevant here.

But the connection between Jewishness and homosexuality may not be restricted simply to Barabas's quasi-feminine character. John Boswell, in *Christianity, Social Tolerance, and Homosexuality*, remarks that "Jews and gay people were often tacitly linked in later medieval law and literature as nonconformists threatening the social order."[30] These prejudices may have played a role in Marlowe's subconscious linkage of Jews and homosexuals.[31] Though Kuriyama does not directly make this claim herself, she strongly suggests it when she argues that "Marlowe, by partially and tentatively adopting the perspective of an 'outsider,' a member of an 'exploited minority,' launches some of his most devastating satirical blasts at the hypocritical Christian society that in his view rejected him and threatened his survival."[32] Possibly Marlowe's growing awareness of his own sexual feelings, which he began to become conscious of during the composition of *Faustus*, frightened him into choosing a protagonist who was not himself directly involved in, or even aspiring to, sexual activity. Nevertheless, the "outsider" figure he chose to portray, and with whom he could strongly identify, indirectly expresses Marlowe's continuing sexual anxieties.

As in *Tamburlaine* and *Doctor Faustus*, we again find evidence of what seems a strong aversion to heterosexual activity in *The Jew of Malta*. Barabas's only reference to his own sexual involvement (there is no reference in the play to a loving relationship with Abigail's mother) is decidedly negative:

> *Bern.* Thou hast committed—
> *Bar.*   Fornication?
> But that was in another country:
> And besides, the wench is dead.
>
> (4.1.39–42)

As the exchange forms one moment in the verbal sparring match between Barabas and the Friars, it is doubtful that the tale is true. Even if it were, the act is regarded only as "fornication," the significance of which is eradicated by the fact of the woman's death. Death seems to be Barabas's way of dealing with the sexual threat, for he takes steps to murder both his daughter Abigail and his adopted son Ithamore when they enter into heterosexual relationships, presumably because they then begin to move outside of the Jew's control. Indeed, Barabas's replacement of Abigail with Ithamore seems already to have begun when he first begins laying his trap for his daughter's lovers Mathias and Lodowick, for it is in this scene, 2.3, that he purchases the Turkish slave. In one sense both Abigail and Ithamore symbolize a part of Barabas's own nature (he calls Ithamore his "second self" [3.4.15]) that he must repress or expunge. As they progress to sexual maturity, Barabas can no longer accept them as part of his own being—he can no longer identify with them. His narcissism prevents him from identifying with them in healthy or positive ways, as Kohut makes clear: "healthy man experiences, and with deepest joy, the next generation as an extension of his own self. It is the primacy of the support for the succeeding generation, therefore, which is normal and human, and not intergenerational strife and [the desire] to kill."[33] Like Tamburlaine, Barabas must exterminate the child (and adopted child) who subconsciously remind him of his own vulnerability, incompleteness, and mortality.

In fact, everyone seeking or engaging in sexual activity that comes within Barabas's sphere of influence is destroyed by him: Mathias and Lodowick are tricked into a mutually fatal duel (though Barabas destroys the latter ostensibly in order to be revenged upon Ferneze, he offers no reason for the destruction of the former); the lecherous Friars are directly or indirectly done away with; and Ithamore and Bellamira (along with her pimp) are poisoned. With the exception of Mathias, all these characters are lured to their deaths by some degree of covetousness or desire for wealth—the flaw that places them in Barabas's power—yet their concomitant "lechery" or sexual desire is significant, for it is Barabas's suppression of his own sexual desires that makes him symbolically more powerful or less vulnerable than they. Barabas seems to delight in destroying those engaged in sexual activity, and his sickening comparison of the nuns swollen with the poisoned porridge to their habitual pregnant state (4.1.6) constitutes a perverse equation of natural process and unnatural death.

Somewhat less disturbing but also dismissive of potentially fulfilling sexual union is Marlowe's parody of romantic conventions on two occasions in the play. In what might best be termed a proleptic parody, the "night scene," during which Barabas recovers his gold, "in its imagery and staging, curiously foreshadows the balcony scene in *Romeo and Juliet*," as Harry Levin points out.[34] The rhetoric here indeed becomes reminiscent of a love scene—"But stay, what star shines yonder in the east? / The loadstar of my life, if Abigail" (2.1.41–42)—but Barabas ends up embracing his gold rather than his daughter. If, as Bawcutt suggests, these lines involve "an irreverent allusion to the Biblical star of Matthew, ii.9,"[35] the parody of the search for the Christ child is ultimately linked to the dehumanizing of Abigail. An even more interesting parody, since it involves Marlowe's reworking of his own earlier lyric, is Ithamore's version of "The Passionate Shepherd to His Love":

> *Bella.* I have no husband, sweet, I'll marry thee.
> *Ith.* Content, but we will leave this paltry land,
> And sail from hence to Greece, to lovely Greece:
> I'll be thy Jason, thou my golden fleece;
> Where painted carpets o'er the meads are hurled,
> And Bacchus' vineyards overspread the world,
> Where woods and forests go in goodly green,
> I'll be Adonis, thou shalt be Love's Queen.
> The meads, the orchards, and the primrose lanes,
> Instead of sedge and reed, bear sugar-canes:
> Thou in those groves, by Dis above,
> Shalt live with me and be my love.
>
> (4.2.93–104)

This parody has been noted in the past, but it has never received the critical attention it deserved until Coburn Freer's analysis:

> Rising out of prose on both sides, this lyric is the most astonishing mixture of garlic and sapphires; so many touches are correct in themselves—starting off without a rhyme, for example, as the poetry machine begins to crank over—that the piece could hardly be improved. Especially notable are the violence of *hurl'd*, with vineyards spreading over the earth in a nightmare worthy of Comus, the crazy geography in having Jason sail to Greece instead of Colchis, and better yet, Dis seated up in heaven. The rapid enumeration of pastoral clichés comes down nicely on *Sugar Canes*, which underscores the childish basis of the fantasy.[36]

Some may express surprise that Marlowe would parody his own poem, but evidently the romantic-pastoral ideal was never one the writer subscribed to in a deeply personal way, and it is even possible to argue that his famous pastoral lyric itself self-consciously parodies its genre. Where he describes the ideal with poetic intensity in *Dido*, his main purpose is to emphasize his characters' surrender to fantasy.

Yet we have seen that in *The Jew* the attack on, or resistance to, sexuality goes deeper than simply a parody of romantic ideals,

and in particular the image of the swollen nuns, "pregnant" with
death, constitutes evidence of the author's disturbed sexual psychology, a mind, as in *Tamburlaine* and *Faustus*, deeply alienated
from its culture's sanctification of the natural. The image, however, is not gratuitously horrifying, for it recalls Faustus swollen
with a self-conceit, struggling to give birth to himself, as Snow
suggests, in his final soliloquy. In *The Jew of Malta* Barabas is faced
with a similar struggle. We first see him in his countinghouse,
which, as we have noted, functions metaphorically as a kind of
womb. He is not really "born," in terms of his struggle for identity, until his wealth is confiscated and he is evicted from his
house. Though he appears an extremely capable and successful
merchant at the beginning of the play, he exists in an essentially
unchallenged state that has a strong element of the fantastic. The
opening soliloquy contains a series of rhetorical tricks that make
it uncertain whether all the fabulous wealth the Jew describes
actually belongs to him or whether it is the imagined possessions
of quasi-mythical Arabians and Moors; while a director must decide exactly what props the actor will be fingering at this moment
(the 1633 text indicates that *"heapes of gold"*[37] lie before him), it is
very difficult to tell from the speech itself where reality ends and
imagination begins:

> Here have I pursed their paltry silverlings.
> Fie, what a trouble 'tis to count this trash!
> Well fare the Arabians, who so richly pay
> The things they traffic for with wedge of gold,
> Whereof a man may easily in a day
> Tell that which may maintain him all his life.
> The needy groom that never fingered groat
> Would make a miracle of thus much coin:
> But he whose steel-barred coffers are crammed full,
> And all his lifetime hath been tired,
> Wearing his fingers' ends with telling it,
> Would in his age be loath to labour so,
> And for a pound to sweat himself to death.
> Give me the merchants of the Indian mines,
> That trade in metal of the purest mould:
> The wealthy Moor, that in the eastern rocks
> Without control can pick his riches up,
> And in his house heap pearl like pebble-stones;
> Receive them free, and sell them by the weight,
> Bags of fiery opals, sapphires, amethysts,
> Jacinths, hard topaz, grass-green emeralds,
> Beauteous rubies, sparkling diamonds,

And seldseen costly stones of so great price
As one of them indifferently rated,
And of a carat of this quantity,
May serve in peril of calamity
To ransom great kings from captivity.
This is the ware wherein consists my wealth:
And thus, methinks, should men of judgement frame
Their means of traffic from the vulgar trade,
And as their wealth increaseth, so enclose
Infinite riches in a little room.

$$(1.1.6-37)$$

The key phrase in the speech is "without control"; Barabas appreciates the lack of restraint in the fantasized Moor, along with the something-for-nothing principle under which he is presumed to operate. The first image of enclosure in the play, the infinite riches in a little room, is thus another narcissistic fantasy of absolute power, untrammeled by the demands of reality. When Calymath arrives demanding the tribute money and Ferneze unscrupulously appropriates Barabas's wealth, the Jew must stop dreaming—idly fingering his wealth in an almost masturbatory manner—and take a more active role in determining his own destiny.

Yet Barabas is not unimpressive in the opening scenes. When the rumor concerning the Turkish envoy upsets the other Jews, Barabas demonstrates the kind of pride we would expect from a Marlovian hero:

See the simplicity of these base slaves,
Who for the villains have no wit themselves
Think me to be a senseless lump of clay
That will with every water wash to dirt!
No, Barabas is born to better chance
And framed of finer mould than common men,
That measure naught but by the present time.

$$(1.2.216-22)$$

He does not accept that he, like other men, dwells in a house of clay, whose foundation is in the dust, as Eliphaz the Temanite states in Job 4:19. He has not been fashioned by the God of Genesis, but presumably through an act of will has molded (or intends to mold) himself. Yet such confidence is built entirely upon his reliance on a secret treasure hoard, on the old pattern of regressive, passive behavior. Only when he learns that he will be denied access into his house do we view truly admirable self-assertion, for after briefly despairing he begins to talk like a potential tragic hero, insisting on his identity in the face of overwhelming circumstances:

> You partial heavens, have I deserved this plague?
> What, will you thus oppose me, luckless stars,
> To make me desperate in my poverty?
> And knowing me impatient in distress,
> Think me so mad as I will hang myself,
> That I may vanish o'er the earth in air,
> And leave no memory that e'er I was?
> No, I will live: nor loathe I this my life;
> And since you leave me in the ocean thus
> To sink or swim, and put me to my shifts,
> I'll rouse my senses, and awake myself.
>
> (1.2.259–69)

In terms of Barabas's struggle for identity, this is the high-water mark of the play.

Water is in fact the element he struggles against: he refuses to "wash to dirt," he courageously chooses to swim rather than sink, but in the end he is boiled to death in a cauldron, the final image of enclosure. Water, symbolic of purification and baptism, becomes a nightmare image since it functions only as a destroyer; in Marlowe's vision baptism can take place only in a symbolic hell,[38] and even then it is not true baptism since it involves not conversion but annihilation. Religion, as Machevil claims, is but a childish toy, and Barabas, after his initial smug vision of his wealth as a product of "the blessings promised to the Jews" (1.1.104), does not waste much time (with a notable exception to be discussed below) petitioning the heavens for aid. Yet, as Steane remarks, "If religion is childish . . . there is a corollary which St Paul teaches: 'when I became a man I put away childish things.'"[39] Barabas fails to become a man, degenerating in a series of cartoon villains, and "childish" religion is vindicated, though farcically, since the Jew's end emblematizes religion's greatest bugbear. Barabas's "birth," like Faustus's, miscarries, and despite the farcical elements in both plays, their tragic plots seem haunted by Christ's metaphor for spiritual rebirth in John 16:21: "A woman when she trauaileth, hathe sorrowe, because her houre is come: but assone as she is deliuered of the childe, she remembreth no more the anguish, for ioye that a man is borne into the worlde." In Marlowe's vision we never get past the anguish, for his men never succeed in giving birth to themselves as *men,* and so the sufferings of sainthood remain only a metaphor for personal trauma.

The Jew of Malta is in some ways even bleaker than *Tamburlaine* and *Doctor Faustus* because becoming a man no longer carries with it any sense of the heroic. In "Marlowe's *'Sound Machevill'*" Catherine Minshull raises the point that Charles Nicholl has recently expanded and explored, that the playwright "would have been familiar with the less savory aspects of government if he had been employed in the secret service."[40] In Marlowe's vision of society, being a man and being a Machiavel amount to the same thing. Many have read *The Jew* as as essentially a study of Machiavellianism,[41] and D. J. Palmer correctly asserts that Barabas "does not come to grief because he is a Machiavel, but because he is not Machiavellian enough."[42] The clearest and most persuasive commentary taking this approach is Minshull's "Marlowe's *'Sound Machevill.'*" According to Minshull, the prologue to *The Jew* "offers a frank, if inflammatory, exposition of Machiavelli's political code," but "Marlowe was being intentionally ironic in presenting Barabas to the audience as an arch-Machiavellian," a role represented in the play not by the Jew but by "Ferneze, who in true Machiavellian fashion is primarily interested in power politics and military matters."[43] By taking advantage of the popular prejudice against Jews and linking it with a popular misconception of Machiavelli ("the stereotype of the underhanded, scheming anti-Christian villain"),[44] Marlowe succeeded in "writing a secret play between the lines of his official play."[45] The play can thus be seen as a joke on its sixteenth-century audience, who, "ignorant of Machiavelli's writings . . . mistook [Marlowe's] caricature of a Machiavellian villain for the real thing."[46]

The task of modern criticism, as well as modern directors, has largely been to uncover the joke, and twentieth-century audiences (assuming Minshull is correct in her conjectures about sixteenth-century ones) seem to have less trouble detecting Ferneze's hypocrisy, since his final couplets—"So, march away, and let due praise be given / Neither to fate nor fortune, but to heaven"— can now come across as "an outrageous irony"[47] rather than a confirmation of a divinely ordained Elizabethan social order. Certainly the contrast between Barabas and Ferneze is crucial to an understanding of the play. However, I would like to suggest a third approach, a kind of dialectical resolution of the presumed sixteenth-century approval of Ferneze's triumph over the villain Barabas, and the modern view of Ferneze as arch-Machiavellian hypocrite. There is no doubt that Marlowe's anti-Christian satire is extremely powerful in the play, and for a full appreciation of the extent of the attack one may read Sanders's commentary.[48] Yet while the Christian society of Malta as a whole is remarkably corrupt, it is questionable whether Ferneze himself is quite the cool, calculating Machiavellian master that more recent criticism has made him out to be. After all, if Barabas did not make the fatal mistake of trusting Ferneze (an action the Governor cannot have foreseen) then Ferneze could expect a fate no better than the one that actually comes to pass for Barabas. In fact, Ferneze rather stupidly fails to inquire into the reason for Barabas's supposed death at the beginning of act 5, when the wiser and more suspicious Del Bosco begins to smell a rat:

> *Bosco.* This sudden death of his is very strange.
> *Fern.* Wonder not at it, sir, the heavens are just.
> Their deaths were like their lives, then think not of 'em.
>
> (1.54–56)

What gives Ferneze a real advantage over Barabas has to do with the distinction between lies and fictions discussed by Coburn Freer in his essay "Lies and Lying in *The Jew of Malta.*" Fictions "require the mutual (if occasionally grudging) consent of all members of a community, and they tend generally to reaffirm established social structures"; lies, on the other hand, "are by definition the expression of attitudes that stand behind or apart from our mutual consent; they are offered by individuals with individual motives . . . and in their most extreme form they would destroy the social fabric altogether."[49] Ferneze's and the other knights' hypocritical "profession" during act 1, scene 2, when Barabas's property is confiscated, receives support from the entire system of beliefs and prejudices embodied in their society; as Freer puts it, "Ferneze and the others . . . are propped up as much by the fictions of their world as by their own inventive lying."[50] In Malta truth becomes irrelevant, and it is appropriate that Ferneze is cast in this scene not only in the role of Caiaphas, as we saw earlier, but also as Pilate, since he remarks, "No, Barabas, to stain our hands with blood / Is far from us and our profession" (145–46). Ferneze's remark here is subsequently contradicted when he suddenly calls upon another fiction—military honor—to justify his breaking faith with the Turks: "Honour is bought with blood, and not with gold" (2.2.56). What is truth, indeed; it certainly does not seem to have much to do with a capable, flexible management of government affairs (a fact demonstrated by the actions of the wily Elizabeth I herself).

Ferneze's role playing is thus facilitated by social fictions, but it is debatable how conscious he is of his own hypocrisy. Emily C. Bartels argues that, because Ferneze himself is under the pressure of other imperialist powers (Turkey and Spain), the play subverts the distinction between dominator and dominated and suggests "imperialism as a self-perpetuating chain reaction."[51] In other words, Ferneze compensates for being taken advantage of by taking advantage of someone else. Yet Bartels questions Ferneze's awareness of his Machiavellian strategies: "the relation between the subject and the object of domination is problematized by Ferneze's complicity in his own subjugation: he misreads domination as alliance and alternately adopts the dictates of both imperializing powers. The play leaves ambiguous how conscious this misreading is on his part, how much a product of blindness or insight, naïveté or cunning."[52] Ferneze is also highly dependent on circumstance. He is an opportunist, knowing how to make the most of the present moment (as when he switches his alliance from the Turks to the Spaniards) as well as knowing how to bide his time (as when he pretends to accept Barabas's offer of reconciliation).

In what amounts to a crucial statement in the play, Barabas lectures Abigail:

> As good dissemble that thou never mean'st
> As first mean truth, and then dissemble it;
> A counterfeit profession is better
> Than unseen hypocrisy.
>
> (1.2.290–93)

If Ferneze's final pretense of friendship with Barabas is undoubtedly a "counterfeit profession," a good deal of his flexibility earlier in the play arises from something like "unseen hypocrisy"; he receives such support from the fictions of his society that he need not be hyperconscious of the roles he is playing. He is undisturbed by the illusory, shifting nature of the human identity he has adopted in the world, since the world is more supportive of him than of Barabas.

Barabas, as the alien in Maltese society, must constantly rely on his own "ruthless individualism."[53] His isolation is actually greater than it need be, for he willfully refuses to acknowledge fraternity with the other Jews of Malta. When they have been summoned to the senate house, Barabas says to his fellow Jews:

> Hum; all the Jews in Malta must be there?
> Ay, like enough; why then, let every man
> Provide him, and be there for fashion sake.
> If anything shall there concern our state,
> Assure yourselves I'll look [*Aside*]—*unto myself.*
>
> (1.1.168–72)

Barabas realizes he must dissemble in order to survive, yet the roles he adopts are always antagonistic and hateful:

> We Jews can fawn like spaniels when we please,
> And when we grin, we bite; yet are our looks
> As innocent and harmless as a lamb's.
> I learned in Florence how to kiss my hand,
> Heave up my shoulders when they call me dog,
> And duck as low as any bare-foot friar,
> Hoping to see them starve upon a stall,
> Or else be gathered for in our synagogue,
> That when the offering-basin comes to me,
> Even for charity I may spit into 't.
>
> (2.3.20–29)

Kuriyama is convincing in her suggestion that Marlowe's identification with Barabas involves a strong sense of "negative identity": "We might recall Erikson's observation that negative identity is associated with the 'ethnic out-group,' the 'exploited minority,' and also with ugliness and evil, four categories into which, in the cultural context of Renaissance England, Barabas clearly falls."[54] Barabas is even willing to accept and elaborate upon the most negative fictions that the Christians in his society have fabricated about the Jews. In his famous speech to Ithamore beginning "As for myself, I walk abroad o' nights / And kill sick people groaning under walls" (2.3.176–201) we assume that the Jew is constructing an imaginative (that is, completely false) personal history from the various fictions of his society. Yet the savage glee with which Barabas identifies with these criminal pursuits leaves him, as a social being, unstable and subject to persecution. Self-fashioning for Barabas is an extremely frenetic activity. Unlike the flexible Ferneze, whose "Machiavellian tactics are employed in the service of the state rather than [the] self,"[55] Barabas can receive no external support for his various projects, outside of his temporary enlistment of Abigail and Ithamore, neither of whom he respects enough as individuals to be able to expect a continuing return of trust. Barabas thus lurches in a much more dangerous way from role to role than the more calmly shifting Ferneze.

It is possible to link Barabas's peculiar brand of aggression—the unfeeling extermination of his own child, for example—to Kohut's concept of "narcissistic rage" to which Donaldson calls attention in his discussion of Tamburlaine's behavior:

> Aggressions employed in the pursuit of maturely experienced causes are not limitless. However vigorously mobilized, their goal is definite: the defeat of the enemy who blocks the way to a cherished goal. . . . The opponent who is the target of our mature aggression is experienced as separate from ourselves, whether we attack him because he blocks us in reaching our object-libidinal goals or hate him because he interferes with the fulfillment of our reality-integrated narcissistic wishes. The enemy, however, who calls forth the archaic rage of the narcissistically vulnerable is seen by him not as an autonomous source of impulsions, but as a *flaw in a narcissistically perceived reality*. He is a recalcitrant part of an expanded self over which he expects to exercise full control and whose mere independence or other-ness is an offense.[56]

The increasing weakness of poetic self-idealization in *The Jew* makes such behavior, I believe, more dramatically "realistic" and disturbing than in *Tamburlaine*. Kohut's analysis sheds light on Barabas's behaviour when Abigail reenters the nunnery:

> I fear she knows ('tis so) of my device
> In Don Mathias' and Lodovico's deaths:
> If so, 'tis time that it be seen into,
> For she that varies from me in belief
> Gives great presumption that she loves me not,
> Or loving, doth dislike of something done.
>
> (3.4.7–12)

Except for the final line, the speech constitutes a fine example of narcissistic reasoning: "she that varies from me in belief" cannot possibly love me. As Bawcutt points out, in "the table of proper names at the end of the Geneva Bible Abigail is translated as 'the fathers ioye,'"[57] and it seems Abigail exists only to reinforce her father's identity and sense of well-being. With Marlovian relationships in general it is helpful to keep in mind Kohut's important point that "object relations are not the same thing as object love.

There are many relationships to other people that have nothing to do with loving other people but that are in the service of narcissistic aims. As a matter of fact, some of the most intense relationships to objects serve narcissistic purposes."[58] This claim is particularly relevant to the behavior of Dido, Tamburlaine, Barabas, and (as we shall see) Edward. But I think it is interesting that in Barabas's final line above, there may be one brief glimmer of a more mature emotion, a sense of guilt that, while she still loves him, she "dislikes of something done." Less attractively, however, this second thought may come to mind not as a realization that he is at fault, but that Abigail may intend to betray him.

In spite of his narcissism, there are nevertheless promising moments in Barabas's career of self-fashioning, such as the heroic assertiveness in the speech "You partial heavens, have I deserved this plague" and the soliloquy that begins act 2:

> Thus, like the sad presaging raven that tolls
> The sick man's passport in her hollow beak,
> And in the shadow of the silent night
> Doth shake contagion from her sable wings,
> Vexed and tormented runs poor Barabas
> With fatal curses towards these Christians.
> The incertain pleasures of swift-footed time
> Have ta'en their flight, and left me in despair;
> And of my former riches rests no more
> But bare remembrance, like a soldier's scar,
> That has no further comfort for his maim.
> O thou, that with a fiery pillar led'st
> The sons of Israel through the dismal shades,
> Light Abraham's offspring, and direct the hand
> Of Abigail this night; or let the day
> Turn to eternal darkness after this.
> No sleep can fasten on my watchful eyes,
> Nor quiet enter my distempered thoughts,
> Till I have answer of my Abigail.

Though histrionic and self-dramatizing, the speech is far more attractive than the sneering, "counterfeit professions" Barabas adopts later to manipulate others. Here he casts himself in a heroic role, and it is an admirable fabrication, one that we feel is necessary in the world; he comes close to creating a viable self, to achieving the desirable state of "unseen hypocrisy." He also takes time out to disengage, to become self-reflecting:

Now I remember those old women's words,

Who in my wealth would tell me winter's tales,
And speak of spirits and ghosts that glide by night
About the place where treasure hath been hid;
And now methinks that I am one of those:
For whilst I live, here lives my soul's sole hope,
And when I die, here shall my spirit walk.

(24–30)

Here Barabas uses fictions, the "winter's tales," to view himself from a different perspective, or in a context different from the more typical, antagonistically self-justifying roles he elsewhere constructs. Particularly interesting in the soliloquy is the prayer to the Jewish God to "Light Abraham's offspring," an epithet that in this context may refer either to Abigail or Barabas himself; it is an attempt at transmuting internalization of a divine ideal. As at various moments in *Tamburlaine*, this God is an act of imagination; but it seems a *positive* act, a source of personal inspiration. The concept of God is subordinated to the individual's own heroic effort, and it is one of the rare moments in the play when Barabas identifies positively and constructively with his cultural background. (His earlier complacent recognition of his riches as a manifestation of the blessings promised to the Jews is less admirable, since at that moment Barabas is still unchallenged, not yet under the pressure to act heroically.)

Despite these glimmers of hope, Barabas shows no further signs of creative self-fashioning; he later can define himself only by a desire to destroy others. In this he resembles Tamburlaine. He acquires his sense of identity and power through his ability to manipulate other people as objects; he never (consciously) considers surrendering to them. The play appears to degenerate into farce more because of Barabas's failure of imagination than Marlowe's. Refusing to recognize others as real people, the Jew, through the mirroring process, becomes less real himself. The action becomes particularly farcical since Barabas, inhabiting a more realistic context than Tamburlaine's romance world, exercises far less control than the earlier hero. He must constantly tidy up the loose ends from each preceding stage of machinations. His comment to the Carpenter in 5.5 is profoundly ironic: "Leave nothing loose, all leveled to my mind" (3). All cannot be leveled to the mind, to complete and instantaneous personal control. In this sense Barabas never fully emerges from the fantasy world he initially inhabits, and, as in *Faustus*, the uncontrolled imagination has its revenge: the hero again is swallowed up by an artifact, a morality emblem.

Yet Barabas, unlike Faustus, has not been obsessed with his eschatological destiny, and his final anguish in the emblematic hell would seem to have little to do with religious retribution, even in a psychological sense—at least with respect to Barabas's psychology. Marlowe appears to be working overtime in *The Jew of Malta* to free himself from any lingering temptation toward religious dependency. Even though Barabas's concept of God remains subordinated to his own effort, the very presence of his prayer in act 2 is remarkable in the context of a play that everywhere else attacks so vigorously the idea that religion could ever help anyone, or that it is anything but monstrous hypocrisy. One senses that Marlowe took a certain perverse pleasure in portraying the fate of the lecherous friars and nuns, in composing Barabas's speech concerning his atrocities on Christians, and in elaborating Ithamore's reply to that speech:

> Once at Jerusalem, where the pilgrims kneeled,
> I strowèd powder on the marble stones,
> And therewithal their knees would rankle so,
> That I have laughed a-good to see the cripples
> Go limping home to Christendom on stilts.
>
> (2.3.210–14)

Behind this sadistic tale lurks the suggestion that those foolish enough to kneel down and submit to religion are deservedly crippled; such devotion simply restricts or damages the individual's personal strength. It is worth noting here that, as several critics have pointed out, the Turks (excluding Ithamore) are the only *truthful* characters in the play, and it is possible to see in Calymath's remark

> I wish, grave governor, 'twere in my power
> To favour you, but 'tis my father's cause,
> Wherein I may not, nay I dare not, dally
>
> (1.2.10–12)

an allusion to Christ's dismissal of his parents' remonstrations in the temple with his statement that he must be about his father's business. If Calymath is a kind of Christ figure, then it is significant that, as the figure of truth, he must be imprisoned and suppressed at the end of the play by the successful politician Ferneze. Significant as well is the fact that Calymath's men are destroyed in a monastery. It is as if Marlowe's realization in *Faustus* of the supreme indifference of God was so devastating that he now must attack the validity of religion, and expose its potential destructiveness, as viciously as possible.

This is perhaps one reason why the plot of *The Jew of Malta* deals so harshly with the unfortunate Abigail. Having realized the extent of her father's treachery, Abigail requests readmittance to the nunnery, claiming that

> experience, purchasèd with grief,
> Has made me see the difference of things.
> My sinful soul, alas, hath paced too long
> The fatal labyrinth of misbelief,
> Far from the Son that gives eternal life.
>
> (3.3.64–68)

She retreats back to what was in fact her original home, which the imagery of the play has associated with the womb. It is a decidedly negative step, not only because of the hypocritical nature of the convent, but because it involves a denial of her need to cultivate an identity in the world. It could be argued that, as a young woman in a patriarchal society, Abigail has few options to pursue, and that, having lost her hopes of marriage to Mathias, she chooses to enter the nunnery, actually in defiance of her father's wishes. However, in the play her choice is presented not in defiant but regressive terms. Dido, Catherine the Queen Mother in *The Massacre at Paris*, and Isabella, particularly in the latter half of *Edward II*, all reveal that Marlowe could artistically conceive of more strong-willed women, although these characters are admittedly partly empowered by their high social standing. That Marlowe was at least familiar with more assertive women from his own class is indicated by Kuriyama's discussion of his two youngest sisters, Ann and Dorothy, who "proved to be exceptionally aggressive."[59]

Abigail cannot escape further "experience" and "grief" if she is to continue to grow and develop as a human being. She complains that she now sees "the difference of things," a phrase that implies the realization, arising mainly from her father's example, that in the world we are not who we pretend to be—well-meaning self-idealization is inevitably disrupted by the often vicious and inconstant nature of social self-fashioning. It is unfortunate that she has had her eyes opened through a deep personal betrayal, for the acceptance of a malleable social persona constitutes a necessary "misbelief" (she does not call it "unbelief") for existence in society. Her decision to surrender prematurely her personal struggle in favor of "the Son that gives eternal life" has a disastrous effect: she in effect sells her *human* birthright for a mess of deadly pottage.

The fact that onstage the pot containing the porridge would resemble the cauldron in which Barabas finally cooks to death links the hero's failure of humanity to Abigail's; and Barabas's final destruction does involve a variation on the basic problem of inadequate humanist self-fashioning shown up by premature self-surrender. Barabas's first "surrender" is a parodic crucifixion and resurrection: having drunk "poppy and cold mandrake juice" (5.1.80), he is taken for dead and thrown over the walls, reviving in time to show the Turks a secret passageway into the town (which, since it is the opening for the "common channels" [89], or sewers, suggests a kind of indirect, anal invasion rather than the phallic violation of towns that Tamburlaine fantastically displayed). A grateful Calymath then creates Barabas the new governor of Malta. Therefore the Jew's machinations, however much difficulty he has had dealing with the loose ends left over from each stage of his intrigues, *seem* finally to have paid off. Yet why does he then make the fatal mistake of trusting Ferneze?

There are two reasons, both related to Barabas's inability to deal with the burden of his own heroic project. The first may be deduced from the doubts he himself enunciates:

> Thus hast thou gotten, by thy policy,
> No simple place, no small authority:
> I now am governor of Malta. True,
> But Malta hates me, and in hating me,
> My life's in danger; and what boots it thee,
> Poor Barabas, to be the governor,
> Whenas thy life shall be at their command?
> No, Barabas, this must be looked into;
> And since by wrong thou got'st authority,
> Maintain it bravely by firm policy,
> At least unprofitably lose it not.
>
> (5.2.27–37)

Does he really fear for his personal safety here? A moment earlier Calymath has given him "To guard thy person, these our Janizaries" (16), and Barabas is intelligent enough to realize that if Malta hates him that much, then simply relinquishing the governorship would not make him any safer. Because of the murky reasoning of this speech, the suspicion arises that Barabas's concern over assassination is really a great rationalization for the fact that, unlike Ferneze, he cannot accept the responsibility of rule. Having accomplished his revenge, he quickly regresses back to the desire to resume his role of merchant, safe in the womblike counting-house, letting others take the enormous risks of sailing on the open seas to obtain wealth for him. He cannot face the truth that power is acquired and maintained only by assuming great responsibility and by taking great risks. Like other Marlovian heroes, he is faced with a simultaneous desire both to exercise and to relinquish control. Yet he does not struggle very long, for in the end it appears he simply lacks personal courage: the admirable line "Maintain it bravely by firm policy" immediately slides into the ignoble, mercenary "At least unprofitably lose it not."

The second reason for his desire to confide in Ferneze has to do with his emotional poverty, a quality that becomes evident when Barabas transfers his need for a second self from Abigail to Ithamore, making him his "only heir":

> O Ithamore, come near;
> Come near, my love, come near, thy master's life,
> My trusty servant, nay, my second self!
> For I have now no hope but even in thee,
> And on that hope my happiness is built.
>
> (3.4.13–17)

Admittedly Barabas does not appear to hold Ithamore in any real affection, for when the slave goes offstage to fetch the pot of rice, Barabas snickers, "Thus every villain ambles after wealth, / Although he ne'er be richer than in hope" (52–53). Yet his overall career suggests that Barabas, though he has assumed the role of a master deceiver, actually deceives himself as to his own emotional needs. He is, after all, far more intimate with Ithamore than we would expect from a Machiavellian manipulator of men. The confidence he places in Ithamore eventually gets him in trouble with Bellamira and Pilia-Borza, so, like Abigail, Ithamore and company must be eliminated through another one of the Jew's colorful contrivances.

Surprisingly, Barabas does not ever learn from his mistakes. At the end of his career he again demonstrates this almost neurotic need to confide in someone. He recalls the prisoner Ferneze, to whom he presents himself "as a friend not known but in distress" (5.2.72). As with Ithamore he becomes positively effusive:

> Governor, I enlarge thee; live with me,
> Go walk about the city, see thy friends.
> Tush, send not letters to 'em, go thyself,
> And let me see what money thou canst make.
> Here is my hand that I'll set Malta free.
> And thus we cast it.
>
> (91–96)

They agree that Barabas will "render . . . The life of Calymath" (79–80) to Ferneze and annihilate the Turkish army. Ferneze exits, and then comes the strangest speech of all, in which Barabas again denies the affection he has just displayed:

> Thus loving neither, will I live with both,
> Making a profit of my policy;
> And he from whom my most advantage comes
> Shall be my friend.
>
> (111–14)

Yet how can he talk about "living with both" when he has just made arrangements to utterly destroy one of the parties? He is deceiving himself in believing he is still practicing Machiavellian policy. It appears as if he has inverted Machiavelli's famous dictum in *The Prince* that it is better to be feared than loved. As Harry Levin remarks:

> [Barabas] is conscious of being hated, and wants to be loved. To be loved—yes, that desire is his secret shame. . . . His hatred is the bravado of the outsider whom nobody loves, and his revenges are compensatory efforts to supply people with good reasons for hating him. Poor Barabas, poor old rich man! That he should end by trusting anybody, least of all the one man who wronged him in the beginning![60]

Barabas has failed in his own role of the perfectly evil villain. In a perverse sense his crawling back into Malta to be revenged after being tossed over the walls—"What, all alone?" (5.1.61)—is really an expression of his need to belong. Underneath the monstrous mask that spouts, "For so I live, perish may all the world" (5.5.10) lies a pitiful individual who never succeeds in taking on either the responsibilities or the lasting relationships of a real man. Barabas's ultimately fragile aggression resembles Marlowe's. According to Baines, Marlowe the arch-iconoclast, the cruel, scornful, and reckless rebel, was not satisfied with seeing the truth of things himself, "but almost into every Company he Com-

eth he perswades men to Atheism willing them not to be afeard
of bugbeares and hobgoblins." It is likely that beneath the injudi-
cious courage and zeal lay a desperate need to belong, to have
company in his campaign to free the world from what haunted
him most.

Barabas's career, perhaps like Marlowe's own, consists of a series of unstable "counterfeit professions" that lead him to a precarious pinnacle, where he is destroyed by a negative and fatal
"unseen hypocrisy": his own lack of awareness of a dark and
complex mixture of accumulated insecurities, fears, and longings,
which could never be released or worked through in more human, natural ways. And while it could hardly be said that Ferneze
shows us Barabas's polar opposite—a warm and loving human
being—those who describe the governor as simply a cool and
ruthless politician ignore the fact that Ferneze, unlike Barabas, is
genuinely grieved for the loss of his child. Reservations about
Lodowick's character should not prevent us from recognizing the
appreciable pain Ferneze suffers at his son's death:

> What sight is this? My Lodowick slain!
> These arms of mine shall be thy sepulchre.
>
> .   .   .   .
>
> Then take them up, and let them be interred
> Within one sacred monument of stone;
> Upon which altar I will offer up
> My daily sacrifice of sighs and tears,
> And with my prayers pierce impartial heavens
> Till they reveal the causers of our smarts. . . .
>
> (3.2.10–34)

The desire to be revenged, if un-Christian, is natural and human,
and in Ferneze's double-crossing of Barabas at the end of the play
the governor is able to merge political and personal advantage-
taking. His prayers *have* been answered (not only in revealing but
also in punishing the perpetrator of the crime) and, if it is very
much a case of God helping those who help themselves, we
should nevertheless hesitate to dismiss Ferneze's last lines in the
play as laughably hypocritical. "Let due praise be given / Neither
to fate nor fortune, but to heaven" may strike modern ears as
gross hypocrisy, yet with respect to Ferneze's own attitude the
statement is perhaps better described as a comforting delusion—
and a necessary one for the maintenance of social stability. Actually, Ferneze has not come out completely on top at the end of
the play, for, as Bartels points out, Del Bosco remains onstage

beside Ferneze in the final scene, reminding us of "the colonizing voice behind the colonizing voice."[61] Ferneze must still deal with the delicate task of both exercising and submitting to authority.

While I think it true that Marlowe identifies very closely with Barabas, I believe it also true that Ferneze, in spite of his failings, represents the kind of man the playwright was working toward, in the sense of admiring or hoping to emulate: the self-possessed yet adaptable individual not tortured by the compromises necessary in human experience, the "difference of things." Ferneze is very much a precursor of the later figures of Navarre and the suddenly competent and mature Edward III in the final scene of *Edward II*. The fact that these characters are sketchily portrayed (and disturbing on their own terms) indicates that Marlowe, in the brief time remaining to him, did not move very far in his artistic and personal realization of this kind of individual. At the time he wrote *The Jew of Malta* Marlowe probably was still very much what Hunter terms a "God-haunted atheist,"[62] that curious condition in which one wants very much to live independent of a concept of God yet remains obsessed by religion's condemnation of self-sufficiency.[63] Marlowe must have been particularly fascinated by the statement of Christ's to which Barabas alludes: "be ye therefore wise as serpentes, and innocent as doues" (Matt. 10:16); it seems a surprisingly Machiavellian thing for Jesus to say. Barabas's version of it—"Now will I show myself to have more of the serpent than the dove; that is, more knave than fool" (2.3.36–37)—reduces, as Bawcutt remarks, "Christ's subtle paradox to a simple alternative, 'cheat or be cheated.'"[64] One suspects a link between Barabas's tendency to reduce things to black and white, to either-or situations, and Marlowe's own struggle against the bleak repent-or-be-damned formula of the Church: it is the struggle to dismiss such doctrine as not only essentially useless but actually seriously detrimental to the constructive development of the self; to replace the bald morality of an overly dogmatic religion with a more flexible and creative dialectic of assertion and surrender. The struggle becomes particularly intense in Marlowe's writing because it involves not only the religious ideas he attacked so vigorously but also his own fears of sexual surrender and a growing realization of his own homosexuality, a potential identity that his society refused to recognize. It is probably not accidental that Barabas's words to Ferneze, "live with me," again allude to Marlowe's own lyric of romantic invitation. Ferneze represents not only a man Marlowe ultimately wanted to become *like*, but also, on a barely subconscious level, one he desired to surrender to sexually.

6

The Massacre at Paris: The Exorcism of Machevil

WHILE IT SEEMS LIKELY THAT READERS WILL CONTINUE TO DIS-
agree as to which of *Tamburlaine, Doctor Faustus,* or *Edward II*
is Marlowe's best play, there will probably always be universal
agreement that *The Massacre at Paris* is his worst. To offer a coherent reading of it would be, as Kuriyama claims, to "seriously
misrepresent a play that is not itself very coherent."[1] Yet the play
is difficult to assess fairly since we possess what is presumably a
reported text, "put together by memorial reconstruction" as H. J.
Oliver conjectures.[2] We are thus left forever wondering how faith-
fully the "singularly crude and unpoetic potboiler"[3] that has come
down to us represents the original form of the play.

In the face of this limitation, and in spite of Oliver's warning
of "how dangerous it is to reach conclusions even about characterizations from such a text,"[4] the play's meaning and its place in
the Marlowe canon can best be understood by exploring the three
main male characters: the Duke of Guise, Navarre, and Henry III.
We have seen the importance of the Barabas/Ferneze contrast in
The Jew of Malta, and in Marlowe's subsequent plays—*The Massacre* and *Edward II*—he moves even further away from the mono-
drama of *Tamburlaine* and *Faustus.* It is therefore wrong to see *The
Massacre* as centered wholly on the Guise, and Kocher falls wide
of the mark when he claims that Marlowe assembles "bloody
deeds from all quarters of his source to construct one of those
titans of evil who so delighted him, and at the same time dimin-
ish[es] the other actors until they scarcely reach to the Guise's
knees."[5] Levin, who also exaggerates the Guise's importance in
the play, nevertheless astutely remarks that if Marlowe "does
nothing else in *The Massacre at Paris,* he exorcises this devil [the
hero as villain] that he has raised [in *The Jew of Malta*]";[6] indeed,
Machevil in the prologue to *The Jew of Malta* mentions the Guise
as one of his incarnations, and in his next play Marlowe strives

175

to defeat and dismiss this narcissistic creation, attempting to replace it with more psychologically viable figures. *The Massacre* is very much a play in which the author works through, or tries to work past, the versions of pathological self-assertion he has previously explored. One alternative the play explores, the ideal figure of Navarre, remains shadowy and unconvincing because he struggles only fitfully against the pre-Oedipal Marlovian matrix of maternal and religious dependency, and his final speech is not quite free from a darker sense of Tamburlainean aggression. At the same time a third figure emerges—the homosexual Henry III—who, in spite of the fact that he also lacks consistency and credibility, embodies more directly Marlowe's psychological concern for socially acceptable individuation. In fact, the simultaneous struggle of both Navarre and Henry III away from pre-Oedipal dependence—they bond homosocially toward the end of the play, as allies against the Guise—may partly explain the play's artistic failure. Marlowe's muse has previously been most effectively inspired by the narcissistic fantasy of absolute control; since he now chooses to exorcise that fantasy, he experiences uncertain poetic inspiration and faces artistic difficulties that he does not resolve until turning to *Edward II,* a play that may be regarded if not as Marlowe's greatest, then certainly as his most honest work.

Before examining the three characterizations in more detail, a discussion of the overall impression created by the play, involving some honesty of our own, is in order. Kocher has stated that Marlowe "is consciously, and perhaps cynically, pandering to the most brutal appetites and prejudices of the Elizabethan spectator."[7] Wilbur Sanders entitles his chapter on *The Massacre* "Dramatist as Jingoist," and suggests the play's badness "raises most pressingly the question of Marlowe's real stature."[8] Douglas Cole, though not as hard on Marlowe as a whole, agrees that *The Massacre* "remains inevitably a crude spectacle of sensationalistic propaganda."[9] More recently Julia Briggs has objected by raising questions that must cross the minds of all Marlowe admirers. In answer to the widespread assumption that the play "is 'obviously' a piece of crude Protestant propaganda," Briggs remarks that the "very obviousness of [this] supposition ought to arouse suspicion, for in Marlowe's dramaturgy things are so seldom exactly what they seem."[10] Later she adds: "Elsewhere [Marlowe's] plays reveal his fascination with morally complex situations—it is hard to understand why this play has traditionally been regarded as the exception."[11] Briggs also cites Judith Weil, who in *Merlin's Prophet* claims that the play's pervading irony is "dependent less upon 'hard' allusions, more upon dramatic structure and implicit ideas," and functions very "obliquely."[12] Weil's argument itself is at times very oblique, though the gist of her discussion may be garnered from her "hypothesis that *The Massacre at Paris* is a satire on the inhuman worldliness of Christian rulers."[13] However, we are on very thin critical ice when Weil remarks: "Never does the obliqueness of [Marlowe's] ironic style appear more irresponsible. *The Massacre at Paris* badly needs a Shavian preface."[14] Even Briggs in her discussion eventually admits that "Whatever reservations may remain with regard to Navarre's fine sentiments or the Guise's gross cynicism, the play's obvious tendency is to invite our approval of the former and our condemnation of the latter."[15] This seems to me the inescapable point—what the play really is trying to do. Thus, while Weil makes several interesting observations during her discussion, I feel it impossible either to accept her thesis that the work is a subtle satire (at least a consistently developed one) or to ignore the strong identification with the Protestant figures in the play. Cole's argument on this point seems to me irrefutable: while "Marlowe had given to the victims of Barabas, with the exception of Abigail, a disreputable coloring which served to minimize any possible sympathy," in *The Massacre at Paris* "the majority of victims are presented as pious and helpless Protestants, fully deserving the audience's complete sympathy."[16] Marlowe clearly has begun to identify more with the victims than the villain-heroes, and in a manner that does not allow for a vigorous satire on all the Christian rulers in the play.

I suggest that Marlowe's strong identification with the "negative identity" of Barabas involved a psychological burden from which he sought artistic release; Barabas's exclamation, "What, all alone?" and his creeping back into Malta reflect Marlowe's own desire to *belong* to a larger group or supporting social structure. *The Massacre* represents an attempt by the playwright to reidentify with his national and religious roots, to reestablish himself as a member of his own community. Unacceptable impulses could then be projected onto an "other"[17]—in this case the French Catholics, especially the Guise. There may be other reasons for Marlowe's identification with the Protestant cause. Kuriyama remarks, "Insofar as Protestantism is indeed a revolt against the paternal authority of the Pope and his hierarchy, Marlowe probably felt a sporadic and transitory identification with the Protestant cause," but adds, "given the play's suggestion that one must be unscrupulous to survive, this identification appears to be quite shallow."[18] I agree that this identification is complicated and in some ways undermined, but I believe that the play suggests—or rather was trying to suggest, as Marlowe originally conceived it— that one need *not* be completely unscrupulous to survive. It is the very idea enunciated by Kuriyama—the distorted Machiavellian vision so energetically explored in *The Jew of Malta*—that Marlowe attempts to move away from in *The Massacre*. In the confused characterizations of Navarre and Henry III the play reveals Marlowe's renewed struggle to create for himself an idealized or at least socially competent masculine self-object. Marlowe had reached a point where he could no longer portray "ruthless individualism" and hypocritical deception as a viable or even dramatically engaging method of personal survival.

We may begin with Marlowe's artistic "exorcism" of the Machiavellian hero-villain. Though some critics have found the Guise admirable or heroic—Steane calls his first soliloquy "one of Marlowe's great speeches," which "starts with a characteristic sense of exciting possibilities opening out"[19]—it is in fact the sense of *pointless* aspiration and violence, the *lack* of exciting possibilities opening out in this speech, that precludes any sympathy we might feel for the character. His first short speech in the play at the beginning of scene 2—"If ever Hymen lour'd at marriage-rites / And had his altars deck'd with dusky lights . . ."—has something of the quality of Barabas's witchlike chant over the poisoned pot of porridge. And if *The Massacre* lacks an Ithamore to undercut the overblown rhetoric ("What a blessing has he given 't! Was ever pot of rice-porridge so sauced?" [3.4.106]), the crude hyperbole is plainly evident from the speech itself. Having it comically undercut would in fact be inappropriate in this play, for, considering Marlowe's greater identification with the victims, there can no longer be anything amusing about the Guise's pathological behavior. Weil points out that the words *resolution* and *revenge* recur as key terms in the play,[20] yet the early scenes of *The Massacre* only emphasize the gratuitous quality of both the Guise's revenge and his resolution. What does he wish to revenge except a royal marriage that had promised to bring peace and harmony to the realm? His resolution can therefore only seem unheroic and maliciously self-serving. Unlike Barabas he is not personally injured at this point in the play, and there is thus no temptation to identify with his heroic project as being at all admirable or even meaningful.

It is worth examining the long soliloquy in more detail. In spite of Steane's admiration and of Oliver's comment that the speech "has a true Marlovian note,"[21] Kuriyama is more accurate when she comments on "its bloated language and its air of smug self-assurance" and adds that "one can recognize, dimly, the familiar features of Tamburlaine's rhetoric, distorted by unnatural swelling, and now accompanied by a most disagreeable stench."[22] Ithamore's "live with me and be my love" speech in The Jew of Malta shows that Marlowe is quite capable of self-parody, and the Guise's soliloquy indeed parodies the rhetoric of Marlowe's earlier aspiring heroes. While the earlier heroes' aspirations were also (though more subtly) undercut in various ways, never has Marlowe portrayed self-definition as such a hollow and pointless act; never has the rhetoric itself come so close to the ridiculous:

> Now, Guise, begins those deep-engender'd thoughts
> To burst abroad those never-dying flames
> Which cannot be extinguish'd but by blood.
> Oft have I levell'd, and at last have learn'd
> That peril is the chiefest way to happiness,
> And resolution honour's fairest aim.
> What glory is there in a common good
> That hangs for every peasant to achieve?
> That like I best that flies beyond my reach.
> Set me to scale the high Pyramides,
> And thereon set the diadem of France,
> I'll either rend it with my nails to naught
> Or mount the top with my aspiring wings,
> Although my downfall be the deepest hell.
>
> (2.31–44)

Here we have the Guise's ostensible object identified—the French "diadem"—though, as Weil points out,[23] we quickly lose sight of it in the following lines. The confusing metaphor involving the diadem set on the "Pyramides" may show, as Oliver argues, "the characteristic refusal to see a middle way,"[24] since the Guise would either mount to the top (on wings) or fall into hell, yet he first talks of either climbing the pyramids or tearing them to pieces—that is, if the "it" in line 42 refers to "Pyramides" as a collective singular, as Oliver argues.[25] However, it is possible to take "it" as referring to the diadem itself, so we get an odd rhetorical conflation of the ends with the means. The confusion here may very well result from faulty reporting. Yet the uncertainty of the antecedent is conceivably deliberate on Marlowe's part, to show the destructiveness—the self-canceling nature—of the Guise's aspirations, since he apparently would destroy both the thing he aspires to and his means of getting to it. A similar suggestion arises when the Duke exclaims:

> For this, my quenchless thirst whereon I build
> Hath often pleaded kindred to the King.
>
> (47–48)

Levin comments on this "curious metaphor which intermixes the acts of construction and consumption"[26] and relates it to the Guise's desire either to climb or to destroy the pyramids. The irony inherent in the Guise's self-destructive stance becomes more apparent when he remarks:

> For this, this head, this heart, this hand and sword,
> Contrives, imagines, and fully executes
> Matters of import, aim'd at by many,
> Yet understood by none:
> For this, hath heaven engender'd me of earth.
>
> (49–53)

Considering the grammatical and metaphoric confusion of the previous lines, the phrase "Yet understood by none" does not come as a surprise, and surely the inescapable assumption here is that "none" includes the Guise himself. The metrical space after the half-line gives us a moment to come to this realization: the Guise really has no idea what he is talking about or aiming at. The antecedent of the frequently repeated "this"—it is presumably at first the French crown, or the act of aspiring toward it—becomes less and less certain as the speech progresses, until he belatedly reminds us (and himself) that he means to "deal [him]self a king" (87).

The speech thus communicates more a sense of uncontrolled restlessness than of steady purpose. There is an emphasis on "engendering" (31, 53), which suggests that the Guise is involved in the same struggle to give birth to himself—to establish a sense of identity—that we have observed with Faustus and Barabas. The trouble is, he seems very confused as to what he identifies with, or defines himself against. At one moment he seems to require the whole earth as his self-object or "other"—"For this, this earth sustains my body's weight" (54)—which modulates into his dream of possessing the French crown—"And with this weight I'll counterpoise a crown" (55)—which itself is replaced by an aimless and juvenile threat—"Or with seditions weary all the world" (56). He gloats over the support he receives from the

Pope and the Queen Mother, and goes on to vaguely identify with thousands of Catholics in "colleges . . . monasteries, priories, abbeys, and halls" (77–78) so that he can speak finally of bringing "the will of *our* desires to end" (84, my emphasis). It is not at all clear, however, how they share a common desire; obviously, they cannot all possess the French crown, though perhaps the Guise egotistically assumes that these men actively support his claim to the throne. Yet if he expects military support from the "thirty thousand able men" (79) and the "thousand sturdy student Catholics" (81), he surely cannot expect it from the "Five hundred fat Franciscan friars and priests" (82); and his earlier rejection of religion makes it clear he does not expect their prayers. The Guise next considers his opponents, beginning with his archenemy:

> Ay, but Navarre, Navarre—'tis but a nook of France,
> Sufficient yet for such a petty King
> That, with a rabblement of his heretics,
> Blinds Europe's eyes and troubleth our estate:
> Him will we—[*Pointing to his sword.*]
>
> (88–92)

If we have thus far been unimpressed by the Guise's rhetoric, this feeble moment certainly validates such a response, since words themselves fail him. He then considers his own countrymen who oppose him, and reacts to this threat by assuming a fantastic Tamburlainean stance that in the more realistic, less poetic context of *The Massacre* only seems ridiculous:

> Give me a look that, when I bend the brows,
> Pale death may walk in furrows of my face;
> A hand that with a grasp may gripe the world.
>
> (97–99)

Yet the image of the superman suddenly falls bathetically into the more mundane one of an eavesdropper who, presumably, actually needs to forestall his enemies' plans:

> An ear to hear what my detractors say . . .
>
> (100)

This is followed by a banal reiteration of the Guise's object of desire:

> A royal seat, a sceptre, and a crown
>
> (101)

and then by a return to hyperbole, the rhetorical force of which is crippled by anacoluthon:[27]

> That those which do behold, they may become
> As men that stand and gaze against the sun.
>
> (102–3)

The Guise concludes:

> The plot is laid, and things shall come to pass
> Where resolution strives for victory.

The only plot we have seen him lay in this scene, however, is the poisoning of the Queen Mother of Navarre. We are left wondering if the Guise has any clearer idea than we do what other "things shall come to pass," and we are mystified by the hollowness of the final line, especially the empty sound of "victory."

As Kuriyama suggests, such language has aptly been described by Wilbur Sanders as "gigantic self-assertions of gigantic non-entities, resounding in a poetic void,"[28] yet Sanders does not consider the possibility that Marlowe was striving for just such an effect. The ironies are too pointed to be accidental. For example, the Guise accuses Navarre of blinding Europe's eyes, but he himself wants to be an exhibitionist sun king whom men "stand and gaze against" and are presumably blinded by. The blindness-sight motif is in fact a crucial one, and I suspect it was more fully developed in the complete text of the play. In scene 2 the Guise says to the Apothecary:

> Go, then, present them [the poisoned gloves] to the Queen of
>   Navarre:
> For she is that huge blemish in our eye
> That makes these upstart heresies in France.
>
> (20–22)

Weil suspects here a "covert reference"[29] to Luke 6:42: "Hypocrite, cast out the beame out of thine owne eye first, & then shalt thou se perfectly, to pul out the mote that is in thy brothers eye."[30] She suggests that the "Guise appears to be a knowing hypocrite, but like Barabas he sometimes seems to fool himself with his professions."[31] I would question, however, if the Duke is con-

scious of the allusion in the above lines, for in the play he characteristically points out the blindness of others while failing to
recognize his own lack of perception or awareness. "For this," he
exclaims in his long soliloquy, "I wake, when others think I sleep"
(2.45), as if he knows and sees more than anyone else, and his
reference to "Matters of import . . . / Yet understood by none"
(51–52) suggests that he believes others do not suspect his evil
designs, an obviously erroneous assumption. There is an interesting recurrence of the seeing-waking motif in the passage from
the Collier leaf,[32] where the Guise stands gloating over the body
of the King's minion, who has cuckolded him, and whom he has
just had murdered. After the Guise's remark—"Revenge it,
Henry, as thou list or dare; / I did it only in despite of thee"
(19.15–16)—the Collier leaf adds the following:

> Fondly hast thou incens'd the Guise's soul,
> That of itself was hot enough to work
> Thy just digestion with extremest shame!
> The army I have gathered now shall aim
> More at thy end than extirpation;
> And when thou think'st I have forgotten this,
> And that thou most reposest on my faith,
> Then will I wake thee from thy foolish dream
> And let thee see thyself my prisoner.[33]

Steane suggests that there is here "the egoist's sense that only *he*
lives a full, waking life; the others dream."[34] However, the great
irony is that throughout the play it is the Guise who lives with
his eyes closed, in a foolish dream. King Henry has no trouble
hoodwinking him at the end by pretending to love him and trust
him, when he has already arranged the Guise's murder:

> *K. Henry.* Cousin, assure you I am resolute—
> Whatsoever any whisper in mine ears—
> Not to suspect disloyalty in thee:
> And so, sweet coz, farewell.
> [*Exit* King *with* Epernoun *and* Captain of the Guard]
> *Guise.* So; now sues the King for favour to the Guise,
> And all his minions stoop when I command.
> Why, this 'tis to have an army in the field.
> Now by the holy sacrament I swear:
> As ancient Romans over their captive lords,
> So will I triumph over this wanton king,
> And he shall follow my proud chariot's wheels.
> *Now do I but begin to look about,*

> And all my former time was spent in vain.
> Hold, sword, for in thee is the Duke of Guise's hope.
>
> (21.44–57, my emphasis)

Marlowe has not portrayed any of his previous heroes or villains as being quite this stupid or blind. The irony of the italicized line could not be more blatant, and it is in fact intensified by the subsequent action. A repentant Third Murderer comes onstage to warn the Guise of the impending ambush. The nobleman decides to proceed, trusting again to the power of his Tamburlainean gaze:

> Yet Caesar shall go forth.
> Let mean conceits and baser men fear death:
> Tut, they are peasants; I am Duke of Guise;
> And princes with their looks engender fear.
>
> (67–70)

In what follows I accept Oliver's interpretation of the action. The Guise exclaims, "As pale as ashes!" at the "ghastly" face of the Third Murderer, and suddenly loses confidence; no godlike entity, he is actually desperately dependent on and sensitive to the mirroring of others. "Nay, then, 'tis time to look about," he says in a cringing attempt to retreat, and the phrase perfectly inverts the sense of his former boastful, "Now do I but begin to look about." The murderers then fall upon him, and he dies ignobly: "To die by peasants, what a grief is this" (81). "*Vive la messe!* Perish Huguenots!" he cries, reminding us of the completely gratuitous nature of the religious murders he has committed, since he has not personally believed in any religion. Although Cole argues that "there is more propaganda value than consistency"[35] in this final curse, there is something psychologically credible about the Guise's inconsistency: we can understand this last-ditch attempt by a dying man to identify with a larger cause, to tack on meaning to an otherwise meaningless struggle.

I therefore believe that, in the context of *The Massacre at Paris*, the Guise's initial rejection of religion is presented as reprehensible, even if its iconoclasm is somewhat akin to Marlowe's own attitudes, and his own personal struggle:

> For this, have I a largess from the Pope,
> A pension and a dispensation too;
> And by that privilege to work upon,
> My policy hath fram'd religion.

Religion: *O Diabole!*
Fie, I am asham'd, however that I seem,
To think a word of such a simple sound,
Of so great matter should be made the ground.

(2.59–66)

It is surely the *groundlessness* of the Guise, in life and in death, that makes us carefully reconsider these lines. With this moment in the speech—and with the irony it produces in light of the Guise's eventual fate—we come close to the divided mind that Marlowe's work as a whole reflects: to assert and define oneself at all costs, ostensibly brooking no limitations, but always with the hesitation, the fear, of isolating oneself from a larger order or pattern of meaning. In spite of Marlowe's vision of the indifference of God in *Faustus* and his attacks on religion in *The Jew of Malta*, he never quite transcends a desire for religious consolation, for the surrender of personal struggle in the arms of a greater being. And if Marlowe in his career moves toward the argument that, for the majority of humankind, God must remain "only" an act of imagination, the playwright (not unlike the Machiavelli of *The Discourses*) nevertheless seems to regard it as a necessary social act, and not always simply as personal hypocrisy.

With the Guise we clearly have a case of failed imagination that results at least in part from his complete rejection of religious identification, his failure to internalize any consistent ideals. Such a rejection leaves him psychologically isolated, forced to depend on sources of support that he must underplay or hypocritically denigrate; he thus relishes his pension from the Pope at the same time that he is "ashamed" of the Pope's religion. In spite of his "gigantic self-assertions," he is hardly self-sufficient, and his reliance on the Pope and Philip of Spain seriously damages his heroic image. He begins to look like a "mere tool":[36]

> *Eper.* Thou able to maintain an host in pay,
> That livest by foreign exhibition!
> The Pope and King of Spain are thy good friends,
> Else all France knows how poor a Duke thou art.

(19.37–40)

The Guise compensates by assuming the grandiose heroic identity of Caesar, a figure the pro-Catholic League pamphlets often compared him to.[37] Yet he seems blind to the tragic fate implied by this identification. For a while he believes himself capable of a superman's career, and his grim joke at the expense of Ramus's life—"*Argumentum testimonii est inartificiale* / To contradict which, I say: Ramus shall die" (9.34–35)—is reminiscent of Tamburlaine's boast that "Will and shall best fitteth Tamburlaine" (part 1, 3.3.41). Yet in his final brief moment of defiance and daring examined above—"Yet Caesar shall go forth. / Let mean conceits and baser men fear death"—he finds, "as Tamburlaine did not, that his emblematic appearance cannot help him."[38] The imagined identity cannot come to terms with reality, and here I disagree with Briggs's assertion that the Guise's death is heroic: "The Guise declares 'Thus Caesar did go forth, and thus he died' (xxi.87)—that is to say, 'thus he went forth bravely, despite warnings' and 'thus he died, treacherously murdered by a trusted friend.'"[39] The Guise as Marlowe portrays him hardly shows genuine courage, and Henry hardly represents Brutus, a trusted friend, for the Guise all along has schemed to destroy him.

The fact is that the Guise has no trusted friends or satisfying personal relationships. His vaguely sexual rapport with the Queen Mother again only serves to cast doubt on his integrity and independence, by raising the question of who is using whom. It is Catherine who speaks the first voice of dissent in the play:

> K. *Char.* Come, mother, let us go to honour this solemnity.
> Q. *Cath.* [*Aside*] Which I'll dissolve with blood and cruelty.
> (1.24–25)

She certainly speaks as an independent agent here, and her later speeches give no evidence that she intends to share the power to which she aspires:

> Tush man, let me alone with him
> To work the way to bring this thing to pass;
> And if he do deny what I do say,
> I'll despatch him with his brother presently,
> And then shall Monsieur [Alençon] wear the diadem.
> Tush, all shall die unless I have my will,
> For while she lives, Catherine will be Queen.
> Come, my Lords, let us go seek the Guise,
> And then determine of this enterprise.
> (14.60–68, which closely parallels 11.37–45)

In light of such speeches the Guise begins to look very much like a pawn of the Queen Mother. He certainly obeys her eagerly:

Be gone, delay no time, sweet Guise.
                              Madam,
I go as whirlwinds rage before a storm.
                                        (11.28–30)

Kuriyama argues that "the Guise may be taken as another of Catherine's sons" and that her final speech "suggests that the Guise is the favored prehomosexual son, her conspirator and confidant."[40] While this theory of the Guise as "prehomosexual" is highly questionable, he does seem to represent the pre-Oedipal, unindividuated self with an unusually strong bond to the Queen Mother. Her response to the Guise's death certainly involves a surprising emotional intensity:

> To whom shall I bewray my secrets now
> Or who will help to build religion?
> . . . .
> But sorrow seize upon my toiling soul,
> For since the Guise is dead, I will not live.
>
>   (21.153–61)

Moreover, Marlowe attaches a strong sense of sexual failure to the Duke's career. Like Tamburlaine, the Guise seems obsessed with his sword's point (2.92, 9.79, 21.57) in a way that suggests a compensatory phallic agression. His marital relations are an embarrassment, since his wife is carrying on an affair with one of the King's minions, Mugeroun—a man whose ambiguous sexual role at court makes him, from the Duke's perspective, an extremely damaging masculine rival. In the scene where the Guise discovers proof of his wife's infidelity there is again an emphasis on sight and eyes, perhaps because this is one of the few times he actually has his eyes opened, and he displays here, albeit briefly, something approaching genuine human suffering. The scene therefore seems more real, more dramatically convincing, than almost any other in the play. The Duchess, thinking of her lover, begins by wishing for a rendezvous in "some place / Where we may one enjoy the other's sight" (15.7–8), a romantic reciprocity that we assume she can never enjoy with her narcissistic husband. The Guise enters and, smelling a rat, insists that he "must see" the "secrets of [her] heart" (19–20). He then castigates her:

> Is all my love forgot which held thee dear,
> Ay, dearer than the apple of mine eye?

> Is Guise's glory but a cloudy mist
> In sight and judgment of thy lustful eye?

(27–30)

In spite of the characteristic emphasis on *his* glory, there is also here a hint of injured affection—"dearer than the apple of mine eye." And while his concern for his image in *her* eyes indicates his need for her as a mirroring self-object, there is also a suggestion that her love and her thoughts, her sight *and* judgment, had been important to him. Yet his final sense of betrayal—"Now I do see that from the very first / Her eyes and looks sow'd seeds of perjury" (37–38)—ironically recalls to us his own treacherous behavior, not to mention his moral blindness and solipsism. He is clearly a man worth betraying, a man who has inspired no affection in others, with the exception of the venomous Queen Mother.

In contrast to the Guise's failed marriage, the brief glimpse we are given of Navarre's married state suggests that it will be one of cooperation and caring. In what seems perhaps an overly schematic fashion, Queen Margaret is shown both tempering her husband's forcefulness and steeling his weakness. When Navarre responds too harshly to his mother's fear of having been poisoned—

> The late suspicion of the Duke of Guise
> Might well have mov'd Your Highness to beware
> How you did meddle with such dangerous gifts

(3.12–14)

—his wife seeks to soften the effect of his speech:

> Too late it is, my Lord, if that be true,
> To blame Her Highness; but I hope it be
> Only some natural passion makes her sick.

(15–17)

Yet when the worst is realized, Navarre displays the Marlovian tendency to premature surrender in which one can hardly overlook the pre-Oedipal implications of simultaneous maternal and religious dependence:

> My mother poison'd here before my face!
> O gracious God, what times are these?
> O grant, sweet God, my days may end with hers,

> That I with her may die and live again.
>
> (21–24)

Margaret now responds with the will to endure which her husband lacks:

> Let not this heavy chance, my dearest Lord,
> (For whose effects my soul is massacred)
> Infect thy gracious breast with fresh supply
> To aggravate our sudden misery.
>
> (25–28)

She thus combines sensitivity or depth of feeling with resolution, and it is significant that such resolution in this instance comes from the woman. Marlowe is apparently moving away from the dichotomy of masculine aggression versus feminine submissiveness established in *Tamburlaine*, but without replacing it with the complete inversion of masculine and feminine roles that occurs periodically in *Dido Queen of Carthage*. And if, in *The Massacre*, Queen Catherine represents female aggressiveness in the extreme, Margaret, unlike Catherine or Dido, displays strength of character without all-consuming willfulness. The Navarre-Margaret relationship promises to be one of mutual cooperation and support rather than a power struggle.

While this reading may seem to attach a great deal of significance to a very brief episode in the play, there are other indications that Marlowe was attempting, in his characterization of Navarre and of those closely associated with him, to portray human beings who succeed in balancing or at least managing their conflicting impulses. Oliver, I believe, comes very close to the heart of what Marlowe was trying to do with Navarre's characterization when he remarks:

Some may see incongruity in the conjunction of ideas when he decides to flee from France:

> I'll muster up an army secretly,
> For fear that Guise, join'd with the King of Spain,
> Might seem to cross me in mine enterprise.
> But God that always doth defend the right
> Will show his mercy and preserve us still
>
> (xiii.37–41)

. . . but Cromwell was neither hypocritical nor irreligious when he gave his famous advice to trust in God and keep your powders dry.[41]

Navarre, like Ferneze, becomes very much a representative of the principle that God helps those who help themselves. I suspect, along with Oliver, that Navarre's character "may have lost some of its complexity in the 'reporting' "[42] and therefore must disagree with those who see him as "the merest patchwork of Protestant commonplaces"[43] or as one who merely spouts "pious platitudes."[44] Navarre's facile faith at the beginning of the play is in fact seriously questioned by the subsequent action. Cole attempts to argue that the play's "outcome is as inevitable as it is orthodox—in fact, it is assured at the very start by the words of Navarre":[45]

> But He that sits and rules above the clouds
> Doth hear and see the prayers of the just,
> And will revenge the blood of innocents
> That Guise hath slain by treason of his heart
> And brought by murder to their timeless ends.
>
> (1.41–45)

Hardly a prophetic "assurance," this speech seems more a case of premature optimism, coming as it does before the massacre itself, when hundreds of Protestants are slaughtered and Navarre barely escapes with his life. What God actually sees and hears remains moot, and "revenge," as Navarre comes to learn, is something he must effect himself. When Cole argues that the scene (12) involving the murder of five or six Protestants at prayers is "obviously intended to increase the indignation of a Protestant audience toward the protagonist [the Guise],"[46] he is undoubtedly correct, but he misses the full significance; for behind this obvious manipulation of audience reactions Marlowe is again questioning the efficacy of prayer (recall Faustus's ironic "Ay, pray for me, pray for me" to the Scholars before his death). With the victory over Joyeux, a matured Navarre can remark, "Thus God, we see, doth ever guide the right, / To make his glory great upon the earth" (18.3–4), but only after he has insisted, before the battle, that "*We must with resolute minds resolve to fight* / In honour of our God and country's good" (16.10–11, my emphasis). Navarre has managed to individuate in a manly sense, and to internalize a religio-political ideal. It is the individual assertion that matters most, but for inspiration and strength Navarre is careful to identify with a larger cause. As Navarre points out, this identification is exactly what the narcissistic Guise lacks: "So he be safe, he cares not what becomes / Of King or country—no, not for them both" (16.42–43). It is interesting to note, however, that by the end of the play Navarre's faith in his own individual assertions seems to have won out over his religious sentiments; as Steane remarks, the "last words of the play are hard and vindictive":[47]

> And then I vow for to revenge his [Henry's] death
> As Rome and all those popish prelates there
> Shall curse the time that e'er Navarre was king
> And rul'd in France by Henry's fatal death!
>
> (24.108–11)

Steane in fact gives a very accurate description of the play's resolution: "We are not left with a fairy-tale world, where all is as it was in the beginning: order re-established and everything happy ever after. What triumphs is a 'good' (as opposed to Machiavellian) political realism, and it is a *hard* and not idyllic re-establishment of order."[48] The ending is thus only guardedly optimistic, for resolution and endurance, rather than love and cooperation, prove to be the necessary ingredients for survival in society. Without any mention of God's guidance or mercy in the final speech, Navarre is in some danger of hardening into the assertive tyranny of a Tamburlainean hero, disposing of prelates as Tamburlaine did kings.

Certainly, however, we are meant to see a triumph of "good" over Machiavellian political realism in Navarre's forthrightness and directness, for even the figure of Henry III has to pay the ultimate price for his employment of Machiavellian tactics in spite of his eventual "conversion." Kocher finds "the contrast between the Anjou of [the massacre] scenes and the sympathetic Henry III of the closing scenes of the play . . . so sharp as to render the character wellnigh unintelligible,"[49] and indeed Henry is not very skillfully developed. Yet the disparate elements in his characterization make him—in relation to Marlowe's own psychological conflicts—the most interesting figure in the play. He at first seems as Machiavellian as the Guise. In his reply to Charles's objection to the massacre, Henry offers a rationale which reveals, according to Kuriyama, "a firmer grasp of the situation,"[50] but it is in fact an evil justification for gratuitous aggression:

> Though gentle minds should pity others' pains,
> Yet will the wisest note their proper griefs,
> And rather seek to scourge their enemies
> Than be themselves base subjects to the whip.
>
> (4.13–16)

Henry displays the same motiveless malignancy during the massacre: "I am disguis'd and none knows who I am, / And therefore mean to murder all I meet" (5.5–6). This action provides a good example of the difference between simple role playing and mature self-fashioning. By temporarily evading the responsibility of maintaining a coherent identity, the young prince is able to practice as much aggression and violence as possible. Such behavior, at an adolescent stage, would appear to have one major advantage: Henry survives while his weak-willed and passive older brother is easily and ruthlessly removed from the picture. Having learned brutal assertiveness, however, Henry also begins to cultivate a certain amount of political savvy and foresight. In his acceptance of the Polish crown (scene 10), Henry "shrewdly assesses the challenge the offer entails,"[51] and also ensures that his inheritance of the French crown will not be prevented. The fact that scene 10 is oddly and ahistorically inserted in the midst of the continuing drama of the massacre suggests that Marlowe was at some pains to highlight the more positive aspects of Henry's character early in the play.

The most interesting aspect of Henry's character is not made apparent until he becomes King of France, and at his coronation declares:

> What says our minions? Think they Henry's heart
> Will not both harbour love and majesty?
> Put off that fear, they are already join'd;
> No person, place, or time, or circumstance
> Shall slack my love's affection from his bent;
> As now you are, so shall you still persist,
> Removeless from the favours of your king.
>
> (14.16–22)

Here is remarkable resolution in a Marlovian context: to harbor both majesty (power) *and* love, and a kind of love that his society is not likely to condone. The speech raises the question whether Henry's behavior represents foolish and irresponsible dotage or a legitimate attempt to balance love and duty.

A brief examination of some of Marlowe's source materials may prove helpful. Briggs points out that the pamphlets of the pro-Catholic League "indulged in the most extravagant character assassinations of Henry III (whom they consistently demoted to 'Henry of Valois') for his failure to adopt their own hard line on the Huguenot issue."[52] Kocher informs us that such publications "spread tales of riot and homosexuality. In its public demands that the mignons be dismissed, the League charged waste of public funds, giving of bad counsel to the King, displacing of the older nobility by these upstarts, and the like. The issue was useful to the League in undermining confidence in the King. Protestants, on the other hand, were faintly apologetic for the mignons, hoping thus to woo Henry away from the League."[53] Marlowe as well is at least "apologetic" for the minions, and while some of Henry's subsequent actions are irresponsible, he shows signs of developing into a mature and competent ruler. His sending of "sweet Joyeux" to do battle with Navarre is reminiscent of the embarrassing Mycetes-Meander rapport in *Tamburlaine,* and his making horns at the Guise is a puerile jest that serves only to incite the Guise and place Mugeroun in more immediate danger. However, he appears to recognize his foolishness quickly, and (though it is too late to save his friend) he thereafter acts with more force and maturity; when confronted with the Guise's recalcitrance, he ironically exclaims:

> Guise, wear our crown, and be thou King of France,
> And as dictator make or war or peace
> Whilst I cry *placet* like a senator!
> I cannot brook thy haughty insolence:
> Dismiss thy camp, or else by our edict
> Be thou proclaim'd a traitor throughout France.
>
> (19.55–60)

Yet the roller coaster ride of our opinion of him continues. Faced with the Guise's dissembling, Henry unfortunately decides to descend to the level of his opponent. His treacherous entrapment of the Duke—as well as the murder of his brother—results eventually in his own betrayal at the hands of the fanatical Friar. With "revenge" recurring as a key word, the law of an-eye-for-an-eye hangs over the action of the play like a dark cloud; witness the exchange between Henry and the Guise's son:

> K. Henry. Boy, look where your father lies.
> G.'s Son. My father slain! Who hath done this deed?
> K. Henry. Sirrah, 'twas I that slew him; and will slay
> Thee too, and thou prove such a traitor.
> G.'s Son. Art thou a king, and hast done this bloody deed?
> I'll be revenged!
>   [*He offereth to throw his dagger.*]
> K. Henry. Away to prison with him! I'll clip his wings
> Or e'er he pass my hands; away with him!

(21.117–24)

The strong suggestion of unending bloodshed perhaps explains
the biblical parody in the coronation scene, when Mugeroun cuts
off the Cutpurse's ear and Henry "forgives" the thief for his offense. As Weil points out,[54] this incident would recall Peter's actions in Gethsemane when Jesus was arrested, and Christ's
admonition (Matt. 26:52): "All that take the sworde, shal perishe
with the sworde." If such a warning forms part of the underlying
message of the play, then Navarre's final emphasis on revenge is
perhaps more ominous than one would first think (and Marlowe's
play surprisingly prophetic, since Navarre himself was eventually
assassinated).

Yet the play elsewhere shows the necessity of individual assertiveness (provided it is controlled and rational) and so it could
hardly be claimed that *The Massacre* advocates a philosophy of
complete nonresistance. Despite the underhanded method of dis-
patching the Guise, this action allows Henry, unlike Charles, to
escape from his mother's domination and to assert his
independence:

> Mother, how like you this device of mine?
> I slew the Guise, because I would be King.
> . . . .
> Cry out, exclaim, howl till thy throat be hoarse,
> The Guise is slain, and I rejoice therefore!
>
> (21.136–49)

Significantly, Henry is helped to this new sense of identity and
power by Epernoun, who first suggests that the Guise be
murdered:

> My Lord, I think, for safety of your royal person,
> It would be good the Guise were made away,
> And so to quite Your Grace of all suspect.
>
> (19.82–84)

Though Henry tells Epernoun, "I will be rul'd by thee" (81), the
King seems far less a mere tool of his friend than Edward II does
of Gaveston. Epernoun appears to be a manly (if sometimes rather
Machiavellian) companion who acts as a positive masculine self-
object for the quickly maturing Henry. In scene 19 Epernoun
manages to aid Henry's reassertion of power over the Guise, but
without seeming to control the King or making him look weak.

Henry now adopts a kind of self-presentation and self-control that suggest the beginnings of more skillfull self-fashioning: "And, Epernoun, though I seem mild and calm, / Think not but I am tragical within" (88–89). To compare him with the two central characters of *The Jew of Malta*, Henry has managed to relinquish the dangerously unstable role playing of Barabas for the calmer, more politically connected and purposeful shifting of Ferneze.

Marlowe's portrayal of intimate friendship between Henry and Epernoun may have been influenced by the pamphlet sources; Briggs states that "explicit accusations of homosexuality were frequently made against the King, *in particular with Epernon*" (my emphasis).[55] Henry apparently moves from an initial stage of irresponsibility and indulgence with a group of minions to a more mature stage where he maintains a constructive and mutually supportive relationship with Epernoun. Epernoun's affection for Henry appears genuine and selfless; he is concerned for Henry's safety and suspicious of the Friar in the final scene, and, when the King is injured, his friend's response reveals a deep attachment:

> *Nav.* [to Henry] Long may you live, and still be King of France.
> *Eper.* Or else die Epernoun.
> *K. Henry.* Sweet Epernoun, thy King must die.
> . . . .
> Ah, Epernoun, is this thy love to me?
> Henry thy King wipes off these childish tears
> And bids thee whet thy sword on Sixtus' bones
> That it may keenly slice the Catholics.
>
> (24.87–99)

Although the text as it has survived does not develop their relationship in great detail, the two men evidently have deeply identified with each other. Though in dying Henry encourages Epernoun in a program of ruthless revenge, this adjuration cannot hide the fact that the King has inspired real, selfless affection in another human being.

While the darker side of manly assertion is present in the portraits of both Henry and Navarre, these characters are brought together in a positive homosocial bond of political and ideological cooperation late in the play when they unite against the Guise. In his portrayal of the alliance of Henry and Navarre, Marlowe's reidentification with his national and religious roots—and, it must be pointed out, Henry's two references to Elizabeth are really the most jingoistic moments of the play—is subtly allied with a sympathetic portrayal of a homosexual king and his faithful lover. Perhaps the more sympathetic treatment of Henry in the Protestant pamphlets contributed, at least subconsciously, to a hope for some kind of social acceptance. Yet *The Massacre at Paris* does not, I believe, reflect a psychological liberation in any modern sense, and the artistic confrontation of overt homosexual feelings in the character of Henry (who after all perishes) leads Marlowe to the emotional excesses, disastrous political conflicts, and intense personal suffering of *Edward II.*

Having examined the three characterizations in some detail, I must add that none is especially convincing or successful. The conversion of Henry from a murderous and unscrupulous young man to a more mature (if still flawed) individual allied with the forces of good is particularly difficult to accept, at least in the shortened form of the play we possess. Marlowe was experiencing such a crucial and difficult transition stage at the moment he wrote *The Massacre* that it is difficult not to accept Kuriyama's general argument that the play's "aesthetic deficiencies originate in [an] underlying . . . [psychological] confusion."[56] *The Massacre* may even, as she suggests, have the "aridity of a futile exercise,"[57] though the play is not without its moments of human affirmation. The scholar Ramus, for example, dies with tragic dignity in the face of the senseless violence embodied by the Guise. Ramus's question to the terrified Taleus, "Wherefore should I fly" (9.6), recalls Faustus's utterance, "Whither should I fly" (2.1.77), but Ramus displays stoic acceptance rather than panic and fear. He even replies calmly and courageously to the Guise's accusation, "And yet didst [thou] never sound anything to the depth" (25), which is in essence a summary of Faustus's failure as a scholar and a man. Marlowe was perhaps originally attracted to this figure because of his intellectual iconoclasm; however, as John Ronald Glenn remarks, "After the bitter anti-Aristotle excesses of his youth, [Ramus] had in fact spent much of his life claiming that he was not opposed to Aristotle at all, but only to the vain scholastics who buried Aristotle under heaps of sterile commentary."[58] We thus again see a pattern of immature self-assertion followed by a more mature recognition of the need for both individual aspiration and an acceptance of authorities external to the self. Marlowe was certainly aware of the development of Ramus's later thought, for the scholar's final dignified defense before being stabbed (40–52) reveals his belief that it was "the marriage of Church and Aristotle which had made academic learning a sterile affair and discouraged thinkers from following their own courses." Ramus's last words, as Glenn states, "are a passionate indictment of the vanity and inconsistency of the Catholic 'Sorbonests' [50], more zealous defending their mountains of quasi-Aristotelian philosophy ('their workes' [51]) than in disseminating knowledge for the purpose of equipping man's reason to serve God."[59] Ramus, who had earlier converted to Protestantism, also reveals his humaneness and moral flexibility by carrying on an intimate relationship with the Catholic Taleus[60] in a society where Catholics and Protestants had become bitter enemies. In spite of the strong Protestant identification in the play, one wonders if Marlowe did not at the same time want to stress that personal qualities rather than religious affiliation determine the worth of an individual. There exists one tantalizing scrap of evidence— outside of the text that has come down to us—that suggests this idea was further developed in the original form of the play. F. P. Wilson informs us that in Thomas Fuller's *Pisgah-Sight of Palestine* (1650), page 95, may be found the following quotation: "I seasonably remember how one being asked in the *Massacre at Paris*, whether he was a *Catholick* or an *Hugonite,* answered *he was a Physician.*"[61]

In light of the homoerotic overtones in the sympathetic portraits of both the Ramus-Taleus and Henry-Epernoun relationships, the play might also contain at least a liminal suggestion that personal qualities rather than *sexual* affiliation determine the worth of an individual. In the final analysis the religious implications of *The Massacre* remain unclear. Ramus's dedication "to the service of the eternal God" (9.52) does not save him (any more than it saves Abigail), Henry dies through a naive belief that "our friars are holy men" (24.23), and even Navarre's final emphasis on personal revenge casts doubts on his future dedication to the Heavenly Father. After *The Massacre* Marlowe appears to abandon his attempt to determine what role God—even as an act of imagination—should play in human experience. In *Edward II* he concentrates almost exclusively on the individual's struggle to maintain and exercise personal control while clamoring for the fulfillment of sexual love. The idea of God recurs briefly as a forgotten dream, though, as we shall see, it still echoes in the emptiness at the core of Marlowe's artistic vision.

7

Edward II: The Illusion of Integrity

BECAUSE OF ITS DIRECT TREATMENT OF HOMOSEXUAL LOVE, *EDWARD II* [1] is a crucial play in the Marlowe canon, and deserves the most careful critical attention. As if intuiting his muse's dependence on narcissistic fantasies, Marlowe again chooses a protagonist who displays marked narcissistic pathology; however, as in *The Jew of Malta* and *The Massacre at Paris,* he explores psychological alternatives through the creation of contrasting characters. While Edward's failure is in fact analyzed fairly objectively in strictly social or political terms, in the final analysis the play remains an emotionally disturbing, even devastating, portrayal of the failure of humanity in general to achieve viable individuation, psychologically reinforcing relationships, and constructive social interaction. Marlowe's darkly secular social vision remains traumatized, uprooted from a traditionally religious worldview but still deeply emotionally and psychologically dependent on its absent spirituality.

Kuriyama remarks in her 1980 study that the play "has sparked no lively controversy. . . . The poet's attitude toward his protagonist, for once, is clear and consistent: our sympathies are encouraged to run fairly close to Kent's."[2] While this statement may be true with respect to the general manipulation of audience sympathies, the play has become, and promises to remain, controversial. Kuriyama does refer to the "generic" dispute over whether *Edward II* is to be regarded as an Elizabethan history play or rather the personal tragedy of an individual who "happens to be the head of a state," as Harry Levin put it.[3] Claude J. Summers, in "Sex, Politics, and Self-Realization in *Edward II*," points out that the play has been dismissed as a proper "history" because of "its failure to promulgate a political lesson compatible with Tudor orthodoxy"; that is, it fails to offer a providential vision of history.[4] While it may appear to some a perversion of postmodern sensibility to assume that such a failure should make the play more, not less, compelling as a work of art, I agree with Summers that "rather than constituting either a flaw or an irrelevancy, the refusal to moralize history is at the heart of both the play's profound political heterodoxy and the personal tragedy of the king."[5]

However, what Summers eventually makes of the king's personal tragedy requires reconsideration. I have remarked, in my previous chapter, that *Edward II* is Marlowe's most honest work, and therefore agree with Kuriyama's statement that it is "the play in which Marlowe seems determined to face his fears most directly."[6] There is in fact other literary evidence of greater personal acceptance on the part of the playwright; assuming that *Hero and Leander* followed *Edward II* relatively closely in time (since by 1592 Marlowe was fast running out of it altogether), it is difficult to believe that a poet who could describe Leander so warmly, and in such loving detail, was still struggling deeply with forbidden sexual impulses. On the other hand, considering that poem from *Leander's* point of view—extrapolating from the myth, the reader foresees the youth's death at the hands of the homosexual Neptune—we might still feel a reservation on the part of the poet with respect to his sense of "homosexual" identity. The fear of loss of "manliness" or personal integrity through homoerotic surrender seems to persist. As the introduction suggested, it is debatable whether a man in the sixteenth century would regard a personal admission of homoerotic attraction as constituting a separate and coherent sexual identity. Citing Alan Bray's *Homosexuality in Renaissance England,* Summers argues that, since "sodomy generally did not denote a specific identity or relate to a particular kind of person, but was considered a temptation to which all men were subject and a symptom of universal dissolution[,] . . . Marlowe's intuition of sexuality as a defining characteristic of personality is all the more remarkable."[7] The intuition referred to here may be more the modern reader's than it is Marlowe's, for *Edward II* is not primarily concerned with asserting homosexual subjectivity, in a revolutionary social sense.

It is true, as Summers contends, that *Edward II* is remarkable for "its resolute failure to condemn homosexuality,"[8] a point established by Purvis Boyette in "Wanton Humour and Wanton Poets: Homosexuality in Marlowe's *Edward II*": "Although Edward is flawed, Marlowe does not locate that flaw in the King's homosexuality."[9] There has in fact been a general consensus, as David Thurn observes, that the play's conflict "is triggered not primarily by the erotic passion that links Edward and Gaveston, but by the violation of class structure represented by Edward's patronage of his lowborn minion."[10] Nevertheless, there have been some attempts to see the sexual issue as central to the play's conflict. The most extreme is Jennifer Brady's argument that Mortimer, apparently threatened by the potential sliding of the homosocial into the homosexual, "approves and vicariously participates in" Edward's murder, which becomes "a phobic, sadistic denigration of homosexual love."[11] Obvious objections to this reading arise: the text makes clear that Mortimer remains ignorant of the method Lightborn uses to kill Edward, and Mortimer himself replies, "his wanton humour grieves not me" to his uncle's oft-quoted speech containing the advice, "Let [Edward] without con-trolment have his will. / The mightiest kings have had their min-ions" (1.4.389–90).[12] The identification of homophobia, however, has persisted, and Viviana Comensoli, citing Dollimore's *Sexual Dissidence*, has argued that while "Mortimer's and the other bar-ons' fear of Gaveston's social climbing follows the common prac-tice in Marlowe's sources, and in early modern society at large, of projecting 'non-sexual fears on to the sexual deviant,' Mortimer's intense hatred of Gaveston's 'baseness' also springs from the fear of being engulfed by something dirty, a common anal fantasy."[13] Comensoli is more convincing when she suggests that Mortimer's equation of Gaveston with Proteus (1.4.410) "confirms that the source of his anxiety is Gaveston's abrogation of the political field through social and sexual fluidity."[14] Mortimer resists and dislikes the "feminine" instability he sees in Gaveston; he displays less homophobia than the more typical Renaissance resistance to ef-feminization. Regarding the play's homoeroticism, Simon Shep-herd reasonably suggests that Edward's behavior is accepted by the two Mortimers only in "the terms on which manliness accepts sodomy,"[15] so that the "allowed sodomy conforms to the estab-lished structures of wealth and class." The significance of such "master and minion" relationships in the literature and social life of early modern England is explored in Bruce R. Smith's *Homosex-ual Desire in Shakespeare's England*. While Smith believes that "Ed-ward and Gaveston play out the roles of 'master' and 'minion,' with all the disparities in power that those roles imply," the critic is forced to conclude that "the role of 'minion' does not quite fit Gaveston," in part because he "enjoys tremendous power."[16] Indeed, to make the relationship fit the master/minion designa-tion in the first place, Smith deliberately obscures the fact that, in Gaveston's allusion to the Hero and Leander myth in the play's opening speech, the favorite has cast Edward in the role of Hero, not of Neptune. Judging by this formula, Edward the "pliant king" fails as a controlling master, and is, as Shepherd remarks, "inconsistently masculine."[17] Jonathan Goldberg objects that, in marking Edward in this way, Shepherd collapses all sexuality into the same sexuality, which in effect becomes a version of critical homophobia; sodomy in the play in fact "allows for difference—sexual difference, gender difference—and allows for ways of conceiving sexual relations and gender construction that cannot be reduced to the normative structure of male/female relations under the modern regimes of heterosexuality."[18] Again this would seem to be attributing to Marlowe a very modern political agenda, although, unlike Summers's, of a constructionist rather than essentialist persuasion.

Most crucial of all with respect to the play's attitude to homosexuality is the problematic issue of the "psychological" or "symbolic" significance of the manner of Edward's death. Kuriyama argues: "Marlowe certainly invites the interpretation first suggested by Empson—that the manner of Edward's death is a Dantesque talion punishment for his sexual transgression."[19] Critics qualify or deny this theory in various ways. Predictably, recent readings such as Brady's offer "sociopolitical" reasons for the method of execution, and attempt to read the play as a critique of society's oppression or persecution of homosexuals. Stephen Guy-Bray, for example, argues that in *Edward II* Marlowe "analyse[s] the way in which society controls sexuality" and that "Edward's attempts to extend legitimacy to a homosexual relationship are the reason for his murder and . . . for the way in which he was killed."[20] Guy-Bray cites Lawrence Danson's article "Continuity and Character in Shakespeare and Marlowe," arguing that the prominence of Edward's social position turns "what might otherwise be seen as eccentricity" into "a sociopolitical offense."[21] This seems to contradict Guy-Bray's later acknowledgment that the barons do not condemn or care about Edward's sexual practices. Danson himself states that "the barons' concern is with the economic and political ramifications of Edward's choices, and all his choices have such ramifications";[22] this does not mean that Edward's sexuality itself becomes a "sociopolitical offense." The king makes very bad choices. Guy-Bray, like Brady, fails to consider Edward's disastrous mismanagement of the affairs of state. Thus, when he argues that "the connection of sexual and social unorthodoxy in Edward provides the tragedy of the play," the term "social unorthodoxy"—because unexplained and unexplored—begins to sound like an evasive euphemism for Edward's political irresponsibility. Guy-Bray does state that the "depth of

[Edward's] love for Gaveston means that it cannot exist covertly beside [his] marriage."[23] The implication here, I think, is that Edward wants something like legitimate marriage with Gaveston, which is impossible in his historical context. However, Edward arranges the marriage between Gaveston and his niece, which implies that, to this extent at least, Edward is prepared to proceed in a socially acceptable manner. It is in my view questionable if what Goldberg regards as the "decentering" power of sodomy in the play was artistically conceived by Marlowe as a radical and intentionally revolutionary form of social interrogation. Bruce Smith offers perhaps the most convincing assessment when, having considered the manner of Edward's death, he concludes: "At issue here is not the fact that Marlowe's Edward is, in psychological terms, a 'homosexual,' or that, in legal terms, he has committed acts of sodomy, but that, in political terms if not physical terms, he has chosen to play the 'boy.'"[24] For various reasons, then, Edward fails as a proper "master," and I am inclined therefore to locate the meaning of Edward's death, and the play as a whole, in something other than a critique of homophobia or social control of sexuality.

To return to the earlier point, I am in general agreement with Summers and Boyette that *Edward II* takes a surprisingly unmoralistic approach to homosexuality, especially in light of the severity of the official morality of the Renaissance, which Alan Bray has described. What needs further examination is not the play's attitude toward homosexuality per se, but rather the way Boyette and Summers view the Edward-Gaveston relationship. Boyette, having considered Edward's vow that he will "either die or live with Gaveston" (1.1.137), remarks that "Edward is fully aware of the stakes in this conflict,"[25] a statement patently untrue since until his death scene Edward is characterized by almost uninterrupted self-delusion. Boyette argues that Marlowe has "internalized the conflict in Edward's heart, whereby Edward perceives his love for Gaveston as the creation of a spiritual wholeness, Eros in union with Anteros"; the critic repeats the point a short while later: "Gaveston affords [Edward] a spiritual wholeness he finds nowhere else, and the effect is a transformation of consciousness that sets him at odds with an unsympathetic world."[26] My initial reaction to the idea of "spiritual wholeness" is to wonder if I have read the same play as Boyette, yet the interpretation would seem possible, for a version of it recurs in Summers's essay:

> [Edward's] attachment to Gaveston represents freedom from responsibility and escape into a world or eroticism at variance with his social

identity, but it is also, and more fundamentally, a quest for selfhood and wholeness. For Edward, self-realization is inextricably linked to communion with another, specifically with Gaveston, to whom his soul is knit [3.2.43]. Thus Gaveston is both a person of sacred worth and a mirror in which the king sees reflected his own possibilities of selfhood.[27]

Edward's attachment to Gaveston certainly represents "freedom from responsibility and escape into a world of eroticism," but the assertion that it is "more fundamentally" a quest for selfhood should give us pause. Summers's emphasis on selfhood is of great importance, since all of Marlowe's plays are "fundamentally" about the quest for selfhood—or, it would be more accurate to say, the failure of such a quest. What is questionable in Summers's assessment is his implied separation of "responsibility" from the quest for selfhood. It is perhaps surprising to see the term in recent criticism at all, monopolized as it has become by the influence of cultural materialism; but "responsibility" remains a key term in Marlowe studies. In *Edward II*, "the refusal to moralize history" in fact intensifies the play's emphasis on personal responsibility, by nullifying the possibility of divine intervention in political and social destiny. The play deals with individuals who succeed or fail to fulfill the roles society has cast them in; that is, they are to an extent socially determined entities, but not completely passive social constructs. The quest for selfhood in the arena of personal relationships is just as much a *responsibility* as is fulfilling one's social duties, and *Edward II* is, in part, about a man who fails on both counts.

The text, however, invites no easy or comfortable moral judgment of the king. The play curiously compels reader and audience to adopt a paradoxical approach. Many will wish to accept Leonora Leet Brodwin's vision of the play as a "culminating treatment of love," in which some apparent conversion, "either actual or purely imaginative, which Marlowe made to homosexual love . . . provided such a release of his sympathies that he could feel empathy with all expressions of love";[28] yet *Edward II* is, in the final analysis, a play in which nobody really loves anybody. Edward is certainly not alone in this respect, for Gaveston, Isabella, and Mortimer also fail to transcend their narcissism. Most of us are probably more willing to identify with Edward than the others in spite of this failing, for a reason that has been succinctly expressed by Clifford Leech. Having quoted the famous exchange between Mortimer and Edward—"Why should you love him whom the world hates so? / Because he loves me more than all the world" (1.4.76–77)—Leech comments: "We know what Gaveston's love is worth, yet this naive—but psychologically profound—utterance of Edward is enough to put us, for the moment, on his side; he becomes an emblem of the human need for love, and of the very human joy when love seems offered."[29] This statement recalls the artistic "release" that Brodwin has identified in the play, yet it is significant that Leech refers to the *need* for love, and the joy when love *seems* offered, for there is no true realization of love in the play. The terms of Leech's analysis ("psychologically profound") suggest, perhaps unfashionably, essentialist belief; nevertheless, I suggest that the reactions, needs, and feelings he addresses are indeed transhistorical. The play does force upon its audience the very question of the nature of love—but only by revealing, finally, love's genuine absence. I therefore find the idea of "spiritual wholeness" between Edward and Gaveston absurd, and not because I react homophobically to the text. It is in fact the *absence* of spiritual wholeness that lies at the heart of the meaning of the play.

I intend to proceed by examining certain problematic characterizations in the play. The conflicted or contradictory nature of the characters has already been intimated in the quotation from Leech, who calls Edward an emblem but refers as well to his psychological profundity; this "emblem" has seemed to at least one reader "Marlowe's most ambitious attempt to create a credible human being."[30] *Edward II*, like all Marlowe's work, is concerned with the tension between art and reality, yet this tension takes on a peculiar manifestation in this play. As in *The Jew of Malta*, *Edward II* explores the idea of role playing in the sense of establishing socially viable, if ultimately illusory, identities, although the vision is now even bleaker than before because being "viable" no longer seems an achievement worth striving for. Self-fashioning seems parodied by characters becoming merely artifacts when they had previously appeared as very "real" people. In *Tamburlaine* the metamorphoses of humans into artifacts is a function of the tyranny of the protagonist; in *Faustus* and *The Jew* it is a function of the hero's failure to achieve legitimate or practical self-fashioning in the physical world, whose rules of survival are in opposition to, or completely undermine, the older morality present in the religious apparatus or echoed in the biblical allusions. In *Edward II* this process—while resembling the pattern of *Faustus* and *The Jew*, without the insistency of the religious reference—at moments seems an inexorable part of the artistic interpretation of reality. The play thus comes close to denying art's ability to give meaning to, or make sense of, experience at all.

The first words of the play are in fact Edward's, although they proceed from Gaveston's mouth, who is quoting a letter from the new king. This dramatic technique is in itself significant, for Edward's failure to speak for himself (here symbolic) underlines his later failure at self-assertion, at establishing an integrated, independent self. This failure is also subtly suggested by the words Edward has chosen: "My father is deceased; come Gaveston, / And share the kingdom with thy dearest friend." There is no reference to his father as "the king" and thus no recognition of the responsibility Edward has inherited. Moreover, there is no sense of mourning over his father's death, in contrast to Edward III's behavior at the end of the play.[31] The loss of a father is not recognized by Edward as a challenge to become himself an independent adult, to go through the "mourning" or suffering of self-development; Edward instead simply replaces one dependency with another. He refuses all Oedipal engagement and remains in a narcissistic state; the opening of the play makes clear his act of "turning away from participation in the conflicts by which sons replace fathers in the world of male responsibilities."[32] The kingdom does not really interest Edward at all, and he is soon willing to leave the "sharing" of the realm to others:

> Make several kingdoms of this monarchy
> And share it equally amongst you all,
> So I may have some nook or corner left
> To frolic with my dearest Gaveston.
>
> (1.4.70–73)

Making several kingdoms of a monarchy is obviously an invitation to political disaster, as *Gorboduc* had emphasized, and the word "frolic" perfectly expresses Edward's infantile fantasy of evading responsibility. It is, however, this childlike quality that partially mitigates our condemnation of him. He never achieves the stature necessary for him to commit a real tragic error, and his career involves the sense of incongruity of a child forced to take on the role of a tragic hero. The irony and poignancy increase at the end because Edward indeed finds himself with nothing but a "nook or corner left," and in that dark and filthy dungeon he certainly cannot frolic.

Edward's final enclosure is thus an ironic answer to his desire to withdraw from the demands of kingship and from adulthood.

With regard to Marlowe's major protagonists, it is surprising that, of a shepherd, a scholar, a merchant, and a king, the last should turn out to be the weakest, and that the character whose field of concern should be the largest—that of governing a kingdom—reduces his interests to the smallest sphere of activity. There seems an inverse relation between the external demands placed on these characters and their ability to accept challenges. Less surprising is that Marlowe's final drama offers another version of the fantasy of power without responsibility, a fantasy we have observed since the prologue to his earliest play. As pointed out in chapter 2, there are interesting parallels between Dido and Edward. Like Dido, Edward's obsessive sexual passion causes him to dismiss his country's welfare:

> *Edward.* How now, what news? Is Gaveston arrived?
> *Mortimer Junior.* Nothing but Gaveston! What means your grace?
> You have matters of more weight to think upon;
> The King of France sets foot in Normandy.
> *Edward.* A trifle! We'll expel him when we please.
>
> (2.2.6–10)

Even the weak Edward, inspired by his rage over Gaveston's death, does indeed temporarily rise to a challenge, but then shows the same indiscriminate and tyrannical disregard for his people that Dido displayed:

> *Mortimer Junior.* Then, Edward, thou wilt fight it to the last,
> And rather bathe thy sword in subjects' blood
> Than banish that pernicious company.
> *Edward.* Ay, traitors all! Rather than thus be braved,
> Make England's civil towns huge heaps of stones
> And ploughs to go about our palace gates.
>
> (3.2.27–32)

From Edward's perspective the provocation seems unjust, and we understand his desire for revenge, but it is more difficult to overlook his disregard for his subjects. In fact, his own complaints about the rebels underline obviously and painfully his sole concerns: "Rebels! Will they appoint their sovereign / His sports, his pleasures, and his company?" (3.1.174–75). Though Wilbur Sanders complains that there is not enough of this kind of commentary, he points out how clearly act 2, scene 2 demonstrates the fact that "high-level political decisions devolve infallibly on the backs of the commonalty":[33]

Mortimer Junior. The idle triumphs, masques, lascivious shows,
And prodigal gifts bestowed on Gaveston
Have drawn thy treasure dry, and made thee weak;
The murmuring commons overstretchèd hath.

. . . .

Lancaster. Thy garrisons are beaten out of France,
And, lame and poor, lie groaning at the gates;

. . . .

The northern borderers, seeing their houses burnt,
Their wives and children slain, run up and down
Cursing the name of thee and Gaveston.

(156–80)

Mortimer's reference to Edward's indulgence in "idle triumphs, masques, [and] lascivious shows" introduces a crucial element in the analysis of Edward's character. A brief review of Marlowe's other major protagonists and their relation to art and poetry will be useful. In the quasi-romance world of *Tamburlaine,* charged with Hermetic idealism, the hero would seem to triumph merely through the power of poetry and rhetoric, though, as I have argued, this apparent power is gradually corroded by the attendant ironies, which finally cause us to question the romance conventions themselves. Yet for much of the play Tamburlaine does not idly boast that "Will and Shall best fitteth Tamburlaine" (part 1 3.3.41); what he wills verbally comes to pass physically. He is thus the polar opposite of Edward, whose threats for the most part are ineffectual, and who laments after his capture, "Well, that shall be shall be; part we must" (4.7.95). Edward in fact resembles the despised Mycetes, although there is now no humor associated with his failure; without the parodic distance of *Tamburlaine,* the realistic context renders the consequences of Edward's actions far more emotionally disturbing. If language has lost its magical power, in Edward it also lacks the secular humanist assertion that can make it meaningful and effective in a social context. Faustus and Barabas represent intermediate stages in this decline of rhetorical might. The apparent power of Faustus's conjurations turns out to be deceptive, and necromancy comes at a terrible price, a loss of self adumbrated in his first seeking out "spiritual" assistance. There is nothing supernatural about Barabas's utterances, since he operates only through the rhetoric of treachery and deception, made comically obvious through the technique of the aside, and psychologically precarious through his alienation from the dominant fictions of his society.

In addition to their varying rhetorical might, the protagonists also operate as playwrights, or at least directors and stage managers. While clearly the master poet of the group, Tamburlaine is also master of stage symbols and theatrical effects. The changing colors of his army's tents indicate his theatrical flair, but even more to the point is his incessant acquisition of self-objects that mirror his prowess and glory, such as the gold and wealth he amasses and exhibits onstage, the crowns he captures, and the human beings he conquers. He uses Bajazeth as a footstool to mount his throne, and parades him around in a cage as a kind of permanent sideshow, a source of entertainment for himself and his companions, conflating for a moment both exhibitionist and voyeuristic perversions. Faustus clearly becomes a director, putting on shows for the German nobility, as well as for his friends in his private study, where he conjures up Helen. Barabas stages the duel between Lodowick and Mathias and then proceeds, with voyeuristic glee, to watch the phallic competition from above. Yet there is a tendency with the later protagonists to get caught up in their own theatrics. Faustus loses self-control in the second conjuration of Helen, and his final agony serves as a play for the devils watching from above (B-text). Barabas must enter as an actor in the French musician interlude (a play that does not go well from the point of view of his evil designs), and of course his last little piece of ingenious staging serves ironically as his own death trap. After examining this process in detail in *The Jew of Malta*, Sara Munson Deats and Lisa S. Starks conclude that "Barabas, functioning simultaneously as playwright, actor, and audience of his own theatrics, both creates fictions and is created by them" through "reciprocal mimesis."[34] Their conclusion reflects the undeniable new historicist assertion that social and cultural "fictions" shape human consciousness, but also I think underlines the question of individual agency, which requires greater emphasis in current critical discourse. In Marlowe we move from protagonists who exercise too much control to ones who exercise too little; in general it may be said that the less episodic, more complicated the action of the plays becomes, the less the protagonists are able to control it, the very dramatic emphasis on absolutely *controlling* the stage action itself indicating a narcissistic preoccupation. Nevertheless, in the process of portraying the psychological failure of these characters, the plays are searching for the possibility of a more constructive involvement of the individual will, as well as greater personal awareness, in this process of "reciprocal mimesis."

What seems to happen to Faustus and Barabas only gradually—getting caught up within theatrical devices rather than controlling them from the outside—happens to Edward from the beginning. As Gaveston muses in the opening scene:

> I must have wanton poets, pleasant wits,
> Musicians that, with touching of a string,
> May draw the pliant king which way I please.
> Music and poetry is his delight;
> Therefore I'll have Italian masques by night,
> Sweet speeches, comedies, and pleasing shows.
>
> (50–55)

Gaveston, rather than Edward, is the director, and while the favorite is out to use the "pliant king," he also wishes to gratify a side of the king's nature that we find attractive. With respect to this speech, Levin points out an important alteration from the source material:

> Marlowe is here refining on Holinshed's description of Edward "passing his time in voluptuous pleasure, and riotous excesse," corrupted by Gaveston, who "furnished his court with companies of iesters, ruffians, flattering parasites, musicians, and other vile and naughtie ribalds, that the king might spend both daies and nights in iesting, plaieing, blanketing [sic], and in such other filthie and dishonorable exercises." Between that medieval brawl and Marlowe's Renaissance pageant, the contrast is brilliantly illuminating.[35]

The change indicates that Marlowe is very much concerned, as in his earlier plays, with the role of art and imagination in experience, yet even more clearly than before we find imagination being used as an escape from or surrogate for experience in the world, rather than a means of mastering it or coming to terms with it. This tendency is stressed when Mortimer remarks:

> When wert thou in the field with banner spread?
> But once! And then thy soldiers marched like players,
> With garish robes, not armour, and thyself,
> Bedaubed with gold, rode laughing at the rest,
> Nodding and shaking of thy spangled crest,
> Where women's favours hung like labels down.
>
> (2.2.181–86)

This is the most obvious example of the sliding of Edward's real duties as king into a parodic, poetic version. The artistic version forms a substitution, rather than a reflection, of Edward's true role as sovereign; as pageantry, therefore, it appears completely hollow.

My reference to Edward's "true role" raises the issue, again related to responsibility, of political, social, and personal integrity. David Thurn argues that the play "stages the consequences of a breakdown in the imaginary constructions that maintain self and state" because "something disturbs the lines of sight by which they constitute themselves."[36] This "something" is eventually identified closely with Gaveston, who "represents the collapse, the murking of the distinctions that ward off threats to identity":

> The figure of Gaveston, with all his extravagant adornments . . . may suggest that the trappings of royal power are themselves nothing more than stage contrivances invested with illusory authority. Even early on, Edward implies as much in his choice of verb when, in a moment of impetuous sobriety, he says he will make Warwick his "chiefest counsellor," and promises that his "silver hairs will more adorn [the] court, / Than gaudy silks or rich embroidery" (1.4.344–46). Edward's minion is the more threatening because he presents the barons, despite their refusal to recognize it, with a kind of mirror image, exposing the ungrounded character of sovereign order.[37]

It is doubtful, however, if the barons experience such philosophically sophisticated new historicist intimations. Power remains for them a very real commodity, and Gaveston, as a drain on that power, a very real and dangerous threat.[38] It is true, as Thurn claims, that Gaveston "undermines the noble claims of natural privilege,"[39] and that sovereign power is exposed as a fiction insofar as the play makes no attempts to portray such power as divinely ordained or inherently natural or right. But given the social structure of the kingdom, and the rights and responsibilities Edward has inherited, it is not enough to insist, as Thurn does, that the play exposes "failures in the *representation* of sovereignty";[40] it is surely, more significantly, a failure in the *exercise* of sovereignty. Recent critical emphasis on ideological control—the hoodwinking of the social order by variously identified hegemonies, who then ride free and easy on the illusions they have created—should not blind us to Marlowe's recognition of the concomitance of responsibility and power. (It has been claimed that the radical Jacobean drama helped destabilize English society to the point of revolution; the process was certainly assisted by, among other things, the ineptitude and inflexibility of the Stuart monarchs. Moreover, Elizabeth I is admired not only because she was a master "showman" but because she was—in spite of her indecisiveness, vanity, and parsimony, and of what from a late-twentieth-century perspective appears the despotic nature of her monarchy—a remarkably intelligent, courageous, and responsible ruler.) Edward in his shallowness regards Warwick's silver hairs as an adornment, but for all we know Warwick may be politically astute and experienced enough to function well as an adviser if Edward chose to use him in this capacity.[41] The silver hairs would then become not just an empty sign or badge of a specious honor, but a meaningful signifier reflecting real, practical worth within the stable "fiction" of a wisely run kingdom.

Criticism of Edward's superficiality may seem gratuitous in the face of the recent demolition of the ideas of personal integrity, interiority, authenticity, and what Dollimore in *Sexual Dissidence* calls the "depth model of the self." Yet it is extremely odd that simple role playing or performative acts have come to be seen as a kind of equivalent to mature self-fashioning, which involves a consistent and lasting commitment to constructive ideals, carefully considers social circumstances and interactions with others (considerations requiring truly *moral* choices), and accepts real responsibility for the role adopted. It is partly increasing theoretical sophistication and, more to the point, effective discursive obfuscation of unethical political agendas that have allowed such counterintuitive assumptions to go unchallenged. To take a typical example of the new historicist questioning of authenticity, let us digress briefly to consider David Scott Kastan's essay "'The King Hath Many Marching in His Coats,' or, What Did You Do in the War, Daddy?" Kastan treats the battle of Shrewsbury in *1 Henry IV*:

> Royal power appears in the play exclusively in represented form. . . . On the battlefield at Shrewsbury the King cannot be distinguished from his representations. Henry's majesty can be effectively mimed. Though Douglas [who has already killed several counterfeit kings] admits to Henry that "thou bearest thee like a king" (5.4.35), royal bearing proves no guarantee of royalty. But the implications of the episode are not merely that Henry unheroically, if prudently, adopts a strategy in the interests of his safety, that appearances are manipulated to disguise the king. They are far more disturbing: that kingship itself is a disguise, a role, an action that a man might play.[42]

However, the overall effect of the second tetralogy is surely to prove to us that kingship is *not* simply an action that a man might play. Henry's overall career disturbs us in the same way that contemporary commentators are so often distressed by the behavior of unscrupulous politicians: they can crudely but effectively manipulate public opinion, they watch the polls, they check which way the wind is blowing. They *do not* take risks in pursuit of strongly held ideals or out of a real commitment to public service; they are interested *only* in getting and maintaining personal power. By introducing numerous counterfeit kings on the battlefield, Henry refracts and pluralizes his kingship in a way that cheapens it. We see—not that *all* kings—but that *this* king is "counterfeit," not because he has usurped the throne but because his *interiority* is not kingly. This interiority may not be essential— Henry must fashion it through decisions, commitments, and acts of will—but it is still a "space" for which he is responsible. Our condemnation of Henry IV is of course not total; in spite of his limitations, Henry IV is clearly far more capable, in terms of practical matters and personal control, than Marlowe's Edward. The skill that Henry displays is a crucial preliminary in self-fashioning[43]—a strengthening of the self in preparation for the greater responsibilities and risks assumed through service to others— and infinitely preferable to Edward's dangerous incompetence.

Returning to Marlowe's play, it must be admitted that Edward does not appear to exceed many of his underlings in shallowness. Marlowe is at some pains to point out their hypocrisy in act 1, where Lancaster bursts out sanctimoniously at the beginning of scene 2:

> What! Will they tyrannize upon the Church?
> Ah, wicked king! accursèd Gaveston!
> This ground which is corrupted with their steps,
> Shall be their timeless sepulchre, or mine.
>
> (3–6)

Subsequently, and almost comically, Mortimer Senior must ask him—as if no one has taken the sentiments in the above speech seriously—"How now, why droops the Earl of Lancaster?" (9). The pouting Lancaster replies, "that villain Gaveston is made an earl" (11), indicating that his dismay arises not from the offense done to the Church but from the fact that the baseborn Gaveston has been promoted to the nobility. The Bishop of Canterbury demonstrates a similar hypocrisy. When asked by Lancaster if he will take up arms against the king, the prelate piously declares, "What need I? God himself is up in arms / When violence is offered to the Church." Mortimer Junior then quickly cuts through this ostensible refusal by immediately interjecting a slightly altered request, "Then will you join with us that be his peers / To banish or behead that Gaveston?" to which the Bishop, revealing his self-interest, pragmatically replies, "What else my lords, for it concerns me near; / The bishopric of Coventry is his" (40–45). However, the exposure of religious hypocrisy does not completely invalidate the political opposition of the barons to Edward. Though motivated by self-interest, the barons remain formidable foes because, as in the speeches in 2.2 (quoted above), the issues they raise are valid and pressing. To raise them at all they must be conscious of them, which apparently is more than can be said for Edward and Gaveston.

The above exchanges suggest, I believe, a peculiar political awareness and competence on the part of the Mortimers, although Mortimer Junior remains the most problematic character in the play. He at first appears less hypocritical than the other barons, and is notable not for a Machiavellian talent at dissembling but for his straightforwardness: he is brash, blunt, and appealingly irascible in a manner that suggests he could have served as a model for Hotspur.[44] It is arguable that the early Mortimer's ability to cut through cant receives a convincing transformation in the later, Machiavellian Mortimer's interruption of Isabella's speech upon their return from France (4.4.14–15), as well as his treatment of Spencer Senior in 4.6: "Take him away; he prates" (73). Though Mortimer here brutally squelches what amounts to a valid (and politically dangerous) point by Spencer Senior, such behavior seems a logical development of Mortimer's earlier brashness and impatience. However, from a humanist perspective, Sanders cannot be completely refuted when he complains that in act 5 "Mortimer's irascible ambivalence is reduced to a monolithic and herculean Machiavellism," which "dramatically and poetically . . . is as much a blind alley as the earlier characterisation of Mortimer was fraught with possibilities."[45] The critic cites the following examples:

> Feared am I more than loved; let me be feared,
> And when I frown, make all the court look pale.
>
> (5.4.50–51)

> Mine enemies will I plague, my friends advance,
> And what I list command who dare control?
>
> (5.4.65–66)

> As for myself, I stand as Jove's huge tree,
> And others are but shrubs compared to me.
>
> (5.6.11–12)

The character of Mortimer seems indeed to have degenerated into a stock Machiavellian villain, whose rhetoric, we may feel, approaches the ridiculous "gigantic self-assertions" of the Duke of Guise. Yet the portrayal of Mortimer is more restrained; like the mower, he has become a talking emblem or artifact, and his reification strains the apparently realistic mode of *Edward II*. The question remains, is this dehumanizing of character a failure of the play or an effect that Marlowe consciously intended?

It is tempting to argue that the dehumanizing of Mortimer is as a result of *his* failure of imagination (of self-fashioning) rather than of *Marlowe's* failure of imagination (of character creation). This might be seen as both a personal and a political failure. Certainly Mortimer's formulaic farewell to Isabella (5.6.58–65) underlines the essential lovelessness of their relationship; as Leech comments, "It would be difficult to find two other lovers in Elizabethan drama who part with words so chill."[46] And Mortimer's earlier valid criticism of Edward's political irresponsibility—because not deeply felt, void of a personal investment of belief or emotion—in a sense constitutes a false, illusory integrity. Having made a career of deconstructing his sovereign's agenda, he finds once the obstacle is removed that he himself stands for precisely nothing, and therefore sinks into a slough of stifling self-regard and treacherous ambition. His use of the unpointed letter to order Edward's murder does suggest his failure to accept responsibility for his own utterances and actions. Marlowe was evidently familiar with this kind of behavior; Mortimer's action accurately reflects Charles Nicholl's observation of the dark world of Elizabethan espionage, where "the things [the agents] did and said are always open to diametrically opposed interpretations."[47] Nevertheless, if Marlowe had wanted to show us the dehumanizing, corrupting effect of political power, he could have portrayed a degeneration more subtle, more consistent with the apparent psychological depth with which he endows other characters.

Isabella, for example, was by earlier critics also regarded as inconsistently developed since she appears as both long-suffering wife and wicked schemer. However, critics such as Summers and Sara Munson Deats have demonstrated that Isabella's transformation is not implausible.[48] As Summers demonstrates, it is Isabella—in her private tête-à-tête with Mortimer—who first suggests that Gaveston be recalled from banishment so that he can be more easily murdered. She is thus thoroughly Machiavellian from the start; a consummate role player, she has adopted the mask of an innocent and long-suffering Queen. As Deats remarks, "from the beginning of the play, Isabella's Griselda mask fits loosely, and a penetrating glance may discern beneath this camouflage a very different kind of woman—a forceful, disciplined, calculating female, fighting with all the weapons in her arsenal to preserve her present status in the state and to regain her lost position in Edward's affections."[49] It is important to recognize that "all the weapons in her arsenal" are of course limited; as a woman in a patriarchal society, she is forced to exercise power indirectly, and her deviousness is at least in part socially constrained. Yet even with this recognition, Isabella does not attract much of our sympathy. Deats's analysis of Isabella is compelling: she demonstrates how cleverly Isabella manipulates the men around her, and how she is largely responsible not only for Gaveston's death but also for Edward's: note how she prods Mortimer at 5.2.42–45. Deats does real justice to the complexity of Isabella's character, as when she carries out an analysis of Isabella's "somewhat obscured motivation."[50] Upon examining the evidence, Deats concludes that "although Isabella's personal ambition and her amorous liaison with Mortimer may be partial inducements for her rebellion, her chief goal is revenge upon the loose, misgoverning, and unfaithful King. Ultimately, therefore, the love that hatcheth death and hate [cf. Kent's remark, 4.6.15] is Isabella's frustrated desire for Edward, not her illicit passion for Mortimer."[51] This analysis may help to explain two of Isabella's speeches (1.4.170–86 and 2.4.15–21) in which she communicates her suffering and, especially in the latter, her apparent love for Edward: "Heavens can witness I love none but you" (2.4.15). Isabella in these speeches has no audience,[52] no one to affect or manipulate; her sentiments must be genuine. She really, in some sense, must love or feel strongly for Edward, as Deats suggests. But we must inquire into the nature of this "love." The idea of enclosure in the lines—"O that mine arms could close this isle about, / That I might pull him to me where I would" (2.4.17–18)—is ominous, since enclosures in Marlowe often have ironic significance. Isabella's desire recalls Dido's dream of retaining Aeneas in her arms even while rich Carthage fleeted upon the sea; it is a fantasy of romantic *control*. What Isabella truly desires, what she truly loves, is her position as queen. That is why, in spite of her sexual attraction for Mortimer, she can never get over her resentment toward Edward, because Mortimer can never quite offer her the security she enjoyed in the first place. Her fear for her security is why she resolves to have Edward murdered: "But Mortimer, as long as he survives, / What safety rests for us, or for my son?" (5.2.42–43). Isabella is primarily in love with what Edward *as king* can offer, or could have offered, her. Her emotional and romantic behavior is another version of the narcissistic manipulation of self-objects.

While the apparent inconsistency of Isabella's transformation may be resolved through a recognition of her talent at role playing and her psychological complexity, it is doubtful whether Mortimer's transformation can be similarly explained. Part of the reason for Marlowe's failure in Mortimer's case may be that, having exorcised the idea of the Machiavellian hero-villain in *The Massacre at Paris*, he is no longer profoundly interested in it, and thus gives it only a rather perfunctory artistic treatment. But this reading ignores the earlier complexity in his character, and a subtler explanation can be offered. It is possible that Mortimer's sudden crystallization into emblem can be related to Marlowe's own realization of the hopelessness of achieving a perfectly "masculine" identity (as Deats remarks in "A Study in Androgyny," Mortimer is the typical "masculine" male);[53] Mortimer is an idealized, (heterosexual) self-object that Marlowe cannot internalize. The sense of failure is countered by reducing such a persona to "only" a stereotype or emblem. This reduction from virile (and to Marlowe probably very attractive) man to stock Machiavellian villain also facilitates the replacement of Mortimer by Edward III, a replacement that, as we shall examine, is not free from the sense of an "artistic" or theoretical solution.

In her discussion of the play Kuriyama remarks that the lack of credibility in some of the characterizations—the awkward shifts—arises from the fact that the "other characters exist primarily as foils to set off the lambent and somewhat tarnished jewel—Marlowe's incompetent and harried King." Kuriyama suggests that the "most glaring of these shifts . . . is in the handling of Spencer and Baldock, who at first appear ambitious and unprincipled, yet burst into poetic lament and stoical resignation when they part from Edward and are led away to their deaths."[54] The "poetic laments" of Spencer Junior and Baldock (4.7.100–112) provide an example of the aestheticizing of death and form a glaring contrast to the way in which Edward suffers his end. A similar example is to be found in Gaveston's death. Deats, referring to the "religious" diction in Gaveston's lines "O, must this day be period of my life, / Centre of all my bliss?" (2.6.4–5) and noting his "yearning cry," "Sweet sovereign, yet I come / To see thee ere I die" (2.5.92–93), argues that he reveals "at least the potential for authentic affection."[55] Kuriyama characteristically offers a less sympathetic reading in her claim that Gaveston's "eagerness to see the King once more before his death is tainted by his obvious hope of saving himself."[56] With respect to the "centre of bliss" quotation, Deats (following Ribner's edition) takes this passage as meaning: "must this day, which should have been centre of all my bliss (through reunion with Edward) become instead the last day of my life." I find this reading doubtful, and with respect to Gaveston's character am inclined to agree with Kuriyama. Whether or not we accept the sincerity of Gaveston's feelings and statements, his final poetic utterances constitute another instance of Marlowe's romanticizing of death in contrast to Edward's horrible murder. But it is Mortimer's demise, which the title of the play refers to as "the tragicall fall," which offers the most significant of such contrasts. Mortimer ends his career with the following farewell:

> Base Fortune, now I see that in thy wheel
> There is a point to which, when men aspire,
> They tumble headlong down. That point I touched,
> And, seeing there was no place to mount up higher,
> Why should I grieve at my declining fall?
> Farewell, fair queen; weep not for Mortimer,
> That scorns the world, and, as a traveller,
> Goes to discover countries yet unknown.

> (5.6.58–65)

Though Steane remarks that this speech "is the only one in the play which is truly heroic,"[57] I agree with Leech that there is "indeed a rather empty rhetoric in Mortimer's acceptance of the turning wheel and his readiness for what may come."[58] The verse sounds formulaic, a made-to-order speech for the tragic hero, and the idea of "undiscovered countries" would not be rendered in terms vigorously appealing to the imagination until Shakespeare wrote *Hamlet*. Certainly we are artistically distanced from Mortimer's death, not only by the conventional rhetoric but by the fact that the execution occurs offstage. His head is brought onstage at the conclusion—perhaps a significant touch of realistic horror—but by this point he has completely devolved into an artifact, a stage prop signifying Edward III's ascendancy.

In contrast, the "emblematic" nature of Edward's death intensifies the horror. This may in part be due to our knowledge "that the 'punishment-fitting-the-crime' aspect of his death is not an invention of Marlowe's to add thematic unity to the play, but the literal truth as recorded in the chronicles."[59] Yet critics have been eager to render Edward's death thematically coherent within Marlowe's play. Bent Sunesen in his essay "Marlowe and the Dumb Show" claims that Gaveston's soliloquy at 1.1.50–70 "has an important status in the tragedy as a kind of emblematic telescoping of the total structure"; like a dumb show, it prefigures the play's course of events by allegorical means.[60] Sunesen suggests that "'one like Actaeon peeping through the grove' is King Edward himself," who is hunted down by his nobles, the "yelping hounds"; they are "the Eumenides of Marlowe's drama . . . a necessary corrective of sin," though still "fundamentally hateful."[61] Deats, in "Myth and Metamorphosis in Marlowe's *Edward II*," adds another dimension to the "allegory" by pointing out that in the Renaissance the "yelping hounds" of the myth were commonly interpreted as "Actaeon's own devouring [sexual] desires." Thus the line "By yelping hounds pulled down and seem to die" (69), suggests "the Elizabethan pun for sexual intercourse, [and] implies that the erotic masque may conclude with a mock murder but actual rape . . . adumbrating the mode of Edward's slaying, which is a grotesque parody of his forbidden sodomy."[62] ("Forbidden," presumably, not so much by the world of the play as by the official morality of Marlowe's time.) Sunesen finds another significance in "seem to die":

> On a deep level of the tragedy there is an overwhelming rightness in that "seem." For in the underlying sacrificial ritual the king as national symbol does not really die. . . . Edward, the guilty individual, must suffer death, it is true; but Edward, the King, the embodiment of the nation, is immortal. . . . That is why, conforming to a common chronicle-play design, the drama does not end with Edward's death but goes on until we have been assured that the monarchy will survive in the firm hold of young King Edward, and the latter has had Mortimer executed, thus demonstrating that the era of purification is over and done with.[63]

Sunesen's emphasis on purification is related to Deats's remark that "the Actaeon analogy stresses *Edward II* as a dramatization of one of man's most univeral myths, the cleansing of the kingdom and the restoring of order through the hunting down and killing of the scapegoat king"; hence "the frequent allegorizing of both the stag and Actaeon as types of Christ."[64]

The problem with such readings is that while they render the play thematically coherent, they are emotionally repellent. From Sunesen's remarks we certainly cannot infer that Edward himself *only* dies symbolically. Paradoxically this symbolic or emblematic

execution is the most *realistic*—and therefore the most disturbing—death scene in English drama. There seems no aesthetic
distancing (apart from the physical masking necessary to stage it)
to mitigate the feelings of violation and terror. Even the pathetic
Richard II is given one last moment of heroic assertiveness, which
serves to place his death throes in a dramatic or artistic context;
in other words, we in the audience are somehow reassured that
what we are watching is another version of "seem to die." Edward's death is not "seem to die"; this is dying—horrible, painful,
unbearable. "O spare me! Or dispatch me in a trice!" (5.5.110) he
pleads, yet his death is prolonged and excruciating, and his terror
fully realized. Much of the horror arises from the portrayal of the
human cost of becoming a symbol, of being sacrificed to an artistic
sense that wants to impose order on or make sense of experience.[65] From a humanist perspective, our reception of the mytho-
logical readings of Sunesen and Deats may parallel our response
to symbolic significances in other literature with a supposedly
historical basis, most notably the Bible (a text Marlowe was obsessed with, but did not embrace). "Real" people often pay an
enormous price in becoming emblems or exempla in symbolically
meaningful narratives. Sunesen's and Deats's references to the
"sacrificial ritual" and the "scapegoat king" evoke a great feeling
of unease: the artistic, or political, or universal significance hardly
"atones" for the individual agony.

Yet I cannot agree with Boyette, who also raises the idea of the
scapegoat king when he remarks that the "rape of Edward . . .
is treated in the play as to make him the archetypal Victim, a
scapegoat for the personal, cultural and social forces that have
repudiated his essential humanity, his decline into flesh—bodies,
music and poetry."[66] "Essential humanity" may in fact be what
Edward possesses too little of, in the sense that he fails both
personally and politically in the construction of this necessary
illusion. Fictions and works of art demand skill, discipline, and
control in their constructions; social fictions also require careful
reading of contexts, an assessment of the relative strengths and
weaknesses both of oneself and others. Edward opts for indulgence in fantasy rather than for skillful artistic control and masterful self-fashioning. What Boyette calls Edward's decline into flesh
is better termed his decline into pure imagination. (Boyette's
definition of "flesh"—"bodies, music and poetry"—is curiously
contradictory.) Edward never acquires the self-cohesion necessary
to function successfully outside the world of fantasy and poetry.
He fails to come to terms with the givens of life—the body, his

inherited personal and social responsibilities, Freud's reality principle. Thus his loss of "humanity," his becoming in the end a
symbol—or perhaps more accurately, his dying at the hands of
one—carries with it a savage sense of poetic justice.

If it can be moralized at all, the "rape" of Edward, the invasion
of his being, suggests less a homophobic society than his own
loss of personal mastery or manliness, his failure to achieve self-
cohesion. Sunesen discusses the issue of manhood in relation to
Edward's vow to make Gaveston "Lord High Chamberlain, / Chief
Secretary to the State and me, / Earl of Cornwall, King and Lord
of Man" (1.1.153–55): "A pun may very well be intended here.
The isle of Man was officially a kingdom; so Edward could actually, in supreme favouritism, confer the title of king upon his
'minion.' Holinshed mentions this detail, and Marlowe, free to
skip such particulars, keeps it, presumably because he feels that
the grand gesture is really a symbolic act, by which Edward de-
livers the complete sovereignty over himself as a private *man* into
Gaveston's hands. . . . The gesture is . . . an abdication of manliness."[67] Edward's relationship with Gaveston is not wrong because it is homosexual but because, to quote from Peter
Donaldson's discussion of *Tamburlaine*, Gaveston is "just another
mirror of a self that must desperately find its reflection . . . rather
than face its own emptiness."[68] Edward's initial greeting of Gaveston—"Knowest thou not who I am? / Thy friend, thy self, another
Gaveston" (1.1.141–42)—is evidence not of a platonic union of
souls but of Edward's complete dependency. Edward does not
have a viable self to offer his love, and therefore their relationship
can in no way proceed as a meaningful dialectic between two
developing personalities. Moreover, I share Leech's view that Edward is mistaken in asserting that Gaveston loves him more than
all the world. Gaveston's lack of real concern for the king becomes
apparent when Edward capitulates to his nobles and agrees to
banish Gaveston, and then attempts to comfort his lover:

> . . . sweet friend, take it patiently.
> Live where thou wilt—I'll send thee gold enough.
> And long thou shalt not stay; or if thou dost,
> I'll come to thee. My love shall ne'er decline.
>
> (1.4.112–15)

Instead of gratefully acknowledging the king's affection, Gaveston can only peevishly reply, "Is all my hope turned to this hell
of grief?" (116), suggesting that Edward's love is not what Gaves-

ton really wants, but rather the social and material advantages that go along with being the king's lover: Gaveston and Isabella, then, are birds of a feather. It is really Edward who has declared the world well lost for love; he projects his own intense needs onto Gaveston. Gaveston functions for Edward, as Abigail for Barabas, as a mirroring self-object, which can be replaced by another—Spencer Junior—just as Barabas replaces Abigail with Ithamore. While Edward is certainly not as adept as Tamburlaine at controlling and arranging the self-objects that surround him, the love he experiences is merely an ineffectual, rather than skillful, manipulation of other people as objects. Such narcissistic love places Edward in the impossible position of needing to control and wanting to relinquish control at the same time. In Kohutian terms, the tension arc between ambitions and ideals within the bipolar self collapses.

Unlike Edward, Gaveston is quite skillful at controlling and arranging his own self-objects. Like Isabella, Gaveston is a good actor, and quite handily adopts the role of Edward's intimate friend and lover, though he makes little real emotional investment in their relationship. This is the view of Toby Robertson, whom I quote because I find particular weight in the opinion of someone who has actually worked closely with the play onstage: "The horrifying power that Gaveston has over him is shown, and Edward becomes like a crawling sycophant; one realizes what is particularly horrifying: Edward is totally in love with Gaveston—is dotty about him—but Gaveston is just using Edward. . . . I think this is all of it for him ["drawing the pliant kind which way I please"]; he does it for his own aggrandizement."[69] It must be acknowledged, however, that other critics have viewed Gaveston more sympathetically. Summers, for example, asserts that "Gaveston does love Edward more than all the world. He rejects the invitation to 'share the kingdom' [1.1.2], finding 'bliss' and 'felicitie' only in the king's embraces."[70] There does seem an awkward incongruity between Gaveston's reference in his opening lines to "him I hold so dear— / The king, upon whose bosom let me die" and his subsequent desire to "draw the pliant king which way I please." Wilbur Sanders remarks that "there is no dramatically realized 'self' in the lines which could mediate between the passionate lover and the cynical opportunist in his character. The two traits are simply juxtaposed and we (or the actor) must make of it what we can."[71] Sanders may be right to suggest that we must "make up Marlowe's mind for him" here; there is something about Gaveston's opening lines that suggest Marlowe's, rather than his character's, artistic "release" (to adopt Brodwin's term again); it is as if Gaveston does not really settle into character until around line 18. However, it is possible that Gaveston, like Edward, is—to borrow a modern cliché—a little in love with the idea of love. Although he is far more self-aware than the king, he is also susceptible to fantasies, to indulging in imaginative dreamworlds. After all, the "Renaissance pageant" of lines 50–70 does come straight out of *his* imagination.

Yet it is the manipulative side of Gaveston's character that soon predominates. This is made immediately apparent in his treatment of the three Poor Men: "But yet it is no pain to speak men fair. / I'll flatter these and make them live in hope" (41–42). Gaveston's "role" becomes more obvious when, in reply to Edward's offer of titles and powers, he humbly replies, "It shall suffice me to enjoy your love" (170); yet a few lines later he is using his new power to seek cruel revenge on the Bishop of Coventry, and to encourage Edward to do so as well. Apparently Edward stupidly misses the obvious irony in Gaveston's acceptance of the king's offers:

> It shall suffice me to enjoy your love,
> Which whiles I have, I think myself as great
> As Caesar riding in the Roman street,
> *With captive kings at his triumphant car.*
>
>   (170–73, my emphasis)

The allusion to Caesar puts Gaveston in the same league as the Guise in *The Massacre at Paris*. In the face of Gaveston's obvious selfishness, I am surprised to find Boyette arguing that the Frenchman appears to be given "even to a kind of ironic honesty about himself and his relations to the King that nobody else in the play achieves. To the modern sensibility, with its concern to avoid hypocrisy, there is a certain disarming frankness in his confession that he pleases the King as the King wants to be pleased so that his own interests can be better served."[72] Boyette's appeal to "modern sensibility" distorts the real dramatic significance of Gaveston's opening soliloquy, which is in fact a "Vice-like announc[ement] of his corruptive tactics to the audience upon his first entrance."[73]

The most unpleasant of Gaveston's "corruptive tactics" is his talent for the sexual manipulation of others. There is evidence in the play that Edward is not the only one Gaveston has used in this way. The exchange between Spencer Junior and Baldock in 2.1 is telling:

> *Spencer Junior.* Baldock, learn this of me: a factious lord
> Shall hardly do himself good, much less us;
> But he that hath the favour of a king
> May with one word advance us while we live.
> The liberal Earl of Cornwall is the man
> On whose good fortune Spencer's hope depends.
> *Baldock.* What, mean you then to be his follower?
> *Spencer Jr.* No, his companion; for he loves me well
> And would have once preferred me to the king.
>
> (6–14)

While both Baldock and Spencer are looking to which side their bread is buttered, Spencer is obviously quite willing to give sexual favors in exchange for social advancement, and acts as if it increases his prestige. He and Gaveston have presumably encountered each other in the past. Gaveston's sexual mercinariness becomes even more apparent in the subsequent dialogue:

> *Baldock.* But he is banished; there's small hope of him.
> *Spencer Junior.* Ay, for a while; but, Baldock, mark the end:
> A friend of mine told me in secrecy
> That he's repealed and sent for back again;
> And even now a post came from the court
> With letters to our lady from the king,
> And as she read, she smiled, which makes me think
> It is about her lover, Gaveston.
>
> (15–22)

Gaveston is willing to play the role not only of the king's intimate friend but also of the lover and husband of the king's niece. Edward's announcement of this marriage in the previous scene comes as something of a shock to the modern reader and audience, and in my mind casts further doubts on Summers's assertion that *Edward II* establishes sexuality as a "defining characteristic of personality." Gaveston is apparently quite flexible sexually, and is not above using either sex for his personal advancement.

Unlike either his lover or his wife, Edward lacks this personal flexibility and skill at role playing. Ironically for a man who gets caught up in theatrics, for the first two-thirds of the play he cannot really *act*, a very necessary talent in the Machiavellian world he inhabits, peopled as it is by "consummate role players and fine dissemblers."[74] Deats points out that Edward shares this particular failing with his brother Kent: "although [they both] attempt to dissemble lest they die [paraphrasing Kent's remark at 4.6.12], they are pathetically ineffectual."[75] Kent has long been recognized as a kind of moral weathervane in the play, a character whose sympathies parallel the audience's. It may in fact have been Marlowe's intention to make him a kind of symbolic "audience" within the play, with whom we identify as a kind of moral center, but whose fate also warns us of our own vulnerability in a Machiavellian society: the point is, disturbingly, that moral sensitivity and emotional involvement make one "impractical" or ineffectual as an actor. Yet while both brothers are weak actors, the charity and concern in Kent's character are contrasted with Edward's self-involvement. The king displays instead an odd combination of naïveté and willfulness, behaving, as critics remark, like a spoiled child. His nobles hardly take his role seriously—since he does not—and act like spoiled children themselves in response, having no compunction in ridiculing their sovereign and interrupting him:

> *Warwick.* O, our heads!
> *Edward.* Ay, yours; and therefore I would wish you grant—
> *Warwick.* Bridle thy anger, gentle Mortimer.
>
> (1.1.118–20)

Admittedly, Edward's designated social role as king is a very difficult and challenging one, but he never appears even to seriously try out for the part. There is never any moment of reflection in the play where he considers altering his behavior. It is only when he is forceably removed from society that he begins his true acting career, ironically signified by the gesture of throwing off his disguise at Neath Abbey: "Hence feignèd weeds, unfeignèd are my woes" (4.7.97). When Leicester proposes to remove Edward in a litter, the king dramatically suggests, with poetic exaggeration, arrangements for his own funeral procession:

> A litter hast thou? Lay me in a hearse,
> And to the gates of hell convey me hence;
> Let Pluto's bells ring out my fatal knell
> And hags howl for my death at Charon's shore.
>
> (87–90)

Edward's histrionic despair here seems only to hasten his own destruction. During his abdication he can only indulge in self-pitying self-dramatizations; his role no longer matters to others since he is being stripped of political power. The abdication becomes a performance in a social void, Edward's "cave of care" (5.1.32). It is an insistence on illusion when the form of the tragedy demands a recognition of "truth"; Edward here achieves no anagnorisis, for he never realizes that his role as king required real responsible action, and was not only a spectacle of power: "But what are kings when regiment is gone / But perfect shadows in a sunshine day?" (26–27). Hypocritically, Edward accuses the woman he has rejected of staining his "nuptial bed with infamy" (31). The king is left with a confusion of signifiers signifying nothing. The crown is in his eyes only a symbol of comfort and privilege to which he clings, rather than a reminder of the responsibility he has abused:

> And in this torment comfort find I none
> But that I feel the crown upon my head;
> And therefore let me wear it yet a while.
>
> (81–83)

He relieves his hatred of Mortimer by ripping up the written name of Mortimer. He fails to realize the truth of his own gesture when, dramatically sending a tear-soaked handkerchief to his queen, he predicts she will not care to read its true "meaning" until it is reinscribed with his own blood: "If with the sight thereof she be not moved, / Return it back and dip it in my blood" (119–20). Death will indeed be the only way Edward manages to inscribe meaning in his social context, into the history of his reign. The ultimate futility of his final performance is underlined by the fact that at one point in the abdication all meaningful signifiers fail him: "The King rageth."

In contrast to Edward's unskillful acting is his son's consummate performance at the end of the play. Edward III is certainly the most crucial minor character in the play. Steane believes that he is the "only character to combine humanity with strength,"[76] and Kuriyama notes that he "shows himself to be both compassionate and just, ordering a swift execution for Mortimer and sending his mother to the Tower for 'further triall' [5.6.79] even though the necessity of committing her reduces him to tears."[77] In an interesting version of this "balancing" thesis, Deats in "A Study in Androgyny" suggests that "the young Edward III may mature to combine the felicitous balance of 'feminine' feeling with 'masculine' firmness that his parents so tragically lacked."[78] (Edward and Isabella have failed, the critic argues, "not through an excess but through a defect in androgyny.") Edward III thus has something in common with Navarre, who shows a potential for balancing conflicting impulses, assertive and passive behavior. Yet the difficulties Marlowe experiences in his portrayal of Navarre have perhaps not been overcome in Edward III. More than one critic has felt that the resolution of the personal and political conflicts in the play is too facile or artful; Edward III seems to fulfill too neatly the role determined—indeed forced upon him—by the formal construction of the play. Thus Claude Summers complains that despite "the rise of Edward III in the final scene, Marlowe's play offers little consolation. His depiction of the world as a solipsistic universe challenges received ideas too completely to be . . . displaced by the perfunctory restoration of order in the final scene."[79] Kuriyama remarks: "If the emergence of young Edward at the end of the play does not particularly inspire or reassure us, we can probably attribute our lack of enthusiasm to the fact that [his] triumph is theoretical, not something that Marlowe feels."[80]

We therefore have a divided response to what is a crucial element in the interpretation of the play. Those supporting the "balancing" thesis make a good case, and we have seen Marlowe begin to formulate the idea of balancing, though less obviously, in *The Jew of Malta* and *The Massacre at Paris*. Marlowe may in fact have "felt" the resolution, at least subconsciously, rather intensely, as a kind of compensatory reassertion of "manhood." Only one scene—significantly, the king's death scene—separates the young Edward who, bullied by Mortimer and coddled by his mother, is unable to save his uncle, and the strong-willed youth who has Mortimer put to death and takes over the reins of government. Dramatically, Marlowe has very carefully arranged for Edward III to regain the control forfeited by his father, both rhetorically and in terms of the stage action. "Traitor, in me my loving father speaks" (5.6.40), he says to Mortimer; Edward has found his true voice, the voice of power, in his son. Unlike his father, Edward III conducts himself with force and authority. He orders the execution of Mortimer; then, when the head is brought back onstage, he orders his father's hearse and his own funeral robes. Thus he consummately manages the final theatrical contrivance, even using, not unlike Tamburlaine, the spoils of victory (Mortimer's head) as a stage prop. Yet he handles the business so skillfully that doubts about the sincerity of his performance may begin to creep in: "Away with her [Isabella]. Her words enforce these tears / And I shall pity her if she speak again" (84–85). (Psychological readings may also raise doubts: although young Edward apparently triumphs in a Freudian sense over a domineering mother, he remains pubescent at the end of the play, and we have no idea how he will deal with his own sexual impulses.) Edward III's final insistence in the play's last lines—"let these tears, distilling from mine eyes, / Be witness of my grief and innocency"— can be interpreted in two ways. Either we have here a perfect *congruency* of inner emotion with outer show, or else Edward's histrionically calling attention to his tears as "witnesses" makes us doubt the sincerity of his grief. Similarly, the phrase "help me to mourn, my lords" (97) also contains an ambiguity. As a *command* it nicely intimates how Edward will combine self-assertiveness with the realization that he must function *with* the cooperation and assistance of those around him. Or, more subversively, it indicates that his grief is not deep or genuine, and he needs help in his show of mourning.

Psychologically then, as Donaldson argues, "the assertive triumph of Edward III resolves none of the questions the play has raised about the human self, and which Edward's sufferings have exemplified. Rather, the final scene is a turn toward superficiality . . . the world of firmer selves, of sons ready to succeed their fathers . . . the world of Oedipal . . . success, is inimical to depth."[81] *Edward II* is a tragedy about the failure of self-fashioning, but it also chillingly suggests that *successful* self-fashioning, especially in the context of a ruthlessly Machiavellian society, may be *only* an act; only the creation of a complex illusion. If, then, self-fashioning is an illusory process, why bother? The answer, clearly, is that it leads to personal competency and personal survival. Yet, depressingly, *Edward II* implies that the most we can obtain is competency and survival in an essentially loveless world. Marlowe's vision never gets past this; he did not live to explore how meaningful self-fashioning could be combined with meaningful and mutually supportive personal and social relationships. However bleak this vision, it is not wrong to call it fundamentally religious, in an Augustinian sense. My approach in this discussion resembles that taken by Mulryne and Fender in "Marlowe and the 'Comic Distance,'" where the critics suggest that the emblems and other symbolic action in the play "do not ratify the realistic action" but instead "act as false leads, promising a falsely comforting 'meaning' which is then discomfited in the realistic action."[82] However, Mulryne and Fender conclude simply that the play functions as a "model of absurdity" and cite Camus as a philosophical basis for an understanding of the play. I contend that the discontinuity evident in the play is best explained by recourse neither to twentieth-century existentialism nor to a materialist explanation of the self as a purely social and cultural construct, but rather to an Augustinian Christianity that continued to haunt Marlowe even as he fought to eradicate it.

Edward's aborted attempts at self-assertion are not infrequently given religious significance. The first person Edward defies in the play, after his joyous reunion with Gaveston, is the Bishop of Coventry, who is rushing off to perform the funeral rites for Edward's father, and on whom Edward "lives to be revenged" (1.1.177) for banishing Gaveston in the first place. Edward orders that the Bishop be humiliated in a manner that foreshadows his own humiliation later in the play.[83] Edward is encouraged in his defiance by Gaveston, who ensures that the king shows no mercy. The subsequent exchange is interesting:

> *Bishop.* For this offense be thou accurst of God.
> *Edward.* Who's there? Convey this priest to the Tower.
>
> (198–99)

The remark "Who's there?" is made to the attendants whom he expects to "convey" the Bishop to prison; yet "Who's there?" refers subversively to the "God" of the previous line, as if Edward were (subconsciously) questioning the existence of God. Ironically the king persists in his assertiveness, his challenge of any external authority (God, Church, duty to dead father), only so he can retain his romantic dependency:

> How fast they run to banish him I love.
> They would not stir, were it to do me good.
> Why should a king be subject to a priest?
> Proud Rome, that hatchest such imperial grooms,
> For these thy superstitious taper-lights,
> Wherewith thy antichristian churches blaze,
> I'll fire thy crazèd buildings and enforce
> The papal towers to kiss the lowly ground.
>
> (1.4.94–101)

Claude Summers in *Christopher Marlowe and the Politics of Power* suggests that in such speeches "Marlowe plays to the violent anti-Roman prejudices of his audience and actually gains sympathy

for Edward."[84] The above speech is very close to one given by the
dying Henry III in *The Massacre at Paris:*

> These bloody hands shall tear his triple crown
> And fire accursed Rome about his ears.
> I'll fire his crazed buildings, and incense
> The papal towers to kiss the holy earth.

(24.60–63)

There may indeed be a plea for sympathy or support in Marlowe's
portrayal of Edward's strongly Protestant sentiments. Yet Edward's defiance is motivated primarily by his desire to please and
possess Gaveston; because of his dependency he never acquires
the personal strength to completely make good on his threats.
Though he appears to triumph temporarily in the middle of the
play, he does so only by transferring his dependency onto Spencer Junior, whom he "marries" by ironically challenging his nobles: "see how I do divorce [*Embraces* Spencer] / Spencer from
me" (3.1.176–77). But Spencer too fails as a source of power; he
can only counsel Edward to "fly, fly" when the Queen and Mortimer return from France (4.5).

In spite of his defiance of the Church's authority, Edward's emotional dependency acquires religious overtones when his career
lies in ruins. A desire for religious consolation, for the surrender
of personal struggle in the arms of a greater being, is expressed
in Marlowe's portrayal of Edward seeking refuge in Neath Abbey,
which carries sexual as well as religious suggestions:

> Father, this life contemplative is heaven—
> O that I might this life in quiet lead!
>
> .   .   .   .
>
>   Good father, on thy lap
> Lay I this head, laden with mickle care.
> O might I never open these eyes again,
> Never again lift up this drooping head,
> O never more lift up this dying heart!

(4.7.20–43)

This scene recalls *Doctor Faustus*, where Faustus ironically lectures
Mephistopheles on "manly fortitude" after the devil laments his
deprivation of everlasting bliss. In Marlowe the dream of heaven
interferes with the individual's attempts to assert "manliness" or
human cohesiveness. Edward's inability to rely on his own integrity or personal strength receives its most poignant and terrifying

expression in the final scene with Lightborn. Here the existence of God has suddenly assumed an all-important role in Edward's mind:

> Yet stay awhile; forbear thy bloody hand,
> And let me see the stroke before it comes,
> That even then when I shall lose my life,
> My mind may be more steadfast on my God.
> . . . .
> I am too weak and feeble to resist;
> Assist me, sweet God, and receive my soul.
>
> (5.5.74–108)

The epithet "sweet," the characteristic Marlovian term of love and endearment, emphasizes Edward's final need for an "other," a lover—a need we all recognize because we all share his terror, not so much of death, but of dying, and of having to do it alone, unassisted.[85] Peter Donaldson remarks that as Edward approaches his end "the evil that befalls him becomes less a matter of a conflict of will, purposes, and personalities, and more a confrontation with an underlying horror inherent in the character of human emotional need."[86] The Lightborn scene carries a further disturbing suggestion of emotional and sexual dependency, which emerges in the interview with director Toby Robertson:

> It wasn't entirely deliberate when I began, but once we were in rehearsal it became clear that this was almost the last "love scene" in the play. . . . We played this with Edward almost lying in Lightborn's lap and sort of crooning to him. He's very gently stroking him and it became like a child asking for love, wanting love, affection. And, of course, this is the trouble—this is what Edward needs. You feel it in the beginning of the play.[87]

Edward's "rape" by Lightborn is a kind of perverse parody of the internalization of the idealized male self-object. Lightborn's name of course suggests Lucifer,[88] and the homoerotic nature of this scene again recalls *Faustus*, where the failure of "manliness" or humanist assertion is linked to an erotic dependency on or desire for the (masculine) supernatural. But Lightborn is an accomplished Machiavel—revealing humanism carried to its darkest extreme—and thus represents the ultimate perversion of the human creative capacity. This figure conflates both the potential evil of human assertion and self-creation, as well as the terror and agony when such assertion and creation fails. God has set up a game that humankind cannot win.

Edward II is thus in a sense a self-consuming artifact, wherein imagination necessarily feeds on and destroys itself: QUOD ME NUTRIT ME DESTRUIT.[89] However skillfully individuals can play their social and political roles, and however effectively they can aesthetically distance themselves from their inevitable mortality, *Edward II* casts all that into doubt by underlining humankind's ultimate failure of self-sufficiency, a dependency, in Marlowe's vision, incapable of romantic or sexual fulfillment. However artful *Edward II*'s resolution—and indeed its entire symmetrical construction—this poetic drama's most memorable and affecting utterance in performance is unquestionably the horrible scream with which Edward dies, an utterance which in effect deconstructs the text. What continues to haunt us in the play is the confused desire for sexual and religious surrender, the dream of premature self-surrender turned to nightmare, the incomplete soul screaming in agony. As in *Doctor Faustus*, the greatest terror of *Edward II* arises from the fact that the illusion most of us necessarily entertain—the essential nature of the human self—is stripped from us before we can bear its loss.

8

Conclusion

THE ESSENTIALLY LOVELESS WORLD PORTRAYED IN *EDWARD II* SEEMS in some ways an inevitable culmination of Marlowe's artistic vision. Indeed, in what was probably his final work he gives hardly a more flattering picture of love: "Love is not full of pity (as men say) / But deaf and cruel where he means to prey" (*Hero and Leander* 2.287–88); Leander preys on Hero presumably as a prelude to being preyed on (and drowned, dissolved) by Neptune. With cruel honesty, Marlowe identifies a deep and dark will to power—neither specifically hetero- or homosexual—that lurks in the heart of sexual "love" and vitiates its lovingness. In the poem the power of brutish desire overwhelms the civilizing tendency of art; in Venus's temple

> . . . you see the gods in sundry shapes,
> Committing heady riots, incest, rapes:
> . . . .
> Jove slyly stealing from his sister's bed,
> To dally with Idalian Ganymede,
> Or for his love Europa bellowing loud,
> Or tumbling with the Rainbow in a cloud;
> Blood-quaffing Mars, heaving the iron net
> Which limping Vulcan and his Cyclops set;
> Love kindling fire, to burn such towns as Troy. . . .
>
> (1.143–53)

It would be wrong, however, to see the poem as simply a celebration of this kind of uncontrolled desire. In spite of its notorious complexity of tone, *Hero and Leander* seems to reflect a new kind of detachment on Marlowe's part, a sardonic maturity. Most intriguing psychologically is that the poem provides one fleeting image of a mature and kindly father:

> Leander's father knew where he had been,
> And for the same mildly rebuked his son,
> Thinking to quench the sparkles new begun.

Yet even such gentleness gives rise to conflict and struggle:

> But love resisted once grows passionate,
> And nothing more than counsel lovers hate.
>
> (2.135–40)

In fact, tenderness seems inevitably to give rise to aggression and violation; in Marlowe's vision it is the inescapable paradox of existence:

> Even as a bird, which in our hands we wring,
> Forth plungeth, and oft flutters with her wing,
> She trembling strove; this strife of hers (like that
> Which made the world) another world begat
> Of unknown joy.
>
> (2.289–93)

The poem recognizes the precariousness of all artistic and intellectual constructs in shaping and constraining the darker forces arising from unfulfilled human emotional and sexual needs. The Destinies are merciless to lovers because they themselves have been abandoned by their lover. Mercury can only temporarily overthrow the patriarchal law of Jupiter in order to facilitate his romantic indulgence, and pays for it with eternal poverty. As a personification of Learning he can still "mount aloft, and enter heaven gate" (1.466), but henceforth in worldly terms he is completely disenfranchised, powerless. Rather than a spiritual exchange between equals, sexual "love" in Marlowe rarely transcends this sense of a vicious cycle of predation, degradation, and revenge—inextricably linked to the assertion and the loss of power.[1]

The absence of mutually supportive or constructive personal relationships in the plays underlines the fictiveness of the human self by denying a major source of support for that illusion: romantic intimacy and reciprocity that makes human life at least temporarily bearable and tenable in an increasingly secular world. Yet in a sense love always fails *because of* the precariousness of the self, a self so insecure that it dare not risk the true surrender of real selfless love. This insecurity is, in a sexual sense, partly related to a tenuous masculinity that sees "acceptable" male sexual activity only in assertive, dominant terms, and resists or fears the possibility of (homo)sexual surrender. This conflict is intensified by a temptation to religious or spiritual surrender of the humanist self that is also strongly resisted, since this self offers the only vehicle for meaningful control and endeavor in secular society, even while such "control" is complicated and compromised, especially in the later plays, by ideological, economic, and sexual determinants that contribute to Marlowe's portrayal of a disrupted, conflicted, and predatory social milieu.

It may be objected that I have desired to have my critical cake and eat it too by putting forth moral cases against Marlowe's protagonists—by criticizing them for failing on human terms—when I have also suggested that those very terms are, in a spiritual or religious sense, called into question. However, if my emphasis on responsibility (taking charge in this world, though not tyrannically) seems to be in tension with the suggestion that Marlowe still suspected—or could never quite escape the belief—that human identity is indeed illusory; this tension is, I believe, very much at the heart of Marlowe's personality and of his plays. The irony of identity is that the individual must struggle to fashion, and is responsible for the integrity of, a self that can never assume complete control of its circumstances, that is partly dependent on and certainly responsible to other selves, and that, according to its (never quite forgotten) mortal and spiritual destiny, must eventually be surrendered. Such a project might seem an exercise in futility were it not for a hope (and the equanimity is probably more the Christian humanist's than Marlowe's) that the integrity the self assumes during this struggle can be incorporated in the final spiritual identity. What remains disturbing, in Marlowe's plays, is that in the self's weakness God's strength does not appear to be guaranteed, contrary to the biblical promise. We find instead various forms of self-delusion (impractical self-fashioning) and the pain and despair of what I have termed the incomplete soul. What remains so deeply compelling about Marlowe's dramatic works, in spite of the devastating bleakness and viciousness of the worlds they portray, is the very human need for a self-fulfilling rather than self-destroying love that they continually evoke. It is this powerful emotional vortex within the plays, although obliquely conveyed, that saves them from being unbearably painful artistic experiences—that, and their exceptional dramatic and poetic achievement.

Marlowe's protagonists experience such great difficulty partly because of their narcissistic confusion as to where the self ends and the "other" begins, almost at times to the extent that the "other" barely exists at all on its own terms. Thus Dido can exclaim incredulously, "The Gods? What Gods" (5.1.128), and Tamburlaine's murky reasoning follows the line of "There is a God, if any God, but anyway I'll do whatever I please" and then a final, shocked, "What daring God torments my body thus?" (part 2 5.3.42). With respect to human "others," Barabas and Edward replace their loved ones as easily as one would exchange a purchase from a department store. This inability to individuate and establish proper "ego boundaries" can be related to the frequency of walls, barriers, and enclosures in the plays, and the acts of breaking them down and retreating behind them. Tamburlaine breaks down walls; Barabas scurries inside the walls of Malta. Faustus bumps his head against the *primum mobile* and then gradually retreats back to the walls of his study, through which he enters the hell-mouth. Edward threatens to make "England's civil towns huge heaps of stones" (3.2.31) and "enforce the papal towers to kiss the lowly ground" (1.4.100–101), but all he ever really wants is to walk with Gaveston about the walls of Tynemouth, and what he finally gets, through complete implosion of the self, is imprisonment and death in a sewage-filled dungeon. The Marlovian self is never stable enough to establish a definite limit, and therefore is either constantly expanding or shrinking.

Marlowe's protagonists fail to fashion themselves with respect to the demands of the external world partly because, through their narcissistic fantasies of omnipotence, they give language and imagination too much power. We generally recognize poetic and figurative language as belonging to the domain of the imagination, where it seems to function in part as compensation for our personal, physical, and temporal limitations. The literalization of metaphor in the plays communicates a sense of the ridiculous or, carried to an extreme, the horrific. With respect to this feature of Marlovian drama, Augustine offers an intriguing commentary. Eugene Vance writes:

> In *De doctrina christiana* (III.v.9), Augustine deepens the link between carnal desire and reading, thereby establishing one of the more complex generative problematics of Western literature, considered as an open-minded inscription of self-thwarting human desire:
>
> > For at the outset, you must be very careful lest you take figurative expressions literally. What the Apostle says pertains to this problem: "For the letter killeth, but the spirit quickeneth." That is, when that which is said figuratively is taken as though it were literal, it is understood carnally. . . . Nor can anything more appropriately be called the death of the soul than that condition in which the thing which distinguishes us from beasts, which is the understanding, is subjected to the flesh in the pursuit of the letter.[2]

In one sense Augustine offers a useful corrective to Hermetic (and materialist) fantasies of absolute rhetorical and discursive control. Human language is not divine language; there is an ontological gap between our language and our being in the world; it is an inevitable condition of our incarnation in the body. A willful disregard of this fact is narcissistic delusion.

Yet Augustinian spirituality is perhaps ultimately yet another version of (displaced) narcissism, since it in a sense short-circuits the humanist project of self-fashioning. Although Augustine emphasized the need for a rigorous program of self-control, of mental and physical discipline, his theological emphasis on grace and human depravity, so quickly institutionalized and politicized, has had extremely unfortunate ideological, political, and psychological effects in Western history. Patrick Grant observes that "from the time of his own acute experience of the bound will, Augustine never flinched in his conviction that saving insight is a gift of grace, and yet . . . Augustine's treatises on original sin, famous for their descriptions of the *massa damnata* and the traducianist notion of evil inherited through the flesh, are stark and fierce reminders of how easily ideas might harden, forced out of touch with the living springs of metaphor."[3] Any society that values individual freedom and development, that refuses to impose "saving insights" from without through institutions and political programs, must take warning at the progressive hardening of Augustine's thought. While our words and images, our aspirations and narratives and dreams, are not absolute powers to be imposed either on our own lives or on the lives of others, the energy for meaningful creation and viable self-fashioning in the world can be supplied by the mediation of our individual efforts and risk taking through the mental and physical processes of experience. The *Confessions*, a favorite work of Reformation piety,[4] offers a compelling but ultimately self-defeating (intentionally from Augustine's perspective) vision of the inadequacy and futility of human rhetorical, imaginative, and creative power. As Vance explains, Augustine begins his commentary on Genesis in book 11 of the *Confessions* by "pleading with God to circumcise his lips so that he may gain the chaste pleasures . . . of understanding God's text." He compares "his tongue to his phallus" and "the hermeneutical performance to erotic love. . . . The 'outer' lies that must be circumcised from his lips are lies uttered externally as verbal or written signs, while the 'inner' occur in the production of that silent, nonverbal language of the soul which precedes the utterance of outward speech; the foreskin of these inner thoughts must also be trimmed in sacrifice before Augustine may enjoy, as he tells God, the 'inside of your words.'"[5] As Vance explains, "any person who speaks his *own* mind can proffer only lies," and "Augustine's plea to be circumcised from both outward and inward lying . . . is as much a plea to transcend his own subjective consciousness as it is a plea to be allowed to speak truly."[6] The impulse is of course antiromantic, stripping the individual human consciousness of meaningful endeavor, assertion, and creativity. The problem is that Augustinianism thus denies the cycle of psychological maturation—denies the recognition that the individual human consciousness cannot *give* to any other, or maintain its competency in a union with any other, unless it is first allowed and encouraged to explore its own powers and limitations.

The Augustinian influence on Marlowe may help to explain why his art is greatly concerned with delusion, with self-indulgent rather than creative or practical uses of imagination, since his emphasis on the perverting power of imagination does in fact have something in common with Augustine's extreme distrust of that faculty. In the *Confessions* Augustine frequently attacks the validity of artistic creation, even though he admits shamefully (in his characteristic way of denying everything that was ever human or attractive about himself) that as a youth he preferred "empty romances," in particular Virgil's *Aeneid,* to "more valuable studies."[7] In book 4 Augustine laments that as a young man he had not yet learned that "man's mind is not the supreme good that does not vary":

> I was struggling to reach you, but you thrust me back so that I knew the taste of death. For *you thwart the proud.* And what greater pride could there be than to assert, as I did in my strange madness, that by nature I was what you are? . . . This is why you thrust me back and crushed my rearing pride, while my imagination continued to play on material forms. Myself a man of flesh and blood I blamed the flesh. I was as fickle as *a breath of wind,* unable to return to you. I drifted on, making my way towards things that had no existence in you or in myself or in the body. They were not created for me by your truth but were the inventions of my own foolish imagination working on material things.[8]

In spite of Augustine's famous struggle with his disease of lust, the imagination and not the body emerges as his most formidable enemy:

> My heart was full of bitter protests against the creations of my imagination, and this single truth [that God could never suffer decay or

hurt or change] was the only weapon with which I could try to drive from my mind's eye all the unclean images which swarmed before it. But hardly had I brushed them aside than, in the flicker of an eyelid, they crowded upon me again.[9]

Similarly, Marlowe's protagonists suffer more from their descent into imagination than their descent into the flesh. Ironically, as a result of their imaginative excesses, their bodies and material circumstances seem to conspire to wreak painful revenges in the whirligig of their careers. Yet, crucially, the body takes revenge because its reality is resisted, because it is not accepted on its own inevitable terms.

Augustine apparently was frustrated by, among other things, the fact that he could not control his erections; this demonstrated for him the corruption of his will. In his unsuccessful struggle with his own humanity—that changing, imperfect, and therefore illusory identity—he postulated the theory of original sin and the depravity of the human race. Ironically through a gigantically perverse act of imagination, he ideologically annihilated the validity of the individual will. I cannot be the first to suspect that Augustine's moment of mystical reconciliation with his mother Monica at Ostia is one of the most significant moments of spiritual narcissism in Western history. The narrative of original sin and atonement is really the great antinarrative, the black hole of all other narratives. As Elaine Pagels points out, most commentators before Augustine saw the theme of the story of Adam and Eve as moral freedom and moral responsibility, not as the instigation of endless depravity.[10] Augustine's doctrine in effect cancels the natural challenges of human growth, loving, and risking inherent in physical existence and physical relationships. Augustine violates his own admonition not to read literally, and the atonement becomes an emblematic surrogate for all other suffering.

At the end of his 1974 study *The Transformation of Sin*, Patrick Grant remarks that while the Augustinian tradition of thought has steadily declined since the Renaissance, "it will no doubt again, in some new formulation, have its say," since "all things contain within themselves the seeds of what opposes them." Paradoxically enough, this tradition of thought has in a sense reemerged in the form of radically antiessential materialist and poststructuralist psychoanalytic discourse. Grant, in a later study, in fact recognizes this development: "We should be careful not to confine an emphasis on the decentered subject to recent theorists such as Lacan, Althusser and [Hillis] Miller. The search for a unified self through the interminable chains of signification and weavings of desire is as familiar in Augustine and Bonaventure as in Lacan and Derrida, as Lacan himself notices."[11] Postmodernist discourses of course do not share with Augustine any concern with spiritual source; their inner, silent language of the soul is "ideology" or "phallocentric logic." Nevertheless, the ethical and moral implications with respect to human identity are disturbingly similar. Dollimore in *Sexual Dissidence*, for example, finds persuasive Jacqueline Rose's psychoanalytic/feminist account of humankind's shifting identity:

> The unconscious constantly reveals the "failure" of identity. Because there is no continuity of psychic life, so there is no stability of sexual identity, no position for women (or for men) which is ever simply achieved. Nor does psychoanalysis see such "failure" as a special-case inability or an individual deviancy from the norm. "Failure" is not a moment to be regretted in a process of adaption, or development into normality, which ideally takes its course . . . Instead "failure" is something endlessly repeated and relived moment by moment throughout our individual histories. . . . Feminism's affinity with psychoanalysis rests above all, I would argue, with this recognition that there is a resistance to identity at the very heart of psychic life.[12]

It may be too obvious at this point to question whether the fact that something is never "simply achieved" should exclude the possibility that it is still deeply worth the effort of achieving. Dollimore's parallel between Renaissance and postmodern conceptions of self in *Sexual Dissidence* is worth consideration: "both despite and because of the obvious and considerable differences, post/modernism is helping us to understand again what the early modern period already knew but in a quite different form: identity is *essentially* informed by what it is not."[13] Yet Dollimore, like other materialists, considers otherness in terms of alienation and threat; his emphasis on the concept of the "perverse dynamic" as an ongoing principle of social interaction in many ways simply perpetuates the savagery, incrimination, and fear truly humane critics should be striving to overcome: "perversion is a concept that takes us to the heart of a fierce dialectic between domination and deviation, law and desire, transgression and conformity; a dialectic working through repression, demonizing, displacement, and struggle."[14] Because of his constant attacks on the depth model of the self, Dollimore cannot perceive of a dialectic of growth and constructive exchange, in which the individual is not a victim of others and of the social order but responsible to them.

In Dollimore's support it would of course be absurd to deny that, even today, gays and lesbians are particularly liable to attack from without because of continuing prejudice and discrimination. Yet it is also impossible to deny that the problem of personal "stability" with respect to sexual desire is universal. This universality is made clear at one moment in Dollimore's analysis of Freud:

> Of other, perverse, activities [Freud] says that they are "ethically objectionable, for they degrade the relationships of love between two human beings from a serious matter to a convenient game attended by no risk and no spiritual participation." . . . [Yet] even as the deviations are being condemned, he complicates the judgement by ascribing a form of idealism to the fantasy life of masturbation, and playfulness to interpersonal perversion. Who, after all, could *not* be tempted by the prospect of sexuality liberated from seriousness, risk, and spiritual participation?[15]

In all honesty Dollimore is right; who could not be so tempted? Yet the fact that the self and human relationships are precarious constructs does not exonerate us from the task of constructing them. Identifying the "single most important concept in material analysis"—praxis—Dollimore remarks in *Radical Tragedy:* "It is a concept which severs the connection between individuality and man, between subjectivity and the human condition. Consequently it rejects the 'tragic' belief in a human essence which by its own nature as well as its relation to the universal order of things, must inevitably suffer."[16] Regrettably, this line of reasoning encourages the conclusion that, if one does suffer, it is always someone else's fault, always the fault of some hegemonic control or oppressive ideology, some unfair discursive formation from without. That psychological growth, self-discipline, risk taking that includes accountability and care all involve inherent "suffering" can be ignored and denied. It is no wonder that Dollimore can claim, in *Sexual Dissidence*, that the "hollowing-out of the deep self is pure pleasure, a release from the subjective correlatives of dominant morality,"[17] but what exactly does this suggest about his critique of the "dominant morality"? Most intriguing of all is his assertion, near the end of the study, that

> to liberate desire from oppression is not—could never be—a matter of resuming or regaining a desire/subjectivity as it existed prior to discrimination. If oppression is imagined as a distortion of the self, then the lifting of oppression might be imagined to result in the self

resuming its natural undistorted form. But . . . *liberated desire would still always be different from its pre-oppression counterpart.* It will bear the history of that oppression, not necessarily as that which disables desire (though it may), but as desire itself. . . . The proposition that the history of sexual oppression will always inhere in the sexual desire of the oppressed, most powerfully in the form of self-oppression, confesses to tragedy.[18]

Here we have a return to "tragedy," which has something to do with the continuance of "self-oppression." But the assertion that liberated desire will always bear the history of its oppression comes close to exonerating the oppressed from *ever* accepting responsibility for the construction of identity. It also raises the nagging suspicion that some materialist critical discourse paradoxically may have a vested interest in the continuance of the oppression it is reacting against: the presence of such oppression is its food, its defining opposition, its reason for being, its (dare I say) very *essence.* Knowing this, and to prevent its deconstruction, it must assert that its proponents will never be whole, never be genuine.

It is because of the above considerations that I have found Kohut's approach particularly compelling. He relates that in his earlier years, while "clinging to Freud's model of the mind depicted as an apparatus that processes forces within a hypothetical space, [he] could find no place for the psychological activities that go by the name of choice, decision, and free will":

Mental-apparatus psychology, governed by the laws of psychic determinism . . . explains a great deal. But while it is true that many psychological activities and interactions lend themselves to being satisfactorily explained within this framework, it is equally true that there are some phenomena that require for their explanation the positing of a psychic configuration—the self—that, *whatever the history of its formation,* has become a center of initiative: a unit that tries to follow its own course.[19]

I have therefore emphasized a humanist concept of selfhood and individual responsibility in this study, while remaining sensitive to social and cultural context. I have done so out of a conviction that the perception of transcultural and transhistorical significance is a critical advantage, not disadvantage—that such perceptions are, in fact, the ultimate goal of even the most historically sensitive analyses. I can even, perhaps a little ironically, find sup-

port from a well-known Marxist literary critic for my humanist
approach:

> The liberal humanist conception of literature sees the act of reading
> as one which engages a universal human subject, one which must
> divest itself of its cultural idiosyncrasies if it is to enter at all deeply
> into this compact. This, in its day, had been a revolutionary idea—a
> strike at the privilege and particularism of the *anciens régimes*, in
> which the notion of a universal humanity, of being able to gain respect
> or a vote or a hearing just because you were human rather than the
> son of a minor Prussian count, was subversive stuff. It is astonishing
> how firmly today's cultural left has repressed the emancipatory side
> of this history, with its Pavlovian reaction to the "unified subject."[20]

It may be objected that my reassertion of a humanist approach
is premature, that I seek to override current legitimate political
agendas; however, it is a pressing question whether the study of
literature as a profession can bear for any great length of time the
denial of the validity of "universalized"—not necessarily "depo-
liticized"—readings. I hope my readings of Marlowe have carried
meaning for all kinds of readers, without oppressing any particular kind.

It is undeniable that Marlowe's plays are concerned to some
degree with various forms of ideological and social oppression
related to the Renaissance social context. Marlowe lived at a time
when the patriarchy of the medieval and Reformation churches
was becoming reinscribed into the patriarchy of the emerging
Enlightenment, a fact that would lead to inestimable suffering for
individuals of both genders and all forms of sexuality. Manliness
in this context is defined in terms too narrow, rigid, and oppressive, and too dependent on the mirroring of feminine passivity,
just as some feminist self-construction is now too dependent on
a simplistic demonization of masculine assertion. But in their exploration of narcissistic disorders the plays gesture in the direction of a more flexible and mature "manliness," a kind of integrity
to which all individuals can aspire. I am aware that some feminist
theory sees the emphasis on individualism as inescapably patriarchal. Linda Hutcheon, quoting Nancy K. Miller, observes that

> feminist theory and practice have problematized even poststructural-
> ism's (unconsciously, perhaps, phallocentric) tendency to see the sub-
> ject in apocalyptic terms of loss or dispersal: instead, they refuse to
> foreclose the question of identity. This refusal is undertaken in the
> name of the (different) histories of women: "Because women have

not had the same historical relation of identity to origin, institution, production, that men have had, women have not, I think, (collectively) felt burdened by too much Self, Ego, Cogito, etc."[21]

Yet (while recognizing that the above assertion may very well misrepresent even the endeavors of many women in the past) the large-scale empowerment of women is certainly a radical change in their history, and it is incredible that those women who have attained highly responsible social and political positions have not now a keen interest in the burden of their Self, Ego, Cogito, et cetera. I do not wish to demean the accomplishment of feminist criticism in Renaissance studies, which has proven invaluable in expanding scholarship to include alternative discourses and texts; it is also, I believe, largely responsible for encouraging a greater freedom and openness in discussions of gender and sexuality in general. Yet female scholars might now also take an increased, not decreased, interest in "canonical" Renaissance texts (Shakespeare's history plays, for example) that treat the challenges and problems inherent in the individual's assumption of secular power, even if these individual characters are predominantly male. Humanist striving itself—the insistence on personal responsibility and integrity—could have been, and still can be at this point in history, more broadly conceived and defined than patriarchy allowed. Even Dollimore briefly entertains the possibility that "a radical humanism might allow difference in the name of the same—since 'we're all ultimately human.'"[22]

While Marlowe was struggling toward a vision of the world where individuals would have more freedom to construct themselves, his plays nevertheless suggest that the achievement of this more flexible dialectic of assertion and surrender would still require skillful "imagining," to be able to judge or foresee one's own strengths and weaknesses, as well as the strengths and weaknesses of those with whom one interacts. The playwright's protagonists fail to make a realistic assessment of these very factors. Their failure, as I have argued, can be related to Marlowe's own religious and sexual conflicts, and his attempts to overcome or resolve them. Unlike Augustine, Marlowe does not cling single-mindedly to a need to somehow realize an unchangeable good beyond his comprehension. At some point in his life Marlowe either found it impossible to put on the armor of God or decided it was not a viable alternative, and was thus faced with having to construct independently an identity even while suspecting its ultimate fictiveness. Given his sexual inclinations and the strictures of his society, this was not an easy task. We cannot underestimate the difficulty of self-fashioning outside the "structure of sacramental and blood relations that normally determine identity."[23] While Mary Beth Rose, reacting against political and social contructionist readings of Renaissance relationships, asserts that "whatever else it may be, love, definitely, is love,"[24] she sees Eros asserting itself and finding its dignity within the socially sanctioned institution of marriage. Homoerotic Eros would find itself, in the Renaissance (and still today), continuously tortured and displaced. Consequently, the predominantly homosexual individual, having no one to share the illusion of self with, would find the illusion that much more difficult to maintain. In such cases, in fact, one would constantly be thrown back on one's own imaginative resources. It is therefore not surprising that Marlowe's characters are given to imaginative indulgence. Arthur Lindley defines Marlovian heroism simply as "a capacity for believing one's own propaganda."[25] However, our attention should be directed not simply to the foolishness of the protagonists but also to a tragic realization that their "propaganda" often receives little support from the fictions of their society. Even Edward's dissipation may be a kind of cathartic expression of Marlowe's own sexual frustration and desperation, though it is certainly no wish fulfillment. If we are poised rather uncertainly, even uncomfortably, between moral evaluations of these characters and a sympathetic identification with their suffering selves, this tension is partly what makes Marlowe's tragedies such a rich and engaging experience for reader and audience. This is what, in effect, makes the four major plays great tragedies.

I have argued that the plays are orthodox in their exposure of human limitation, but heterodox in their treatment of traditional religious doctrine. Thus, in spite of my emphasis on responsibility, my iconoclastic, psychological readings place me in the romantic camp; and, though I recognize that "authenticity" is largely constructed by the individual under the pressure of various social and physical limitations, I am not willing to give up the term, just as I am not willing to abandon the distinction between hypocrisy and sincerity, between courageous risk taking and cowardly, indirect manipulation. However, the irony of identity is a complex irony that refuses to delineate or morally distinguish assertive and passive behavior according to religious or social codes. If Marlowe's protagonists misuse their imagination, or delude themselves into believing their own unrealistic propaganda, we can understand and sympathize. Experience forces us all to create our own propaganda, even while some of us can choose, with less effort or with less sense of integrity, to buy into already established agendas. Inevitably all our choices involve risks and repercussions that unpredictably determine the extent to which our projects of self-fashioning turn into comedy or tragedy. That is why the Divine Creator in Marlowe turns out to be a rather unlovable bystander, as he waits in the wings—or rather, in keeping with the Elizabethan theater, as he sits on one side of the stage as privileged spectator—watching us make ourselves only so we can unmake ourselves.

To return now to the Donne lyric with which I began, Marlowe was very intent on the voyage of self-assertion *westward*, but he also kept, as I have suggested, an image somewhere in his mind of what he had turned his back on. As Kyd informs us, the story of the prodigal son had a fascination for Marlowe, who claimed "That the prodigall Childes portion was but fower nobles, he held his purse so neere the bottom in all pictures, and that it either was a iest or els fowr nobles then was thought a great patrimony not thinking it a parable."[26] Behind Marlowe's own jest here— and clearly the story was for him a very significant parable—lies a bitterness not surprising in light of the ideas explored in this study. If, according to God's scheme, having *returned* to the father's house is so much better than having never left at all, Marlowe was quite prepared to make the effort, yet not without a certain despair concerning the paucity of personal resources some individuals set out with, a resentment at how poorly the father furnishes his children for the arduous journey. What is truly remarkable, and deeply impressive, about Marlowe's personal career is the amount of courage he displayed in the midst of his anxiety and doubt. He pursued surely one of the most dangerous of activities—employment in the secret service—at the same time that he became a popular and successful playwright. Unlike some of his characters, Marlowe did not attempt to escape the "real" world. If he did in truth die cursing and blaspheming, one cannot help admiring his energy and tenacity.

The remarkable irony, however, is that, *like* Faustus, Barabas, and Edward, Marlowe ended his career by becoming a kind of unwilling artifact in a morality fable. I am referring of course to works such as Thomas Beard's *Theatre of Gods Iudgements* (1597) and Edmunde Rudierde's *The Thunderbolt of Gods Wrath against Hard-Hearted and stiffe-necked sinners* (1618), the titles of which sufficiently indicate their authors' interpretations of the moral significance of Marlowe's death. Still, Marlowe deserves honor rather than revilement for his great artistic achievement and his "tenacity." His struggle was, I believe, based on a conviction that any idea of religious truth must in some way be tested against what the self experiences in this world; that is, the self owes its first allegiance to its own sanity and survival, and cannot ignore either the social skills or the emotional and sexual needs that factor in this survival. The versions of pathology and despair that Marlowe explored often reveal an intense criticism of the ideologies and hypocrisies of his society, of the cultural limitations that prevented him from achieving some form of psychological and social stability. Yet the plays move us most intensely not as social criticism but as tragedy, because they reveal on a deeper level a struggle against great odds on the part of the playwright himself—involving, through sympathetic identification and participation, the reader or spectator—to emerge a more mature and adaptable, but a no less creative, human being.

Notes

Chapter 1. Introduction

1. Stephen Greenblatt, *Renaissance Self-Fashioning: From More to Shakespeare* (Chicago: University of Chicago Press, 1980), 2.

2. Augustine, Sermon 169, quoted in Peter Brown, *Religion and Society in the Age of Saint Augustine* (London: Faber and Faber, 1972), 30; Greenblatt, *Renaissance Self-Fashioning*, 2.

3. Scott Peck, *The Road Less Traveled* (New York: Touchstone, 1978), 97.

4. William Kerrigan and Gordon Braden, *The Idea of the Renaissance* (Baltimore: Johns Hopkins University Press, 1989), 122.

5. Pico della Mirandola, *Oration on the Dignity of Man*, trans. A. Robert Caponigri (Washington, D.C.: Regnery Gateway, 1956), 7–9.

6. Kerrigan and Braden, *The Idea of the Renaissance*, 122.

7. Patrick Grant, *The Transformation of Sin: Studies in Donne, Herbert, Vaughan, and Traherne* (Montreal: McGill-Queen's University Press; Amherst: University of Massachusetts Press, 1974), 26.

8. Pico, *Oration on the Dignity of Man*, 10–11.

9. Grant, *The Transformation of Sin*, 38.

10. Greenblatt, *Renaissance Self-Fashioning*, 256, 257.

11. Catherine Belsey, *The Subject of Tragedy: Identity and Difference in Renaissance Drama* (London: Methuen, 1985), 223.

12. Ibid., 54.

13. Catherine Belsey, *John Milton: Language, Gender, Power* (Oxford: Basil Blackwell, 1988), 104.

14. See especially the final chapter of Jonathan Dollimore, *Radical Tragedy: Religion, Ideology, and Power in the Drama of Shakespeare and His Contemporaries* (Chicago: University of Chicago Press, 1984).

15. Ibid., 155.

16. Ibid., 163, 168.

17. Paul Kocher, *Christopher Marlowe: A Study of His Thought, Learning, and Character* (1946; reprint, New York: Russell and Russell, 1962), 4.

18. A. D. Wraight, *In Search of Christopher Marlowe* (London: Macdonald and Co., 1965), 5.

19. A more recent treatment of Marlowe's religious dissidence than Kocher's may be found in Michael Keefer's 1604 edition of *Doctor Faustus* (Peterborough, Ontario: Broadview Press, 1991), xxii–xxxiii.

20. Charles Nicholl, *The Reckoning: The Murder of Christopher Marlowe* (New York: Harcourt Brace and Co., 1992), 129.

21. Roy Kendall, "Richard Baines and Christopher Marlowe's Milieu," *English Literary Renaissance* 24, no. 3 (1994): 525.

22. Ibid., 536.

23. Nicholl, *The Reckoning*, 310.

24. Kendall, "Richard Baines and Christopher Marlowe's Milieu," 541.

25. Kocher, *A Study of His Thought*, 33–68.

26. J. B. Steane, *Marlowe: A Critical Study* (Cambridge: Cambridge University Press, 1964), 23.

27. Frederick S. Boas, *Christopher Marlowe: A Biographical and Critical Study* (Oxford: Clarendon Press, 1940), 112.

28. Ibid.

29. I must add here, as an aside, that I believe Charles Nicholl's claim that the treatise was a deliberate plant is one of the weakest points in his argument (*The Reckoning*, 284–89), and suggests he is straitjacketed by his own conspiracy theory. It is not certain that the only reason for arresting Kyd was to incriminate Marlowe, and had someone actually wished to do so, surely a more contemporary and directly politically incriminating document could have been chosen.

30. William Dinsmore Briggs, "On a Document Concerning Christopher Marlowe," *Studies in Philology* 20 (1923): 153.

31. Quoted in Wraight, *In Search of Christopher Marlowe*, 311.

32. W. D. Briggs, "On a Document Concerning Christopher Marlowe," 156.

33. Ibid., 157.

34. M. C. Bradbrook, *The School of Night: A Study in the Literary Relationships of Sir Walter Raleigh* (1936; reprint, New York: Russell and Russell, 1965).

35. Eleanor Grace Clark, *Ralegh and Marlowe* (1941; reprint, New York: Russell and Russell, 1965).

36. Kocher, *A Study of His Thought*, 7–18.

37. Wraight, *In Search of Christopher Marlowe*, 164.

38. Hilary Gatti, "Bruno's Heroic Searcher and Marlowe's *Doctor Faustus*," *Rinascimento* 26 (1986): 99–138.

39. John Bakeless, *The Tragicall History of Christopher Marlowe* (Cambridge: Harvard University Press, 1942), 1:127, 129.

40. James Robinson Howe, *Marlowe, Tamburlaine, and Magic* (Athens: Ohio University Press, 1976).

41. Eugenio Garin, *Medioevo e Rinascimento* (Bari: G. Laterza and F., 1954), 151; Howe's translation, *Marlowe, Tamburlaine, and Magic*, 11.

42. Howe's translation of Ficino's *Théologie Platonicienne*, vol. 1, trans. Raymond Marcel (Paris, 1964), 229; Howe, *Marlowe, Tamburlaine, and Magic*, 11.

43. This theme has been explored by, among other critics, Joel B. Altman, who in *The Tudor Play of Mind: Rhetorical Inquiry and the Development of Elizabethan Drama* (Berkeley: University of California Press, 1978) argues that "Marlowe's plays are literally dramatized *suppositions*, each examining in its own way the ability of the human wit to 'grow a second nature,' as Sidney puts it—to discover and sustain a true universe" (322).

44. Stephen Greenblatt, "Marlowe and Renaissance Self-Fashioning," in *Two Renaissance Mythmakers: Christopher Marlowe and Ben Jonson*, ed. Alvin Kernan (Baltimore: Johns Hopkins University Press, 1977), 63.

45. Emily C. Bartels, *Spectacles of Strangeness: Imperialism, Alienation, and Marlowe* (Philadelphia: University of Pennsylvania Press, 1993), xv.

46. Kerrigan and Braden remark that Greenblatt "seems to posit an ideal of independent self-fashioning far purer than anything ever seriously proposed for Renaissance individualism—something close indeed to Hegel's *unendende Subjectivität*—so that the concluding revelation of its insupportability is something of a set-up" (*The Idea of the Renaissance*, 223 n. 27).

47. Bartels, *Spectacles of Strangeness*, 24.

48. Ibid., 8.

49. Sigmund Freud, *Civilization and Its Discontents*, trans. James Strachey (New York: Norton, 1961), 72–73.

50. Stephen Frosh, *The Politics of Psychoanalysis* (New Haven: Yale University Press, 1987), 49, quoting N. O. Brown, *Life against Death* (Middletown, Conn.: Wesleyan University Press, 1959), 25.

51. David D. Gilmore, *Manhood in the Making: Cultural Concepts of Masculinity* (New Haven: Yale University Press, 1990), 28.

52. Debora Kuller Shuger, *Habits of Thought in the English Renaissance: Religion, Politics, and the Dominant Culture* (Berkeley: University of California Press, 1990), 223.

53. Peter S. Donaldson, "Conflict and Coherence: Narcissism and Tragic Structure in Marlowe," in *Narcissism and the Text: Studies in Literature and the Psychology of Self*, ed. Lynne Layton and Barbara Ann Schapiro (New York: New York University Press, 1986).

54. Stephen Frosh, *Identity Crisis: Modernity, Psychoanalysis, and the Self* (New York: Routledge, 1991), 101.

55. Donaldson, "Conflict and Coherence," 36.

56. Ibid., 36-37.

57. Ibid., 37.

58. See the introduction to *Narcissism and the Text: Studies in Literature and the Psychology of Self* by Lynne Layton and Barbara Ann Schapiro.

59. Introduction to *The Future of Psychoanalysis*, ed. Arnold Goldberg (New York: International Universities Press, 1983), xiii.

60. John Russell, *Hamlet and Narcissus* (Newark: University of Delaware Press, 1995), 16.

61. Katharine Eisaman Maus, *Inwardness and Theater in the English Renaissance* (Chicago: University of Chicago Press, 1995), 27, 28.

62. Ibid., 31.

63. Lyndal Roper, *Oedipus and the Devil: Witchcraft, Sexuality and Religion in Early Modern Europe* (London: Routledge, 1994), 13.

64. Thomas Greene, "The Flexibility of the Self in Renaissance Literature," in *The Disciplines of Criticism: Essays in Literary Theory, Interpretation, and History*, ed. Peter Demetz, Thomas Greene, and Lowry Nelson, Jr. (New Haven: Yale University Press, 1968), 249. Although clearly from a patriarchal perspective, Erasmus's statement recalls Simone de Beauvoir's similar statement about women; the parallel, however, raises pressing and challenging questions concerning both the socialization of and individual responsibility for personal identity.

65. Gilmore, *Manhood in the Making*, 11.

66. Donaldson, "Conflict and Coherence," 37.

67. Keith Wrightson, *English Society, 1580–1680* (London: Hutchinson, 1982), 13.

68. L. G. Salingar, "The Social Setting," in *The Age of Shakespeare*, vol. 2 of the New Pelican Guide to English Literature, ed. Boris Ford (London: Penguin, 1982), 17.

69. Nicholl, *The Reckoning*, 113.

70. Ibid., 266.

71. Giordano Bruno, lib. I, cap. 7, quoted in Wraight, *In Search of Christopher Marlowe*, 172.

72. See also Gatti, "Bruno's Heroic Searcher and Marlowe's *Doctor Faustus*," 104–5. Gatti writes of "the emergence of a new concept of knowledge, which becomes the right and possession of anyone capable of pursuing and achieving it. Bruno was prepared to follow this concept to an openly heretical conclusion, reducing the prophets, saints and Christ himself to the same level as other exceptionally learned men" (105).

73. Wraight, *In Search of Christopher Marlowe*, 173.

74. Quoted by Clark, *Ralegh and Marlowe*, 386.

75. Dollimore, *Radical Tragedy*, 162–63.

76. Roper, *Oedipus and the Devil*, 16–17.

77. William Blackburn, "'Heavenly Words': Marlowe's Faustus as a Renaissance Magician," *English Studies in Canada* 4 (1978): 4.

78. Kerrigan and Braden, *The Idea of the Renaissance*, 125.

79. See William H. Halewood, *The Poetry of Grace* (New Haven: Yale University Press, 1970), 56.

80. Richard Waswo, *Language and Meaning in the Renaissance* (Princeton: Princeton University Press, 1987), 253–54.

81. Kocher, *A Study of His Thought*, 119.

82. William Leigh Godshalk, "Marlowe's *Dido, Queen of Carthage*," *ELH* 38 (1971): 2–3.

83. J. B. Steane, introduction to *Christopher Marlowe: The Complete Plays* (Harmondsworth, U.K.: Penguin Books, 1969), 15.

84. Harry Levin, *Christopher Marlowe: The Overreacher* (1952; reprint, London: Faber and Faber, 1961), 34.

85. Claude J. Summers, "Sex, Politics, and Self-Realization in *Edward II*," in *"A Poet and a filthy Play-maker": New Essays on Christopher Marlowe*, ed. Kenneth Friedenreich, Roma Gill, and Constance Kuriyama (New York: AMS Press, 1988), 222.

86. Alan Bray, *Homosexuality in Renaissance England* (London: Gay Men's Press, 1982), 16-17.

87. Eve Sedgwick, *Epistemology of the Closet* (Berkeley: University of California Press, 1990), 62.

88. Northrop Frye, *The Great Code: The Bible and Literature* (Toronto: Academic Press Canada, 1982), 154.

89. Roper, *Oedipus and the Devil*, 43–44.

90. It is interesting to note as well that this tradition of manly Protestantism continues in England and its empire during later centuries. David D. Gilmore points out that "an obsessive moral masculinization in the English-speaking countries went beyond mere mortals of the day to Christ himself, who was portrayed in turn-of-the-century [1900] tracts as 'the supremely manly man,' athletic and aggressive when necessary, no 'Prince of Peace-at-any-price.' . . . Pious and articulate English Protestants loudly proclaimed their muscular religion as an antidote to what Charles Kingsley derided as the 'fastidious maundering, die-away effeminacy' of the High Anglican Church" (*Manhood in the Making*, 18).

91. Sedgwick, *Epistemology of the Closet*, 40.

92. Ibid.

93. Michel Foucault, *The History of Sexuality*, vol. 1, *An Introduction* (1976), trans. Robert Hurley (New York: Pantheon, 1978), 105–6; Bruce R. Smith, *Homosexual Desire in Shakespeare's England: A Cultural Poetics* (Chicago: University of Chicago Press, 1991), 5–6.

94. Sedgwick, *Epistemology of the Closet*, 40–41.

95. Smith, *Homosexual Desire in Shakespeare's England*, 27.

96. Valerie Traub, *Desire and Anxiety: Circulations of Sexuality in Shakespearean Drama* (London: Routledge, 1992), 9.

97. Ibid., 10.

98. I find this suggestion, for example, implicit in many of the arguments in Gregory Bredbeck's *Sodomy and Interpretation: Marlowe to Milton* (Ithaca: Cornell University Press, 1991). See my review, *Seventeenth-Century News* 52 (1994): 16–18.

99. Traub, *Desire and Anxiety*, 7.

100. Greenblatt, "Marlowe and Renaissance Self-Fashioning," 56.

101. Mary Beth Rose, *The Expense of Spirit: Love and Sexuality in English Renaissance Drama* (Ithaca: Cornell University Press, 1988), 8.

102. Bray, *Homosexuality in Renaissance England*, 61.

103. Ibid., 57, 71, 76.

104. Quoted in Kocher, "Marlowe's Atheist Lecture," in *Marlowe: A Collection of Critical Essays*, ed. Clifford Leech (Englewood Cliffs, N.J.: Prentice-Hall, 1964), 160.

105. Smith, *Homosexual Desire in Shakespeare's England*, 196.

106. Constance Brown Kuriyama, *Hammer or Anvil: Psychological Patterns in Christopher Marlowe's Plays* (New Brunswick, N.J.: Rutgers University Press, 1980), 120.

107. Valerie Traub has asserted that if, "as Thomas Laqueur argues, the Galenic paradigm which dominated sixteenth- and seventeenth-century medicine understood men to originate as female, then the fear of a reverse teleology—of being turned back into a woman—may have been a common masculine fantasy" (*Desire and Anxiety*, 51). Debora Kuller Shuger has criticized this argument's dependence on Laqueur, since Laqueur in fact makes "exactly the opposite point: on the single-sex model, women could turn into men (the womb could 'get out' and become a penis); the reverse was not considered possible" ("Excerpts from a Panel Discussion," in *Renaissance Discourses of Desire*, ed. Claude Summers and Ted-Larry Pebworth [Columbia: University of Missouri Press, 1993], 269). It is perhaps better to cut the Gordian knot of the whole Galenic inversion question with Lyndal Roper's recognition that "what Laqueur is actually describing is the discourse of medical theory. It is not apparent that it was by means of such theory that early modern people understood their bodies. Rather, their culture rested on a very deep apprehension of sexual difference as an organizing principle of culture—in religion, work, magic and ritual" (*Oedipus and the Devil*, 16). I am thus not suggesting that Renaissance men feared that they would literally turn into women, but that they would fail to fulfill the culturally imposed demands of manliness, and thus be construed, to their shame, as "womanly" (weak, unstable, dependent).

108. See Smith, *Homosexual Desire in Shakespeare's England*, 194–96.

109. John Boswell points out, for example, that even in ancient Rome, whose citizens "were extraordinarily dispassionate about sexuality," a "very strong bias appears to have existed against passive sexual behaviour on the part of an adult male citizen. . . . Apart from general questions of gender expectations and sexual differentiation, the major cause of this prejudice appears to have been a popular association of sexual passivity with political impotence" (*Christianity, Social Tolerance, and Homosexuality* [Chicago: University of Chicago Press, 1980], 62, 74).

110. Like the majority of commentators, I am treating *Dido Queen of Carthage* as wholly by Marlowe, and not as a collaboration by Marlowe and Nashe. Thematically and poetically, it strikes me as thoroughly Marlovian.

111. Leonora Leet Brodwin, "*Edward II*: Marlowe's Culminating Treatment of Love," *ELH* 31 (1964): 139–55.

112. Steane, *Marlowe: A Critical Study*, 337–62.

113. Ibid., 347, quoting Mahood, *Poetry and Humanism* (London: Jonathan Cape, 1950), 54.

114. Steane, *Marlowe: A Critical Study*, 346.

CHAPTER 2. *DIDO QUEEN OF CARTHAGE:* TENUOUS MANHOOD

1. H. J. Oliver, ed., Introduction to *Dido Queen of Carthage and The Massacre at Paris* (Cambridge: Harvard University Press, 1968), xxxiv. All quotations of the play will be from this edition.

2. For example, Clifford Leech, grossly oversimplifying Virgil's masterpiece, remarks with respect to the play, "Vergil, the legendarily orthodox spokesman for imperial Rome, [Marlowe] twisted into ironic comedy," yet he admits that J. B. Steane, a critic he highly admires, sees the play "in terms of high tragedy" (*Christopher Marlowe: Poet for the Stage*, ed. Anne Lancashire [New York: AMS Press, 1986], 37, 41). See also Oliver's introduction to the Revels edition.

3. Kuriyama, *Hammer or Anvil*, 61.

4. Ibid., 53.

5. Heinz Kohut, *The Restoration of the Self* (New York: International Universities Press, 1977), 177.

6. Ibid., 185–86.

7. Ibid., 180.

8. Ibid., 187–88 n. 8.

9. Frosh, *Identity Crisis*, 101.

10. Ibid., 103–4.

11. Kohut, *The Restoration of the Self*, 172.

12. Layton and Schapiro, introduction to *Narcissism and the Text* (New York: New York University Press, 1986), 5.

13. Kohut, *The Restoration of the Self*, 180–81.

14. Kuriyama, *Hammer or Anvil*, 53.

15. See ibid., 54.

16. All quotations of the *Aeneid* are from the translation by Robert Fitzgerald (New York: Vintage Books, 1983).

17. Kuriyama, *Hammer or Anvil*, 55.

18. See, for example, Godshalk, "Marlowe's *Dido, Queen of Carthage*," 5.

19. Bakeless, *The Tragicall History of Christopher Marlowe* 2:62.

20. Mary Elizabeth Smith,"*Love Kindling Fire": A Study of Christopher Marlowe's "The Tragedy of Dido Queen of Carthage"* (Salzburg: Universität Salzburg, 1977), 9.

21. J. R. Mulryne and Stephen Fender, "Marlowe and the 'Comic Distance,'" in *Christopher Marlowe: Mermaid Critical Commentaries*, ed. Brian Morris (London: Ernest Benn, 1968), 52.

22. Virgil's Aeneas as well only observes the Priam-Pyrrhus sequence (from the palace rooftop?), although he is not initially saved from the murderous Pyrrhus by Venus, as Marlowe's Aeneas is.

23. Kohut, *The Restoration of the Self*, 227.

24. Ibid., 246.

25. Kuriyama, *Hammer or Anvil*, 72.

26. Steane, *Marlowe: A Critical Study*, 45.

27. Mulryne and Fender, "Marlowe and the 'Comic Distance,'" 50.

28. See ibid., 51–52.

29. Ibid., 52.

30. M. E. Smith, *"Love Kindling Fire,"* 7.

31. Malcolm Bowie, *Freud, Proust, and Lacan: Theory as Fiction* (Cambridge: Cambridge University Press, 1987), 115.

32. Lacan, *The Seminar of Jacques Lacan: Freud's Papers on Technique, 1953–1954* (New York: Norton, 1988), 16.

33. Garry M. Leonard, *Reading "Dubliners" Again: A Lacanian Perspective* (Syracuse: Syracuse University Press, 1993), 6.

34. Bowie, *Freud, Proust and Lacan*, 116.

35. Jonathan Dollimore, *Sexual Dissidence: Augustine to Wilde, Freud to Foucault* (Oxford: Clarendon Press, 1991), 281.

36. Leonard, *Reading Dubliners Again*, 13-14.

37. Ibid., 14.

38. Layton and Schapiro, introduction to *Narcissism and the Text*, 6.

39. Oliver, ed., *Dido Queen of Carthage and The Massacre at Paris*, 53.

40. *Hero and Leander*, 1.167–68, in *Christopher Marlowe: The Complete Poems and Translations*, ed. Stephen Orgel (Harmondsworth, U.K.: Penguin Books, 1971).

41. Leech, *Christopher Marlowe: Poet for the Stage*, 39.

42. Don Cameron Allen, "Marlowe's *Dido* and the Tradition," in *Essays on Shakespeare and Elizabethan Drama in Honor of Hardin Craig*, ed. Richard Hosley (Columbia: University of Missouri Press, 1962), 68.

43. Godshalk, "Marlowe's *Dido, Queen of Carthage*," 16.

44. Ibid.

45. Ibid., 8.

46. Marjorie Garber, "Closure and Enclosure in Marlowe," in *Two Renaissance Mythmakers: Christopher Marlowe and Ben Jonson*, ed. Alvin Kernan (Baltimore: Johns Hopkins University Press, 1977), 7.

47. Ibid., 8.

48. Oliver, ed., *Dido Queen of Carthage and The Massacre at Paris*, 56.

49. Kuriyama, *Hammer or Anvil*, 60; Kris, *Psychoanalytic Explorations in Art* (New York: International Universities Press, 1952), 182, 185, 214.

50. Kuriyama, *Hammer or Anvil*, 75.

51. Brian Gibbons, "Unstable Proteus: Marlowe's *The Tragedy of Dido Queen of Carthage*," in *Christopher Marlowe: Mermaid Critical Commentaries*, ed. Brian Morris (London: Ernest Benn, 1968), 45–46.

52. Kocher, *A Study of His Thought*, 103.

CHAPTER 3. *TAMBURLAINE THE GREAT:* TENUOUS GODHOOD

1. Kohut, *The Kohut Seminars on Self Psychology and Psychotherapy with Adolescents and Young Adults*, ed. Miriam Elson (New York: Norton, 1987), 82.

2. Kuriyama, *Hammer or Anvil*, 1.

3. I am endorsing Leech's view that "rather than imagining Marlowe as driven to a Second Part after the first performance of Part I, we may think of him as seeing during the composition of Part I the need for a larger compass—just as, it has been suggested, Shakespeare did in writing *Henry IV*" [*Christopher Marlowe: Poet for the Stage*, 67]. The prologue to part 2 does indeed sound like the work of a hack, or, perhaps as Leech suggests, the stationer Richard Jones.

4. Belsey, *The Subject of Tragedy*, 29.

5. Mulryne and Fender, "Marlowe and the 'Comic Distance,'" 54.

6. Ibid., 53–54.

7. Barber, "The Death of Zenocrate: 'Conceiving and Subduing Both,'" *Literature and Psychology* 16 (1966): 16.

8. Kuriyama, *Hammer or Anvil*, 8.

9. Ibid., 19.

10. All quotations of the play are from *Tamburlaine the Great*, ed. J. S. Cunningham (Baltimore: Johns Hopkins University Press, 1981).

11. Robert Kimbrough, "*1 Tamburlaine*: A Speaking Picture in a Tragic Glass," *Renaissance Drama* 7 (1964): 22.

12. Belsey, *The Subject of Tragedy*, 29.

13. Greenblatt, *Renaissance Self-Fashioning*, 194.

14. Clark, *Ralegh and Marlowe*, 229–30.

15. Wraight, *In Search of Christopher Marlowe*, 135.

16. Richard A. Martin, "Marlowe's *Tamburlaine* and the Language of Romance," *PMLA* 93 (1978): 248, 251.

17. Judith Weil, *Christopher Marlowe: Merlin's Prophet* (Cambridge: Cambridge University Press, 1977).

18. Johannes Birringer, *Marlowe's "Dr. Faustus" and "Tamburlaine": Theological and Theatrical Perspectives* (Frankfurt: Verlag Peter Lang, 1984).

19. Cunningham's phrase in his introduction (39) to describe Judith Weil's approach in *Merlin's Prophet*.

20. As has frequently been observed, the sense of comic deflation may have been much stronger in the original form of the play, since the printer Richard Jones admitted: "I have (purposely) omitted and left out some fond and frivolous gestures, digressing (and in my poor opinion) far unmeet for the matter, which I thought might seem more tedious unto the wise than any way else to be regarded, though (haply) they have been of some vain, conceited fondlings greatly gaped at, what times they were showed upon the stage in their graced deformities." Quoted in Leech, *Poet for the Stage*, 61.

21. Birringer, *Marlowe's Dr. Faustus and Tamburlaine*, 87.

22. Kuriyama, *Hammer or Anvil*, 14.

23. Ibid.

24. Dollimore, *Sexual Dissidence*, 56.

25. Levin, *Christopher Marlowe: The Overreacher*, 65.

26. Dollimore, *Radical Tragedy*, 112.

27. Howe, *Marlowe, Tamburlaine, and Magic*, 42.

28. Cunningham, introduction, 11.

29. Bruno, *Five Dialogues on Cause, Principle, and Unity*, trans. Jack Lindsay (New York: International Publishers, 1962), 131; quoted in Howe, *Marlowe, Tamburlaine, and Magic*, 43.

30. Bruno, *Heroic Frenzies*, trans. P. E. Memmo (Chapel Hill: University of North Carolina Press, 1966), 108–9; quoted in Howe, *Marlowe, Tamburlaine, and Magic*, 48.

31. Nicholl, *The Reckoning*, 194.

32. Ibid., 210.

33. Ibid., 196-197.

34. Ibid., 201.

35. Ibid., 215.

36. Barber, *Creating Elizabethan Tragedy*, ed. Richard P. Wheeler (Chicago: University of Chicago Press, 1988), 76.

37. George Geckle, *"Tamburlaine" and "Edward II": Text and Performance* (London: Macmillan, 1988), 59.

38. As Mark Thornton Burnett writes, "according to some psychological theories [citing Armando R. Favazza, *Bodies under Siege: Self-Mutilation in Culture and Psychiatry* (Baltimore and London: Johns Hopkins University Press, 1987), 136], skin-cutting signals the symbolic creation of female genitalia" (*"Tamburlaine* and the Body," *Criticism* 33 [1991]: 44). Thornton argues that "Tamburlaine's condition worsens when he lances his arm."

39. Norman Rabkin, "Marlowe's Mind and the Heart of Darkness," in *"A Poet and a filthy Play-maker": New Essays on Christopher Marlowe*, ed. Kenneth Friedenreich, Roma Gill, and Constance B. Kuriyama (New York: AMS Press, 1988), 14–15.

40. Ibid., 21.

41. Kuriyama, *Hammer or Anvil*, 219.

42. William Urry, *Christopher Marlowe and Canterbury*, ed. Andrew Butcher (London: Faber and Faber, 1988), 41.

43. Kuriyama, *Hammer or Anvil*, 232.

44. Summers, "Sex, Politics, and Self-Realization in *Edward II*," 237.

45. Donaldson, "Conflict and Coherence," 38-39.

46. Ibid., 40.

47. Ibid., 38.

48. Ibid., 39.

49. B. R. Smith, *Homosexual Desire in Shakespeare's England*, 33.

50. Barber, "The Death of Zenocrate: 'Conceiving and Subduing Both,'" 19.

51. B. R. Smith, *Homosexual Desire in Shakespeare's England*, 33.

52. Ibid., 59.

53. Dollimore, *Sexual Dissidence*, 183.

54. Greenblatt, "Marlowe and Renaissance Self-Fashioning," 56.

55. Donaldson, "Conflict and Coherence," 45.

56. Ibid., 46.

57. Kimberley Benston, "Beauty's Just Applause: Dramatic Form and the Tamburlanian Sublime," in *Modern Critical Views: Christopher Marlowe*, ed. Harold Bloom (New York: Chelsea House Publishers, 1986), 221.

58. Mary Beth Rose, *The Expense of Spirit*, 21.

59. Benston, "Beauty's Just Applause," 222.

60. Mary Beth Rose, *The Expense of Spirit*, 21.

61. Ibid., 40.

62. Donaldson, "Conflict and Coherence," 52.

63. Garber, "Closure and Enclosure in Marlowe," 8.

64. Mulryne and Fender, "Marlowe and the 'Comic Distance,'" 54

65. Burnett, *"Tamburlaine* and the Body," 32.

66. Ibid., 34.

67. Ibid., 37.

68. Kohut, *The Restoration of the Self*, 237.

69. Donaldson, "Conflict and Coherence," 46.

70. Ibid., 47.

71. Birringer, Marlowe's "Dr. Faustus" and "Tamburlaine," 147–48.

72. Weil, Merlin's Prophet, 137.

73. Simon Shepherd, Marlowe and the Politics of Elizabethan Theatre (Brighton: Harvester Press, 1986), 150.

74. Ibid., 151-52.

75. Camus, "Hope and the Absurd in the World of Franz Kafka," in Kafka: A Collection of Critical Essays, ed. Ronald Gray (Englewood Cliffs, N.J.: Prentice-Hall, 1962), 148; Mulryne and Fender, "Marlowe and the 'Comic Distance,'" 50.

76. Roy W. Battenhouse, Marlowe's "Tamburlaine": A Study in Renaissance Moral Philosophy (Nashville, Tenn.: Vanderbilt University Press, 1941), 258.

77. Greenblatt, Renaissance Self-Fashioning, 202.

78. Kuriyama, Hammer or Anvil, 9.

79. Steane, Marlowe: A Critical Study, 114–15.

80. Ian Gaskell, "2 Tamburlaine, Marlowe's 'War against the Gods,'" English Studies in Canada 11 (1985): 186.

81. Steane, Marlowe: A Critical Study, 115.

82. Ibid., 114–15.

83. Alternatively, these religious scruples may involve the more traditionally Puritan anxiety arising from the individual's responsibility for establishing and maintaining his own personal relationship with God. An interesting article taking this approach is G. K. Hunter's "The Beginnings of Elizabethan Drama: Revolution and Continuity," Renaissance Drama, n.s., 17 (1986): 29–52. Hunter remarks that the "Reformed individual was . . . continually caught up as a protagonist in the largest and most terrifying drama that can be imagined, required to struggle and ask and decide and achieve, in a Satanic world, and without any external mediation" (37). He sees the "attitude of mind depicted [in Tamburlaine] . . . as an atheistic version of the Lutheran soul in its search for justification through faith—atheistic because in this case the believer has simply excluded God from the equation and concentrated his faith on himself" (39). I have traced Marlowe's religious ideology to other, more heterodox sources because I find even in the orthodoxy of the Reformed churches an emphasis on mediation. Calvin, for example, remarks: "For though, strictly speaking, faith ascends from Christ to the Father, yet he [Christ in John 14:1] suggests that though it were even fixed on God, yet it would gradually decline unless he interposed to preserve its stability. The majesty of God is otherwise far above the reach of mortals, who are like worms crawling upon the earth" (On the Christian Faith, ed. John T. McNeill [Indianapolis: Bobbs-Merrill, 1957], 55).

84. Samuel C. Chew, The Crescent and the Rose: Islam and England during the Renaissance (1937; reprint, New York: Octagon, 1965), 396.

85. Kocher, A Study of His Thought, 88.

86. Chew, The Crescent and the Rose, 405.

87. See ibid., 406–22.

88. Greenblatt, Renaissance Self-Fashioning, 202.

89. Gaskell, "Marlowe's 'War against the Gods,'" 189.

90. Johnstone Parr argued many years ago that Tamburlaine dies from a malignant "distemper" of a febrile nature, "brought on as a result of his fiery temperament" ("Tamburlaine's Malady," PMLA 59 [1944]: 698). However, Parr's reading does not attempt to explain the coincidence of Tamburlaine's challenge and the sudden onset of the distemper.

91. Donaldson, "Conflict and Coherence," 53.

92. Gatti, "Bruno's Heroic Searcher and Marlowe's *Doctor Faustus*," 130.

93. Kohut, *The Kohut Seminars*, 81. According to Kohut, the failure to internalize an external self-object leads to problems with the management of the reality principle, since when an external object is internalized, there eventually occurs a necessary loss involving the "recognition that the ideal is not [completely] ideal."

Chapter 4. *Doctor Faustus:* The Exorcism of God

1. Howe, *Marlowe, Tamburlaine, and Magic*, 145.

2. William Blackburn, "'Heavenly Words': Marlowe's Faustus as a Renaissance Magician," *English Studies in Canada* 4 (1978): 3.

3. Ibid.

4. Ibid., 5.

5. Ibid.

6. Birringer, in *Marlowe's "Dr. Faustus" and "Tamburlaine": Theological and Theatrical Perspectives*, argues that "Faustus' inability to proceed towards repentance, to see God as a God of mercy, clearly indicates the typical blindness and insecurity of a reprobate" (164). Michael Keefer, in his 1604–version edition of the play, cites Dollimore's argument in *Radical Tragedy* that *Faustus* is an exploration of "subversion through transgression" (Dollimore 109), which interrogates the "Calvinistic theological orthodoxy of Elizabethan England" (Keefer xlvii). It is not conclusive, however, that an Elizabethan audience would have assumed Faustus's reprobation, as Keefer implies in his introduction. Calvinism in England was to develop into a more "watered down" version (see Halewood, *The Poetry of Grace*, 56–57); moreover, a good deal of the population of England was still Catholic. Dollimore in fact suggests that the more extreme Calvinist position was under serious scrutiny in Elizabethan England:

> If there is one thing that can be said with certainty about this period it is that God in the form of "mere arbitrary will omnipotent" could not "keep men in awe." We can infer as much from many texts, one of which was Lawne's *Abridgement* of Calvin's *Institutes*, translated in 1587—around the time of the writing of *Dr Faustus*. The book presents and tries to answer [not very successfully, Dollimore goes on to argue] . . . objections to Calvin's theology. (118)

Books such as Lawne's were presumably motivated by a need to refute a general interrogation already at work in Marlowe's society. The view of *Doctor Faustus* as itself simply a critique of the oppressive ideology of predestination I find reductive. For dramaturgical reasons, I have some sympathy with King-Kok Cheung's assertion in "The Dialectic of Despair in *Doctor Faustus*" that Faustus's despair in the play, rather than being incontrovertible evidence of reprobation, "works dialectically to keep alive the possibility of salvation" and "keeps the play alive with suspense and tension" ("A Poet and a filthy Play-maker," 193–94). Nevertheless, my belief that the play is overall a radical interrogation of Christian belief leads me to emphasize, as do those who see it as a direct critique of predestination, those elements that tend to undermine rather than confirm religious faith.

7. The A-text is now certainly back in favor, and Keefer summarizes the case against the proponents of the B-text—in particular, W. W. Greg—who were

often guided by their own "ideological prejudices" in making editorial decisions. Yet Keefer also raises the question of whether "an element of fashion is involved . . . in the current swing among editors of *Doctor Faustus* towards the A version of the play" (xx), and does not, for me, quite dispel the doubts concerning the "ideological prejudices" of more recent editors. I do not intend a lengthy discussion of the textual problem, but will make the following observations. Keefer offers very convincing evidence of "ideologically-motivated revision" in the B-text; yet he also claims that "some at least of [Greg's] repeated claims for the priority of B's readings over A's are justified" (lxvii). In the new Revels edition, the editors David Bevington and Eric Rasmussen reach the following conclusion:

> Because the B-text incorporates a thorough if intermittent reworking of concept and language, it deserves to be treated as a text by itself. All the evidence adduced here, on the other hand, points to the A-text as closer in most ways to the original work of Marlowe and his collaborator (though the B-text remains an important witness in critical editing and offers a few clearly superior readings, along with a host of indifferent variants that may in some cases by authorial) (*Doctor Faustus*, A-and B-texts [Manchester: Manchester University Press, 1993], 77).

Unable to ignore the persuasive and powerful arguments of recent critics and editors, I bow to the current preference for the A-text; however, I am also unable to ignore the intriguing fact that the B-text, as Keefer, Bevington, and Rasmussen admit, occasionally contains superior readings and variants that may be authorial. Thus it is safe to conclude that reader, scholar, and director should be familiar with both A- and B-texts of Marlowe's most famous play. While I agree with those critics who find *Faustus* an interrogative, unorthodox text, I have difficulty with generalizations that dismiss the B-text as less interrogative than the A-text. It may be more heavily censored than A, but the B-text in some points seems quite amenable to fairly radical interpretation. I will therefore quote from the new Revels edition of the play, edited by Bevington and Rasmussen, which contains both A and B; unless otherwise indicated, quotations will be from the A-text, but I will also consider the B-text where it offers evidence relevant to my argument. This approach, I must admit, is not quite what Bevington and Rasmussen have in mind when they assert that both texts "continue to deserve our divided attention" (that is, separate consideration). However, it seems to me inevitable that as long as the content of the original Marlovian text remains in any doubt, critics will continue to speculate and draw concurrently from both A and B in their arguments. I belong to the minority that feels there are elements found only in the B-text that are too good, and that seem too Marlovian, to abandon.

     8. Quoted from W. W. Greg, ed., *Marlowe's "Doctor Faustus": Parallel Texts* (Oxford: Clarendon Press, 1950).

     9. Max Bluestone, *"Libido Speculandi*: Doctrine and Dramaturgy in Contemporary Interpretations of Marlowe's *Doctor Faustus*," in *Reinterpretations of Elizabethan Drama*, ed. Norman Rabkin (New York: Columbia University Press, 1969), 77.

     10. See Gatti, "Bruno's Heroic Searcher and Marlowe's *Doctor Faustus*," 134–35.

     11. This literalization of metaphor, the reification of Faustus's psychological disintegration as physical dismemberment, is so typically Marlovian that I am inclined to accept the penultimate scene in the B-text, where the Scholars discover Faustus's remains, as Marlowe's.

12. Kuriyama, *Hammer or Anvil*, 100.

13. Kohut, *The Restoration of the Self*, 243.

14. Robert S. Wallerstein, "Self Psychology and 'Classical' Psychoanalytic Psychology: The Nature of Their Relationship," in *The Future of Psychoanalysis*, ed. Arnold Goldberg (New York: International Universities Press, 1983), 35, 38.

15. Kohut, *The Kohut Seminars*, 79.

16. Ibid.

17. Donaldson, "Conflict and Coherence," 60.

18. Frosh, *Identity Crisis*, 82–83.

19. Ibid., 85.

20. C. L. Barber, "'The form of Faustus's fortunes good or bad,'" *Tulane Drama Review* 8, no. 4 (1964): 93; Lily B. Campbell, "*Doctor Faustus*: A Case of Conscience," *PMLA* 67, no. 2 (1952): 219–39.

21. Barber, "The form of Faustus's fortunes," 95–96.

22. Halewood, *The Poetry of Grace*, 45.

23. The reading suggested by Bluestone, "*Libido Speculandi*," 35–36.

24. Edward Snow, "*Doctor Faustus* and the Ends of Desire," in *Two Renaissance Mythmakers: Christopher Marlowe and Ben Jonson*, ed. Alvin Kernan (Baltimore: Johns Hopkins University Press, 1977), 105.

25. Ibid., 90.

26. All biblical quotations are from the Geneva Bible, a facsimile of the 1560 edition (Madison: University of Wisconsin Press, 1969).

27. As Bevington and Rasmussen suggest, "try" here can mean "subject to severe test or strain" and note that most editors accept the B1 reading "tire."

28. Shepherd, *Marlowe and the Politics of Elizabethan Theatre*, 96.

29. Greenblatt, *Renaissance Self-Fashioning*, 196.

30. Ibid., 197.

31. See Greg, *Parallel Texts*, 330.

32. According to the *Oxford Dictionary of Quotations*, 2d ed. (London: Oxford University Press, 1953), 10, the origin of this quotation is unknown. It is "*said to have been traced to a lost treatise of Empedocles. Quoted in the Roman de la Rose, and by S. Bonaventura in Itinerarius Mentis in Deum, cap v. ad fin.*"

33. Weil, *Merlin's Prophet*, 62; Birringer, *Marlowe's "Dr. Faustus" and "Tamburlaine,"* 179.

34. Snow, "Marlowe's *Doctor Faustus* and the Ends of Desire," 70.

35. Kuriyama, *Hammer or Anvil*, 120.

36. Kay Stockholder, "'Within the massy entrailes of the earth': Faustus's Relation to Women," in "*A Poet and a filthy Play-maker: New Essays on Christopher Marlowe,*" ed. Kenneth Friedenreich, Roma Gill, and Constance B. Kuriyama (New York: AMS Press, 1988), 218.

37. Kuriyama, *Hammer or Anvil*, 121.

38. Bray, *Homosexuality in Renaissance England*, 19–21.

39. Blackburn, "'Heavenly Words,'" 3–5.

40. Bray, *Homosexuality in Renaissance England*, 24, 25.

41. Levin, *Christopher Marlowe: The Overreacher*, 138.

42. Kuriyama, *Hammer or Anvil*, 121.

43. Ibid., 122.

44. *Doctor Faustus*, ed. John D. Jump (Cambridge: Harvard University Press, 1962), app. 2, 127.

45. Stockholder, "Within the massy entrailes of the earth," 206.

46. Ibid.

47. See Greg, "The Damnation of Faustus," in *Marlowe: A Collection of Critical Essays*, ed. Clifford Leech (Englewood Cliffs, N.J.: Prentice-Hall, 1964), 103–6.

48. The absence of parental, particularly paternal, affection is most clearly hinted at in Marlowe's source: "John Faustus, born in the town of Rhode . . . his father a poor husbandman and not able well to bring him up; but having an uncle at Wittenberg, a rich man and without issue, took this J. Faustus from his father and made him his heir; insomuch that his father was no more troubled with him." (*Damnable Life*, quoted in *Doctor Faustus*, ed. Jump, app. 2, 123).

49. Stockholder, "Within the massy entrailes of the earth," 208.

50. Bevington and Rasmussen argue (1) that the "possibility that Greene may have pioneered in bringing a famous magician on stage seems implausible in view of Greene's other blatant attempts to capitalise on Marlowe's success, as in *Alphonsus, King of Aragon* (1587–8) and its nearly parodic depiction of the overreacher Tamburlaine." Partly because *Friar Bacon* does not seem to me a poor imitation of *Faustus* (it is, in fact, one of the most underrated Renaissance plays), I can entertain the possibility that Greene's magician play pre-dated Marlowe's.

51. Robert Greene, *Friar Bacon and Briar Bungay*, in *Drama of the English Renaissance*, ed. Russell A. Fraser and Norman Rabkin (New York: Macmillan, 1976), 1: 360.

52. Fredson Bowers, as cited by Bevington and Rasmussen, claims that "Arethusa's arms are spoken of . . . as 'azured' by the blue reflection in the water [Arethusa was metamorphosed into a fountain] of the sky" (191). In this case, the image involves a pleasurable mirroring or internalization of the romantic self-object.

53. "The ironic echo of the angelic announcement of Christ's birth, 'I bring you good tidings of great joy' (Luke ii.10)," Bevington and Rasmussen, eds., *Doctor Faustus*, 139.

54. Snow, "*Doctor Faustus* and the Ends of Desire," 72.

55. Wilbur Sanders, *The Dramatist and the Received Idea: Studies in the Plays of Marlowe and Shakespeare* (Cambridge: Cambridge University Press, 1968), 242.

56. Roper, *Oedipus and the Devil*, 44.

57. Joel Altman also argues for a "certain conflation in Marlowe's mind of the arts of poetry and magic—a development not surprising, given his concern with the capacity of the imagination to 'invent' reality." See *The Tudor Play of Mind*, 374 n. 47.

58. Blackburn, "'Heavenly Words,'" 4.

59. Ibid., 6.

60. Ibid.

61. Ibid.

62. This process is most fully explored by G. K. Hunter in "Five-Act Structure in *Doctor Faustus*," *Tulane Drama Review* 8, no. 4 (1964): 77–91.

63. Blackburn, "'Heavenly Words,'" 8.

64. Shepherd, *Marlowe and the Politics of Elizabethan Theatre*, 99.

65. Ibid., 100.

66. Ibid., 102.

67. Ibid.

68. Jump, ed., *Doctor Faustus*, 88.

69. Bluestone, "*Libido Speculandi*," 70.

70. Keefer, ed., *Doctor Faustus*, a 1604-edition, 140.

71. Bevington and Rasmussen, eds., *Doctor Faustus*, A- and B-texts, 188.

72. Edward Snow's term in "Ends of Desire." See also Barber's discussion in "The form of Faustus's fortunes," 106–13, where the play's oral imagery is explored.

73. Barber, "The form of Faustus's fortunes," 93.

74. Snow, "*Doctor Faustus* and the Ends of Desire," 93.

75. Since these characters are, as quoted above from Snow, "imperturbably suspended" in the "ontological void" that tortures Faustus. While it might be objected that my phrase "natural grace" is a historically inaccurate conception, or at least ahistorically applied, A. S. P. Woodhouse in fact finds in Spenser's use of the term "grace" various levels of meaning in addition to the strictly theological one of "God working inwardly upon the will and infusing power." Grace may also manifest as "God's overflowing bounty in bestowing outward benefits or in intervening as providential care in the natural order" and as "native endowment or . . . natural excellence" ("Nature and Grace in *The Faerie Queene*," in *Elizabethan Poetry: Modern Essays in Criticism*, ed. Paul J. Alpers [New York: Oxford University Press, 1967], 355). It was certainly possible for some Elizabethans, in spite of the Calvinist influence in their religious thought, to conceive of more benign, and more calmly continuous, relationships between spiritual and physical existence.

76. Snow, "*Doctor Faustus* and the Ends of Desire," 102.

77. Margaret O'Brien, "Christian Belief in *Doctor Faustus*," ELH 37 (1970): 10–11.

78. Joseph Summers, *George Herbert: His Religion and Art* (Cambridge: Harvard University Press, 1968), 127.

79. Ibid., 128.

80. It is interesting to note that the lowest panel of the East Window of Corona in Canterbury Cathedral, a window "occupying a position only second in dignity and importance [in the cathedral]" (Bernard Rackham, *The Ancient Glass of Canterbury* [London: Lund Humphries and Co., 1949], 73) is a representation of the Grapes of Eshcol: "Two of the returning [Israelite] spies carry on a staff between them 'a branch with one cluster of grapes.' Inscribed: . . . [in Latin] ('This one refuses to look back at the cluster, the other thirsts to see it; Israel knows not Christ, the Gentile adores him')" (75). Marlowe undoubtedly was familiar with this window as a child. In what may very well have been his next play after *Faustus*, he identifies closely with the "Israelite" Barabas over the Gentiles who oppose him.

CHAPTER 5. *THE JEW OF MALTA:* THE FAILURE OF CARNAL IDENTITY

1. M. M. Mahood, *Poetry and Humanism* (London: Jonathan Cape, 1950), 74.

2. G. K. Hunter, "The Theology of Marlowe's *The Jew of Malta*," *Journal of the Warburg and Courtauld Institutes* 27 (1964): 213.

3. Sara Munson Deats, "Biblical Parody in Marlowe's *The Jew of Malta*: A Re-Examination," *Christianity and Literature* 37 (1988): 27, 39.

4. All quotations of *The Jew of Malta* are from the Revels edition, ed. N. W. Bawcutt (Manchester: Manchester University Press, 1978).

5. See ibid., 82–83, n. 99–100.

6. All biblical quotations are from the Geneva Bible.

7. Deats, "Biblical Parody in Marlowe's *The Jew of Malta*," 33, 34.

8. Ibid., 42.

9. Ibid., 32.

10. Hunter, "The Theology of Marlowe's *The Jew of Malta*," 214.

11. Ibid., 219.

12. Kuriyama, *Hammer or Anvil*, 160.

13. A. J. A. Waldock, *"Paradise Lost" and Its Critics* (Cambridge: Cambridge University Press, 1962), 54.

14. Deats, "Biblical Parody in Marlowe's *The Jew of Malta*," 42.

15. Hunter, "The Theology of Marlowe's *The Jew of Malta*," 213–14.

16. *The English Poems of George Herbert*, ed. C. A. Patrides (London: J. M. Dent and Sons, 1974), 176.

17. Deats, "Biblical Parody in Marlowe's *The Jew of Malta*," 37–38.

18. Ibid., 38.

19. Ibid., 39.

20. Bawcutt, ed., *The Jew of Malta*, 137.

21. Deats, "Biblical Parody in Marlowe's *The Jew of Malta*," 39.

22. Kuriyama, *Hammer or Anvil*, 140.

23. Ibid., 149.

24. Ibid., 141.

25. Ibid., 154.

26. Hunter, "The Theology of Marlowe's *The Jew of Malta*," 221–25.

27. *Tamburlaine*, part 1, 5.1.177.

28. Sanders, *The Dramatist and the Received Idea*, 42.

29. Freud, "Little Hans," *Penguin Freud Library* (Harmondsworth, 1977) 8:336n. Quoted in Jeremy Tambling, "Abigail's Party: 'The Difference of Things' in *The Jew of Malta*," in *In Another Country: Feminist Perspectives in Renaissance Drama*, ed. Dorothea Kehler and Susan Baker (Metuchen, N.J.: Scarecrow Press, 1991), 102.

30. John Boswell, *Christianity, Social Tolerance, and Homosexuality*, commentary to fig. 9; see also pp. 15–16.

31. *The Jew of Malta* is not the only time in literature that Jewishness has been used as a cover for a homosexual figure. Garry Wills in his article "*Oliver Twist*: Love in the Lower Depths," *New York Review of Books* 36, no. 16 (26 October 1989): 60–67, discusses how Dickens used Fagin's Jewishness (taking advantage, like Marlowe, of popular prejudice) as a mask for his character's pederasty.

32. Kuriyama, *Hammer or Anvil*, 150.

33. Heinz Kohut, "Introspection, Empathy and the Semicircle of Mental Health," *International Journal of Psychoanalysis* 63 (1982): 404.

34. Levin, *Christopher Marlowe: The Overreacher*, 92.

35. Bawcutt, ed., *The Jew of Malta*, 100.

36. Coburn Freer, "Lies and Lying in *The Jew of Malta*," in *"A Poet and a filthy Play-maker": New Essays on Christopher Marlowe*, ed. Kenneth Friedenreich, Roma Gill, and Constance B. Kuriyama (New York: AMS Press, 1988), 156.

37. *The Famous Tragedy of the Rich Jew of Malta*, 1633, reproduced by Scolar Press, 1970.

38. The cauldron is, as Hunter demonstrates, "a traditional image of hell" ("The Theology of Marlowe's *The Jew of Malta*," 234).

39. Steane, *Marlowe: A Critical Study*, 174.

40. Catherine Minshull, "Marlowe's 'Sound Machevill,'" *Renaissance Drama*, n.s., 13 (1982): 52.

41. In "*The Jew of Malta* and the Critics: A Paradigm for Marlowe Studies," *Papers on Language and Literature* 13 (1977): 321–24, Kenneth Friedenreich surveys critics who have adopted this approach.

42. D. J. Palmer, "Marlowe's Naturalism," in *Christopher Marlowe: Mermaid Critical Commentaries*, ed. Brian Morris (London: Ernest Benn, 1968), 174.

43. Minshull, "Marlowe's '*Sound Machevill*,'" 40, 41.

44. Ibid., 53.

45. Ibid., 51.

46. Ibid., 53. Minshull's most interesting historical point is that the Elizabethan ruling class, more enlightened than the average theatergoer, would probably have approved of Marlowe's play, since "it was to the authorities' advantage that a popular misconception of Machiavelli should flourish to obscure the import of Machiavelli's works as an analysis of [actual] statecraft" (52).

47. As it did in a Royal Shakespeare Company revival discussed by James L. Smith in "*The Jew of Malta* in the Theatre," in *Christopher Marlowe: Mermaid Critical Commentaries*, ed. Brian Morris (London: Ernest Benn, 1968), 19.

48. Both chap. 3 and app. A in Sanders, *The Dramatist and the Received Idea*.

49. Freer, "Lies and Lying in *The Jew of Malta*," 143, 144.

50. Ibid., 160.

51. Emily Bartels, "Malta, the Jew, and Fictions of Difference: Colonial Discourse in Marlowe's *The Jew of Malta*," *English Literary Renaissance* 20 (1990): 8.

52. Ibid.

53. Freer, "Lies and Lying in *The Jew of Malta*," 160.

54. Kuriyama, *Hammer or Anvil*, 150.

55. Deats, "Biblical Parody in Marlowe's *The Jew of Malta*," 43.

56. Kohut, "Thoughts on Narcissism and Narcissistic Rage," in *The Psychoanalytic Study of the Child*, vol. 27 (1972), ed. Ruth S. Eissler, Anna Freud, et al. (New York: International University Press, 1973), 385–86. Quoted in Donaldson, "Conflict and Coherence," 51.

57. Bawcutt, ed., *The Jew of Malta*, 89.

58. Kohut, *The Kohut Seminars*, 10.

59. Kuriyama, *Hammer or Anvil*, 220.

60. Levin, *Christopher Marlowe: The Overreacher*, 99.

61. Bartels, "Colonial Discourse in Marlowe's *The Jew of Malta*," 16.

62. Hunter, "The Theology of Marlowe's *The Jew of Malta*," 240.

63. I would disagree, however, with Hunter's statement that Marlowe was "simultaneously fascinated and horrified by the apparent self-sufficiency of the fallen world" ("The Theology of Marlowe's *The Jew of Malta*," 240). This assumes a kind of orthodoxy that I do not believe Marlowe possessed. He was certainly fascinated by the world's "self-sufficiency," but not at all horrified by it. The tension in his work arises from personal doubts and fears concerning his own ability to become self-sufficient.

64. Bawcutt, ed., *The Jew of Malta*, 107.

CHAPTER 6. *THE MASSACRE AT PARIS:* THE EXORCISM OF MACHEVIL

1. Kuriyama, *Hammer or Anvil*, 94.

2. Oliver, ed., *Dido Queen of Carthage and The Massacre at Paris* lix. All references to the play will be from this edition.

3. Levin, *Christopher Marlowe: The Overreacher*, 106.

4. Oliver, ed., *Dido Queen of Carthage and The Massacre at Paris*, lv.

5. Paul Kocher, "François Hotman and 'The Massacre at Paris,'" *PMLA* 56 (1941): 368.

6. Levin, *Christopher Marlowe: The Overreacher*, 103–4.

7. Kocher, "François Hotman and 'The Massacre at Paris,'" 368.

8. Sanders, *The Dramatist and the Received Idea*, 36.

9. Douglas Cole, *Suffering and Evil in the Plays of Christopher Marlowe* (Princeton: Princeton University Press, 1962), 155.

10. Julia Briggs, "Marlowe's *Massacre at Paris:* A Reconsideration," *Review of English Studies* 34 (1983): 258–59.

11. Ibid., 260.

12. Weil, *Christopher Marlowe: Merlin's Prophet*, 82.

13. Ibid., 102.

14. Ibid., 85.

15. Briggs, "Marlowe's *Massacre at Paris:* A Reconsideration," 273.

16. Cole, *Suffering and Evil*, 144.

17. In a recent reading of the play as "history," Andrew M. Kirk calls attention to the importance of the "otherness" of France in English historical accounts. French history acts as a "mirror" of mutability for the English historiographers, but the mutability is "demystified, thereby resisting the tendency of other descriptions, such as in the *Mirror for Magistrates*, to depict earthly instability and change as caused by inexorable and inexplicable fortune. Instead, historical mutability and disorder result from the historical actors, who function as agents that engender the chaos around them. [*The Massacre at Paris*], which depicts the reigns of two kings and the beginning of a third, offers French kings as sources of disorders" ("Marlowe and the Disordered Face of French History," *Studies in English Literature* 35, no. 2 [1995]: 197). While Kirk's readings of the play's characters, especially the Guise, are questionable, since he elides some of the more disturbing elements of the play to give an "objective" account of Marlowe's construction of French history, his reading is important in its recognition of the emphasis on kingly responsibility and the dangers of human inconstancy and vacillation, as depicted in Renaissance plays that treat French history.

18. Kuriyama, *Hammer or Anvil*, 91.

19. Steane, *Marlowe: A Critical Study*, 239.

20. Weil, *Merlin's Prophet*, 84.

21. Oliver, ed., *Dido Queen of Carthage and The Massacre at Paris*, 99.

22. Kuriyama, *Hammer or Anvil*, 82-83.

23. Weil, *Merlin's Prophet*, 86.

24. Oliver, ed., *Dido Queen of Carthage and The Massacre at Paris*, lxxiii.

25. Ibid., 100.

26. Levin, *Christopher Marlowe: The Overreacher*, 106.

27. Though one wonders if Oxberry's emendation, cited by Oliver (104), does not likely reflect what Marlowe originally wrote: "That those which do behold them may become."

28. Kuriyama, *Hammer or Anvil*, 83; Sanders, *The Dramatist and the Received Idea*, 32.

29. Weil, *Merlin's Prophet*, 87.

30. All biblical quotations are from the Geneva Bible.

31. Weil, *Merlin's Prophet*, 87.

32. See Frederick S. Boas, *Christopher Marlowe: A Biographical and Critical Study* (Oxford: Clarendon, 1940), app. to chap. 10, 168–71, for a discussion of this manuscript fragment.

33. Quoted in Boas, *Christopher Marlowe*, 170.

34. Steane, *Marlowe: A Critical Study*, 238.

35. Cole, *Suffering and Evil*, 148.

36. Kuriyama, *Hammer or Anvil*, 87.

37. See Kocher, "Contemporary Pamphlet Backgrounds for Marlowe's *The Massacre at Paris*," *Modern Language Quarterly* 8 (1947): 155.

38. Weil, *Merlin's Prophet*, 98.

39. Briggs, "Marlowe's *Massacre at Paris*: A Reconsideration," 266.

40. Kuriyama, *Hammer or Anvil*, 88.

41. Oliver, ed., *Dido Queen of Carthage and The Massacre at Paris*, lxv.

42. Ibid., lxvi.

43. Kocher, "Contemporary Pamphlet Backgrounds," 316.

44. Cole, *Suffering and Evil*, 156.

45. Ibid., 150.

46. Ibid., 151.

47. Steane, *Marlowe: A Critical Study*, 245.

48. Ibid., 244.

49. Kocher, "François Hotman," 367–68.

50. Kuriyama, *Hammer or Anvil*, 78. Kuriyama presumably finds such an argument politic since "survival depends on striking first and hardest" (77), yet the Protestants have assembled in Paris to celebrate a wedding, not to attack the Catholics!

51. Kuriyama, *Hammer or Anvil*, 78.

52. Briggs, "Marlowe's *Massacre at Paris*: A Reconsideration," 263.

53. Kocher, "Contemporary Pamphlet Backgrounds," 169.

54. Weil, *Merlin's Prophet*, 97.

55. Briggs, "Marlowe's *Massacre at Paris*: A Reconsideration," 264.

56. Kuriyama, *Hammer or Anvil*, 93.

57. Ibid.

58. John Ronald Glenn, "The Martyrdom of Ramus in Marlowe's *The Massacre at Paris*," *Papers on Language and Literature* 9 (1973): 375.

59. Ibid., 376.

60. Taleus is referred to as "Ramus' bedfellow" in the play (9.12). Alan Bray in "Homosexuality and the Signs of Male Friendship in Elizabethan England," *History Workshop Journal* 29 (1990), warns us not to jump to any conclusions: "This was a society where most people slept with someone else and where the rooms of a house led casually one into the other and servants mingled with their masters. Such a lack of privacy usually made who shared a bed with whom into a public fact" (4). Marlowe, however, seems eager to include a reference to their intimate relationship. As John Ronald Glenn points out, "At the time of Ramus's murder, Audomorus Talaeus (Omer Talon, 1510–1562) had been dead ten years, as Marlowe surely knew. . . . Talaeus was well known as Ramus's lifelong friend and collaborator. . . . Talaeus had spent much of his life as Ramus's disciple, publishing Ramus's ideas and defending him against critics" ("The Martyrdom of Ramus," 371). If we are willing to credit a homoerotic potential in their relationship, then Ramus, like Henry, becomes an instance of Marlowe seeking sympathy for a figure with propensities like his own. As Glenn

points out, Ramus emerges as the central Protestant victim during the massacre because his is the only scene that Marlowe chooses to expand.

61. F. P. Wilson, *"The Massacre at Paris* and *Edward II,"* in *Marlowe: A Collection of Critical Essays,* ed. Clifford Leech (Englewood Cliffs, N.J.: Prentice-Hall, 1964), 128.

CHAPTER 7. *EDWARD II:* THE ILLUSION OF INTEGRITY

1. As I remarked in the introduction, I have followed Ellis-Fermor's chronology of Marlowe's plays, agreeing in general with the reasons elaborated by Leonora Leet Brodwin in her essay *"Edward II:* Marlowe's Culminating Treatment of Love."* It is worth mentioning here one point raised by Julia Briggs that, in addition to my remarks in the previous chapter, strongly suggests that *Edward II* followed *The Massacre at Paris.* Briggs comments on the "striking parallels" developed in a "notorious" Catholic League pamphlet by Jean Boucher entitled *Histoire tragique et mémorable de Pierre de Gaveston,* published in July 1588. Boucher in his preface "makes explicit" the analogy between Gaveston and Epernoun, both corrupters of kings, and warns Henry III of Edward's fate, who died impaled upon "une broche rouge de feu" (Briggs, "Marlowe's *Massacre at Paris:* A Reconsideration," 264). It seems likely that the parallel drawn by Boucher prompted Marlowe, for his subsequent dramatic endeavor, to turn to Holinshed in order to investigate the details of Edward's reign.

2. Kuriyama, *Hammer or Anvil,* 175.

3. Levin, *Christopher Marlowe: The Overreacher,* 110.

4. Summers, "Sex, Politics, and Self-Realization in *Edward II,"* 222.

5. Ibid.

6. Kuriyama, *Hammer or Anvil,* 195.

7. Summers, "Sex, Politics, and Self-Realization in *Edward II,"* 238.

8. Ibid., 222.

9. Purvis Boyette, "Wanton Humour and Wanton Poets: Homosexuality in Marlowe's *Edward II," Tulane Studies in English* 22 (1977): 43.

10. David Thurn, "Sovereignty, Disorder, and Fetishism in Marlowe's *Edward II," Renaissance Drama,* n.s., 21 (1990): 116.

11. Jennifer Brady, "Fear and Loathing in Marlowe's *Edward II,"* in *Sexuality and Politics in Renaissance Drama,* ed. Carole Levin and Karen Robertson (Lewiston, N.Y.: Edwin Mellen Press, 1991), 177.

12. All quotations of the play are from the Revels edition, ed. Charles R. Forker (Manchester: Manchester University Press, 1994).

13. Viviana Comensoli, "Homophobia and the Regulation of Desire: A Psychoanalytic Reading of Marlowe's *Edward II," Journal of the History of Sexuality* 4 (1993): 193; Dollimore, *Sexual Dissidence,* 237.

14. Comensoli, "Homophobia and the Regulation of Desire," 193.

15. Shepherd, *Marlowe and the Politics of Elizabethan Theatre,* 204.

16. B. R. Smith, *Homosexual Desire in Shakespeare's England,* 211, 213.

17. Shepherd, *Marlowe and the Politics of Elizabethan Theatre,* 204.

18. Jonathan Goldberg, *Sodometries: Renaissance Texts, Modern Sexualities* (Stanford, Calif.: Stanford University Press, 1992), 128–29.

19. Kuriyama, *Hammer or Anvil,* 178.

20. Stephen Guy-Bray, "Homophobia and the Depoliticizing of *Edward II," English Studies in Canada* 17 (1991): 126, 131.

21. Ibid., 130.

22. Lawrence Danson, "Continuity and Character in Shakespeare and Marlowe,"*Studies in English Literature* 26 (1986): 223.

23. Guy-Bray, "Homophobia and the Depoliticizing of *Edward II*," 131.

24. Smith, *Homosexual Desire in Shakespeare's England*, 220–21.

25. Boyette, "Wanton Humour and Wanton Poets," 40.

26. Ibid., 40, 41.

27. Summers, "Sex, Politics, and Self-Realization," 233.

28. Brodwin, "*Edward II*: Marlowe's Culminating Treatment of Love," 155.

29. Leech, *Christopher Marlowe: Poet for the Stage*, 134.

30. Kuriyama, *Hammer or Anvil*, 181.

31. See Sara Munson Deats's article, "Marlowe's Fearful Symmetry in *Edward II*," in "*A Poet and a filthy Play-maker: New Essays on Christopher Marlowe*, ed. Kenneth Friedenreich, Roma Gill, and Constance B. Kuriyama, 241–62, for a discussion of the structure of the play as two symmetrical halves containing significant parallels and contrasts.

32. Donaldson, "Conflict and Coherence," 54.

33. Sanders, *The Dramatist and the Received Idea*, 126.

34. Sara Munson Deats and Lisa S. Starks, "'So neatly plotted, and so well perform'd': Villain as Playwright in Marlowe's *The Jew of Malta*," *Theatre Journal* 44 (1992): 388.

35. Levin, *Christopher Marlowe: The Overreacher*, 114.

36. Thurn, "Sovereignty, Disorder, and Fetishism," 117.

37. Ibid., 129–30.

38. James Voss, in "*Edward II*: Marlowe's Historical Tragedy," *English Studies* 63 (1982): 517–30, argues that the danger posed by Gaveston "is neither merely legal nor symbolic, for the wealth he has acquired represents a potential threat to the barons' military hegemony." Gaveston's influence promises to radically alter the kingdom's power structure: "Whereas traditionally power was more or less equally balanced between central and regional forces, between the king and peers, Edward's elevation of Gaveston signifies a decisive increase of the king's power and authority at the expense of the nobility and at odds with accepted practice" (521).

While the historical implications are interesting, Voss's reading as a whole implies a validity to Edward's political struggle that the play itself does not support; in Marlowe the "increase in the king's power and authority at the expense of the nobility" is sought only to facilitate Edward's self-indulgence (Voss terms it, again it seems to me euphemistically, a "nontraditional lifestyle consciousness" [523]). Edward has no plans to use the increased power creatively or responsibly, for the good of his kingdom.

39. Thurn, "Sovereignty, Disorder, and Fetishism," 130.

40. Ibid., 131.

41. In fact, Holinshed describes Warwick "reverentially as 'a man of great counsell and skilfull prouidence,'" as Forker observes in his introduction (52).

42. David Scott Kastan, "The King Hath Many Marching in His Coats,' or, What Did You Do in the War, Daddy?," in *Shakespeare Left and Right*, ed. Ivo Kamps (New York: Routledge, 1991), 252–53.

43. Although this summary will necessarily constitute a gross simplification of one of his most fascinating achievements, in the second tetralogy Shakespeare (inspired initially by *Edward II*) has taken the king as archetype of the self and explored the development from narcissism (Richard II) to crudely effective but

superficial self-fashioning (Henry IV) to a more mature, if still deeply disturbing and problematic, attainment of a highly integrated self (Henry V).

44. See Sanders, *The Dramatist and the Received Idea*, 133 and n. 17.

45. Ibid., 133.

46. Leech, *Christopher Marlowe: Poet for the Stage*, 142.

47. Nicholl, *The Reckoning*, 113.

48. Claude J. Summers, "Isabella's Plea for Gaveston in Marlowe's *Edward II*," *Philological Quarterly* 52 (1973): 308–10; Sarah Munson Deats, "*Edward II*: A Study in Androgyny," *Ball State University Forum* 22 (1981): 30–41.

49. Deats, "A Study in Androgyny," 32.

50. Ibid., 34.

51. Ibid.

52. With the possible exception (depending on the director's decision) of 2.4.15, which is apparently uttered to Edward as he breaks away from her and leaves the stage.

53. Deats, "A Study in Androgyny," 35.

54. Kuriyama, *Hammer or Anvil*, 180.

55. Deats, "A Study in Androgyny," 40.

56. Kuriyama, *Hammer or Anvil*, 184.

57. Steane, *Marlowe: A Critical Study*, 217.

58. Leech, *Christopher Marlowe: Poet for the Stage*, 142.

59. Mulryne and Fender, "Marlowe and the 'Comic Distance,'" 60–61.

60. Bent Sunesen, "Marlowe and the Dumb Show," *English Studies* 35 (1954): 248.

61. Ibid., 246.

62. Sara Munson Deats, "Myth and Metamorphosis in Marlowe's *Edward II*," *Texas Studies in Literature and Language* 22 (1980): 311.

63. Sunesen, "Marlowe and the Dumb Show," 248.

64. Deats, "Myth and Metamorphosis," 311.

65. As noted in chap. 4, the horror of literalized metaphor is also present in the B-text of *Faustus*, when the Second Scholar cries, "here are Faustus's limbs, / All torn asunder by the hand of death." To recognize that Faustus's identity or self-image is disintegrating psychologically is disturbing, but to find out he has actually been torn to pieces physically is horrifying. However, this mutilation happens in the hiatus between two scenes, whereas in *Edward II* we are forced to sit through the king's agonizing death.

66. Boyette, "Wanton Humour and Wanton Poets," 48.

67. Sunesen, "Marlowe and the Dumb Show," 244–45.

68. Donaldson, "Conflict and Coherence," 46.

69. Toby Robertson, interview, "Directing *Edward II*," *Tulane Drama Review* 8, no. 4 (1964): 178–79.

70. Summers, "Sex, Politics, and Self-Realization," 233.

71. Sanders, *The Dramatist and the Received Idea*, 134.

72. Boyette, "Wanton Humour and Wanton Poets," 43.

73. Deats, "Marlowe's Fearful Symmetry," 248.

74. Deats, "Myth and Metamorphosis," 316.

75. Ibid.

76. Steane, *Marlowe: A Critical Study*, 213.

77. Kuriyama, *Hammer or Anvil*, 207.

78. Deats, "A Study in Androgyny," 41.

79. Summers, "Sex, Politics, and Self-Realization," 236.

80. Kuriyama, *Hammer or Anvil*, 208-9.

81. Donaldson, "Conflict and Coherence," 58.

82. Mulryne and Fender, "Marlowe and the 'Comic Distance,'" 62.

83. See Deats, "Marlowe's Fearful Symmetry," 248.

84. Summers, *Christopher Marlowe and the Politics of Power* (Salzburg: Universität Salzburg, 1974), 167–68.

85. It is worth noting here that Kuriyama finds Mortimer's final speech not flat or formulaic but impressive, because he courageously faces those unknown countries *alone*: "Mortimer, like Edward, is most attractive when he bows to forces he cannot control, although Mortimer, whose personality was stronger to begin with, bows with more manly grace, declining to submit himself, like the weaker, 'feminine' characters, to God" (*Hammer or Anvil*, 200).

86. Donaldson, "Conflict and Coherence," 58.

87. Robertson, "Directing *Edward II*," 179.

88. The name Lightborn "is neither more nor less than an Anglicization of 'Lucifer'" (Levin, *Christopher Marlowe: The Overreacher*, 124).

89. The Latin motto on the Corpus Christi portrait of Marlowe. A. D. Wraight observes that the sentiment is echoed in Shakespeare's Sonnet 73: "Consum'd with that which it was nourish'd by" (*In Search of Christopher Marlowe*, 68). In Marlowe's play it is significant that Lightborn, symbolic of the perversion of the human creative capacity, is himself killed immediately after performing the "climactic" murder of his career.

CHAPTER 8. CONCLUSION

1. It would be naive, however, to suggest this vision is peculiar to Marlowe. See Camille Paglia's *Sexual Personae: Art and Decadence from Nefertiti to Emily Dickinson* (New Haven: Yale University Press, 1990) for a disturbing and controversial, but challenging and fascinating, treatment of sado-masochism in Western art and literature.

2. Eugene Vance, *Mervelous Signals: Poetics and Sign Theory in the Middle Ages* (Lincoln: University of Nebraska Press, 1986), 9–10.

3. Patrick Grant, *Literature and Personal Values* (New York: St. Martin's Press, 1992), 37.

4. Halewood, *Poetry of Grace*, 41.

5. Vance, *Mervelous Signals*, 7.

6. Ibid., 9.

7. Augustine, *Confessions*, trans. R. S. Pine-Coffin (Harmondsworth, U.K.: Penguin Books, 1961), 34.

8. Ibid., 86–87.

9. Ibid., 133.

10. Elaine Pagels, *Adam, Eve, and the Serpent* (New York: Vintage Books, 1988).

11. Grant, *Literature and Personal Values*, 100–101.

12. Jacqueline Rose, *Sexuality in the Field of Vision* (London: Verso, 1986), 90–91; Dollimore, *Sexual Dissidence*, 257.

13. Dollimore, *Sexual Dissidence*, 282.

14. Ibid., 103.

15. Ibid., 188-89.

16. Dollimore, *Radical Tragedy*, 157.

17. Dollimore, *Sexual Dissidence*, 311.

18. Ibid., 325.

19. Kohut, *The Restoration of the Self*, 244–45.

20. Terry Eagleton, "Discourse and Discos: Theory in the Space Between Culture and Capitalism," *Times Literary Supplement*, no. 4763, (15 July 1994).

21. Linda Hutcheon, afterword to *Remembering Postmodernism: Trends in Recent Canadian Art*, by Mark A. Cheetham (Toronto: Oxford University Press, 1991), 119, quoting Nancy K. Miller, "Changing the Subject: Authorship, Writing, and the Reader," *Feminist Studies/Critical Studies*, ed. Teresa de Lauretis (Bloomington: Indiana University Press, 1986), 106.

22. Dollimore, *Sexual Dissidence*, 78.

23. Greenblatt, "Marlowe and Renaissance Self-Fashioning," 56.

24. M. B. Rose, *The Expense of Spirit*, 11.

25. Arthur Lindley, "The Unbeing of the Overreacher: Proteanism and the Marlovian Hero," *Modern Language Review* 84 (1989): 16.

26. Quoted in Boas, *Christopher Marlowe*, 243.

Bibliography

Allen, Don Cameron. "Marlowe's *Dido* and the Tradition." In *Essays on Shakespeare and Elizabethan Drama in Honor of Hardin Craig*, edited by Richard Hosley. Columbia: University of Missouri Press, 1962.

Altman, Joel B. *The Tudor Play of Mind: Rhetorical Inquiry and the Development of Elizabethan Drama*. Berkeley: University of California Press, 1978.

Augustine. *Confessions*. Translated by R. S. Pine-Coffin. Harmondsworth, U.K.: Penguin Books, 1961.

Bakeless, John. *The Tragicall History of Christopher Marlowe*. 2 vols. Cambridge: Harvard University Press, 1942.

Barber, C. L. *Creating Elizabethan Tragedy: The Theater of Marlowe and Kyd*. Edited by Richard P. Wheeler. Chicago: University of Chicago Press, 1988.

———. "The Death of Zenocrate: 'Conceiving and Subduing Both.'" *Literature and Psychology* 16 (1966): 15–24.

———. "The Form of Faustus' Fortunes Good or Bad." *Tulane Drama Review* 8, no. 4 (1964): 92–119.

Bartels, Emily C. "Malta, the Jew, and Fictions of Difference: Colonial Discourse in Marlowe's *The Jew of Malta*." *English Literary Renaissance* 20 (1990): 1–16.

———. *Spectacles of Strangeness: Imperialism, Alienation, and Marlowe*. Philadelphia: University of Pennsylvania Press, 1993.

Battenhouse, Roy W. *Marlowe's "Tamburlaine": A Study of Renaissance Moral Philosophy*. Nashville, Tenn.: Vanderbilt University Press, 1941.

Belsey, Catherine. *John Milton: Language, Gender, Power*. Oxford: Basil Blackwell, 1988.

———. *The Subject of Tragedy: Identity and Difference in Renaissance Drama*. London: Methuen, 1985.

Benston, Kimberley. "Beauty's Just Applause: Dramatic Form and the Tamburlanian Sublime." In *Modern Critical Views: Christopher Marlowe*, edited by Harold Bloom. New York: Chelsea House Publishers, 1986.

Birringer, Johannes. *Marlowe's "Dr. Faustus" and "Tamburlaine": Theological and Theatrical Perspectives*. Frankfurt: Verlag Peter Lang, 1984.

Blackburn, William. "'Heavenly Words': Marlowe's Faustus as a Renaissance Magician." *English Studies in Canada* 4 (1978): 1–14.

Bluestone, Max. "*Libido Speculandi* : Doctrine and Dramaturgy in Contemporary Interpretations of Marlowe's *Doctor Faustus*." In *Reinterpretations of Elizabethan Drama*, edited by Norman Rabkin. New York: Columbia University Press, 1969.

Boas, Frederick S. *Christopher Marlowe: A Biographical and Critical Study*. Oxford: Clarendon Press, 1940.

Boswell, John. *Christianity, Social Tolerance, and Homosexuality.* Chicago: University of Chicago Press, 1980.

Bowie, Malcolm. *Freud, Proust, and Lacan: Theory as Fiction.* Cambridge: Cambridge University Press, 1987.

Boyette, Purvis. "Wanton Humour and Wanton Poets: Homosexuality in Marlowe's *Edward II.*" *Tulane Studies in English* 22 (1977): 33–50.

Bradbrook, M. C. *The School of Night: A Study in the Literary Relationships of Sir Walter Raleigh.* 1936. Reprint, New York: Russell and Russell, 1965.

Brady, Jennifer. "Fear and Loathing in Marlowe's *Edward II.*" In *Sexuality and Politics in Renaissance Drama,* edited by Carole Levin and Karen Robertson. Lewiston, N.Y.: Edwin Mellen Press, 1991.

Bray, Alan. "Homosexuality and the Signs of Male Friendship in Elizabethan England." *History Workshop Journal* 29 (1990): 1–19.

———. *Homosexuality in Renaissance England.* London: Gay Men's Press, 1982.

Bredbeck, Gregory W. *Sodomy and Interpretation: Marlowe to Milton.* Ithaca: Cornell University Press, 1991.

Briggs, Julia. "Marlowe's *Massacre at Paris* : A Reconsideration." *Review of English Studies* 34 (1983): 257–78.

Briggs, William D. "On a Document Concerning Christopher Marlowe." *Studies in Philology* 20 (1923): 153–59.

Brodwin, Leonora Leet. "*Edward II*: Marlowe's Culminating Treatment of Love." *ELH* 31 (1964): 139–55.

Brown, Peter. *Religion and Society in the Age of Saint Augustine.* London: Faber and Faber, 1972.

Burnett, Mark Thornton. "*Tamburlaine* and the Body." *Criticism* 33 (1991): 31–47.

Calvin, John. *On the Christian Faith.* Edited by John T. McNeill. Indianapolis: Bobbs-Merrill, 1957.

Cheung, King-Kok. "The Dialectic of Despair in *Doctor Faustus.*" In *"A Poet and a filthy Play-maker": New Essays on Christopher Marlowe,* edited by Kenneth Friedenreich, Roma Gill, and Constance B. Kuriyama. New York: AMS Press, 1988.

Chew, Samuel C. *The Crescent and the Rose: Islam and England during the Renaissance.* 1937. Reprint, New York: Octagon Books, 1965.

Clark, Eleanor Grace. *Ralegh and Marlowe.* 1941. Reprint, New York: Russell and Russell, 1965.

Cole, Douglas. *Suffering and Evil in the Plays of Christopher Marlowe.* Princeton: Princeton University Press, 1962.

Comensoli, Viviana. "Homophobia and the Regulation of Desire: A Psychoanalytic Reading of Marlowe's *Edward II.*" *Journal of the History of Sexuality* 4 (1993): 175–200.

Danson, Lawrence. "Continuity and Character in Shakespeare and Marlowe." *Studies in English Literature* 26 (1986): 217–34.

Deats, Sara Munson. "Biblical Parody in Marlowe's *The Jew of Malta* : A Re-Examination." *Christianity and Literature* 37 (1988): 27–48.

———. "*Edward II*: A Study in Androgyny." *Ball State University Forum* 22 (1981): 30–41.

———. "Marlowe's Fearful Symmetry in *Edward II.*" In *"A Poet and a filthy Playmaker"*: *New Essays on Christopher Marlowe*, edited by Kenneth Friedenreich, Roma Gill, and Constance B. Kuriyama. New York: AMS Press, 1988.

———. "Myth and Metamorphosis in Marlowe's *Edward II.*" *Texas Studies in Literature and Language* 22 (1980): 304–21.

Deats, Sara Munson, and Lisa S. Starks. "'So neatly plotted, and so well perform'd': Villain as Playwright in Marlowe's *The Jew of Malta.*" *Theatre Journal* 44 (1992): 375–89.

Dollimore, Jonathan. *Radical Tragedy: Religion, Ideology, and Power in the Drama of Shakespeare and His Contemporaries.* Chicago: University of Chicago Press, 1984.

———. *Sexual Dissidence: Augustine to Wilde, Freud to Foucault.* Oxford: Clarendon Press, 1991.

Donaldson, Peter S. "Conflict and Coherence: Narcissism and Tragic Structure in Marlowe." In *Narcissism and the Text: Studies in Literature and the Psychology of the Self,* edited by Lynne Layton and Barbara Ann Schapiro. New York: New York University Press, 1986.

Donne, John. *The Complete English Poems.* Edited by A. J. Smith. Harmondsworth, U.K.: Penguin Books, 1971.

Eagleton, Terry. "Discourse and Discos: Theory in the Space between Culture and Capitalism." *Times Literary Supplement* no. 4763 (15 July 1994).

Ellis-Fermor, U. M. *Christopher Marlowe.* London: Methuen, 1927.

Foucault, Michel. *The History of Sexuality.* Vol. 1, *An Introduction* (1976). Translated by Robert Hurley. New York: Pantheon, 1978.

Freer, Coburn. "Lies and Lying in *The Jew of Malta.*" In *"A Poet and a filthy Playmaker"*: *New Essays on Christopher Marlowe*, edited by Kenneth Friedenreich, Roma Gill, and Constance B. Kuriyama. New York: AMS Press, 1988.

Freud, Sigmund. *Civilization and Its Discontents.* Translated by James Strachey. New York: Norton, 1961.

Friedenreich, Kenneth. "*The Jew of Malta* and the Critics: A Paradigm for Marlowe Studies." *Papers on Language and Literature* 13 (1977): 318–35.

Frosh, Stephen. *Identity Crisis: Modernity, Psychoanalysis, and the Self.* New York: Routledge, 1991.

———. *The Politics of Psychoanalysis.* New Haven: Yale University Press, 1987.

Frye, Northrop. *The Anatomy of Criticism.* Princeton: Princeton University Press, 1957.

———. *The Great Code: The Bible and Literature.* Toronto: Academic Press Canada, 1982.

Garber, Marjorie. "Closure and Enclosure in Marlowe." In *Two Renaissance Mythmakers: Christopher Marlowe and Ben Jonson,* edited by Alvin Kernan. Baltimore: Johns Hopkins University Press, 1977.

Gaskell, Ian. "2 *Tamburlaine,* Marlowe's 'War against the Gods.'" *English Studies in Canada* 11 (1985): 178–92.

Gatti, Hilary. "Bruno's Heroic Searcher and Marlowe's *Doctor Faustus.*" *Rinascimento* 26 (1986): 99–138.

Geckle, George L. *"Tamburlaine" and "Edward II": Text and Performance.* London: Macmillan, 1988.

Geneva Bible, A facsimile of the 1560 edition. Introduction by Lloyd E. Berry. Madison: University of Wisconsin Press, 1969.

Gibbons, Brian. "Unstable Proteus: Marlowe's *The Tragedy of Dido Queen of Carthage*." In *Christopher Marlowe: Mermaid Critical Commentaries*, edited by Brian Morris. London: Ernest Benn, 1968.

Gilmore, David D. *Manhood in the Making: Cultural Concepts of Masculinity*. New Haven: Yale University Press, 1990.

Glenn, John Ronald. "The Martyrdom of Ramus in Marlowe's *The Massacre at Paris*." *Papers on Language and Literature* 9 (1973): 365–79.

Godshalk, William Leigh. "Marlowe's *Dido, Queen of Carthage*." *ELH* 38 (1971): 1–18.

Goldberg, Arnold, ed. *The Future of Psychoanalysis: Essays in Honor of Heinz Kohut*. New York: International Universities Press, 1983.

Goldberg, Jonathan. *Sodometries: Renaissance Texts, Modern Sexualities*. Stanford, Calif.: Stanford University Press, 1992.

Grant, Patrick. *Literature and Personal Values*. New York: St. Martin's Press, 1992.

———. *The Transformation of Sin: Studies in Donne, Herbert, Vaughan, and Traherne*. Montreal: McGill-Queen's University Press; Amherst: University of Massachusetts Press, 1974.

Greenblatt, Stephen. "Marlowe and Renaissance Self-Fashioning." In *Two Renaissance Mythmakers: Christopher Marlowe and Ben Jonson*, edited by Alvin Kernan. Baltimore: Johns Hopkins University Press, 1977.

———. *Renaissance Self-Fashioning: From More to Shakespeare*. Chicago: University of Chicago Press, 1980.

Greene, Robert. *Friar Bacon and Friar Bungay*. In *Drama of the English Renaissance*, edited by Russell A. Fraser and Norman Rabkin. New York: Macmillan, 1976. 1:357–82.

Greene, Thomas. "The Flexibility of the Self in Renaissance Literature." In *The Disciplines of Criticism: Essays in Literary Theory, Interpretation, and History*, edited by Peter Demetz, Thomas Greene, and Lowry Nelson, Jr. New Haven: Yale University Press, 1968.

Greg, W. W. "The Damnation of Faustus." In *Marlowe: A Collection of Critical Essays*, edited by Clifford Leech. Englewood Cliffs, N.J.: Prentice-Hall, 1964.

Guy-Bray, Stephen. "Homophobia and the Depoliticizing of *Edward II*." *English Studies in Canada* 17 (1991): 125–33.

Halewood, William. *The Poetry of Grace*. New Haven: Yale University Press, 1970.

Herbert, George. *The English Poems of George Herbert*. Edited by C.A. Patrides. London: J. M. Dent and Sons, 1974.

Howe, James Robinson. *Marlowe, Tamburlaine, and Magic*. Athens: Ohio University Press, 1976.

Hunter, G.K. "The Beginnings of Elizabethan Drama: Revolution and Continuity." *Renaissance Drama*, n.s., 17 (1986): 29–52.

———. "Five-Act Structure in *Doctor Faustus*." *Tulane Drama Review* 8, no. 4 (1964): 77–91.

———. "The Theology of Marlowe's *The Jew of Malta*." *Journal of the Warburg and Courtauld Institutes* 27 (1964): 211–40.

Hutcheon, Linda. Afterword to *Remembering Postmodernism: Trends in Recent Canadian Art*, by Mark A. Cheetham. Toronto: Oxford University Press, 1991.

Kastan, David Scott. "'The King Hath Many Marching in His Coats,' or, What Did You Do in the War, Daddy?" In *Shakespeare Left and Right*, edited by Ivo Kamps. New York: Routledge, 1991.

Kendall, Roy. "Richard Baines and Christopher Marlowe's Milieu." *English Literary Renaissance* 24, no. 3 (1994): 507–51.

Kerrigan, William, and Gordon Braden. *The Idea of the Renaissance.* Baltimore: Johns Hopkins University Press, 1989.

Kimbrough, Robert. "*1 Tamburlaine:* A Speaking Picture in a Tragic Glass." *Renaissance Drama* 7 (1964): 20–34.

Kirk, Andrew M. "Marlowe and the Disordered Face of French History." *Studies in English Literature* 35 (1995): 193–213.

Kocher, Paul. *Christopher Marlowe: A Study of His Thought, Learning, and Character.* 1946. Reprint, New York: Russell and Russell, 1962.

———. "Contemporary Pamphlet Backgrounds for Marlowe's *The Massacre at Paris*." *Modern Language Quarterly* 8 (1947): 151–73, 309–18.

———. "François Hotman and 'The Massacre at Paris.'" *PMLA* 56 (1941): 349–68.

———. "Marlowe's Atheist Lecture." In *Marlowe: A Collection of Critical Essays*, edited by Clifford Leech. Englewood Cliffs, N.J.: Prentice-Hall, 1964.

Kohut, Heinz. "Introspection, Empathy and the Semicircle of Mental Health." *International Journal of Psychoanalysis* 63 (1982): 395–407.

———. *The Kohut Seminars on Self Psychology and Psychotherapy with Adolescents and Young Adults.* Edited by Miriam Elson. New York: Norton, 1987.

———. *The Restoration of the Self.* New York: International Universities Press, 1977.

———. "Thoughts on Narcissism and Narcissistic Rage." In *The Psychoanalytic Study of the Child*, Vol 27 (1972), edited by Ruth S. Eissler, Anna Freud et al. New York: International Universities Press, 1973.

Kris, Ernst. *Psychoanalytic Explorations in Art.* New York: International Universities Press, 1952.

Kuriyama, Constance Brown. *Hammer or Anvil: Psychological Patterns in Christopher Marlowe's Plays.* New Brunswick, N.J.: Rutgers University Press, 1980.

Lacan, Jacques. *The Seminar of Jacques Lacan: Freud's Papers on Technique, 1953–1954.* New York: Norton, 1988.

Layton, Lynne, and Barbara Ann Schapiro. Introduction to *Narcissism and the Text: Studies in Literature and the Psychology of the Self.* Edited by Lynne Layton and Barbara Ann Schapiro. New York: New York University Press, 1986.

Leech, Clifford. *Christopher Marlowe: Poet for the Stage.* Edited by Anne Lancashire. New York: AMS Press, 1986.

Leonard, Garry M. *Reading "Dubliners" Again: A Lacanian Perspective.* Syracuse: Syracuse University Press, 1993.

Levin, Harry. *Christopher Marlowe: The Overreacher.* 1952. London: Faber and Faber, 1961.

Lindley, Arthur. "The Unbeing of the Overreacher: Proteanism and the Marlovian Hero." *Modern Language Review* 84 (1989): 1–17.

Machiavelli, Niccolò. *The Discourses.* Edited by Bernard Crick. Translated by Leslie J. Walker. Harmondsworth, U. K.: Penguin Books, 1983.

———. *The Prince.* Translated by George Bull. Harmondsworth, U. K.: Penguin Books, 1982.

Mahood, M. M. *Poetry and Humanism.* London: Jonathan Cape, 1950.

Marlowe, Christopher. *The Complete Poems and Translations.* Edited by Stephen Orgel. Harmondsworth, U.K.: Penguin Books, 1971.

———. *Dido Queen of Carthage and The Massacre at Paris.* Edited by H. J. Oliver. Cambridge: Harvard University Press, 1968.

———. *Doctor Faustus.* Edited by John D. Jump. Cambridge: Harvard University Press, 1962.

———. *Doctor Faustus* A 1604-version ed. Edited by Michael Keefer. Peterborough, Ontario: Broadview Press, 1991.

———. *Doctor Faustus, A- and B-texts.* Edited by David Bevington and Eric Rasmussen. Manchester: Manchester University Press, 1993.

———. *Edward the Second.* Edited by Charles R. Forker. Manchester: Manchester University Press, 1994.

———. *The Jew of Malta.* Edited by N. W. Bawcutt. Manchester: Manchester University Press, 1978.

———. *Marlowe's "Doctor Faustus": Parallel Texts.* Edited by W. W. Greg. Oxford: Clarendon Press, 1950.

———. *Tamburlaine the Great.* Edited by J. S. Cunningham. Baltimore: Johns Hopkins University Press, 1981.

Martin, Richard A. "Marlowe's *Tamburlaine* and the Language of Romance." *PMLA* 93 (1978): 248–64.

Maus, Katharine Eisaman. *Inwardness and Theater in the English Renaissance.* Chicago: University of Chicago Press, 1995.

Minshull, Catherine. "Marlowe's 'Sound Machevill.'" *Renaissance Drama,* n.s., 13 (1982): 35–53.

Mulryne, J. R., and Stephen Fender. "Marlowe and the 'Comic Distance.'" In *Christopher Marlowe: Mermaid Critical Commentaries,* edited by Brian Morris. London: Ernest Benn, 1968.

Nicholl, Charles. *The Reckoning: The Murder of Christopher Marlowe.* New York: Harcourt Brace and Co., 1992.

O'Brien, Margaret. "Christian Belief in *Doctor Faustus.*" *ELH* 37 (1970): 1–11.

Oxford Dictionary of Quotations. 2d ed. London: Oxford University Press, 1953.

Pagels, Elaine. *Adam, Eve, and the Serpent.* New York: Vintage Books, 1988.

Paglia, Camille. *Sexual Personae: Art and Decadence from Nefertiti to Emily Dickinson.* New Haven: Yale University Press, 1990.

Palmer, D. J. "Marlowe's Naturalism." In *Christopher Marlowe: Mermaid Critical Commentaries,* edited by Brian Morris. London: Ernest Benn, 1968.

Parr, Johnstone. "Tamburlaine's Malady." *PMLA* 59 (1944): 696–714.

Peck, Scott. *The Road Less Traveled.* New York: Touchstone, 1978.

Pico della Mirandola. *Oration on the Dignity of Man.* Translated by A. Robert Caponigri. Washington, D.C.: Regnery Gateway, 1956.

Rabkin, Norman. "Marlowe's Mind and the Heart of Darkness." In *"A Poet and a filthy Play-maker": New Essays on Christopher Marlowe,* edited by Kenneth Friedenreich, Roma Gill, and Constance B. Kuriyama. New York: AMS Press, 1988.

Rackham, Bernard. *The Ancient Glass of Canterbury.* London: Lund Humphries and Co., 1949.

Robertson, Toby. Interview by John Russell Brown. "Directing *Edward II.*" *Tulane Drama Review* 8, no. 4 (1964): 174–83.

Roper, Lyndal. *Oedipus and the Devil: Witchcraft, Sexuality, and Religion in Early Modern Europe.* London: Routledge, 1994.

Rose, Mary Beth. *The Expense of Spirit: Love and Sexuality in English Renaissance Drama.* Ithaca: Cornell University Press, 1988.

Russell, John. *Hamlet and Narcissus.* Newark: University of Delaware Press, 1995.

Salingar, L. G. "The Social Setting." In *The Age of Shakespeare.* Vol. 2 of the New Pelican Guide to English Literature, edited by Boris Ford. London: Penguin, 1982.

Sanders, Wilbur. *The Dramatist and the Received Idea: Studies in the Plays of Marlowe and Shakespeare.* Cambridge: Cambridge University Press, 1968.

Sedgwick, Eve. *Epistemology of the Closet.* Berkeley: University of California Press, 1990.

Shepherd, Simon. *Marlowe and the Politics of Elizabethan Theatre.* Brighton: Harvester Press, 1986.

Shuger, Debora Kuller. "Excerpts from a Panel Discussion." In *Renaissance Discourses of Desire,* edited by Claude Summers and Ted-Larry Pebworth. Columbia: University of Missouri Press, 1993.

———. *Habits of Thought in the English Renaissance: Religion, Politics, and the Dominant Culture.* Berkeley: University of California Press, 1990.

Smith, Bruce R. *Homosexual Desire in Shakespeare's England: A Cultural Poetics.* Chicago: University of Chicago Press, 1991.

Smith, James L. "*The Jew of Malta* in the Theatre." In *Christopher Marlowe: Mermaid Critical Commentaries,* edited by Brian Morris. London: Ernest Benn, 1968.

Smith, Mary Elizabeth. *"Love Kindling Fire": A Study of Christopher Marlowe's "The Tragedy of Dido Queen of Carthage."* Salzburg: Universität Salzburg, 1977.

Snow, Edward A. "*Doctor Faustus* and the Ends of Desire." In *Two Renaissance Mythmakers: Christopher Marlowe and Ben Jonson,* edited by Alvin Kernan. Baltimore: Johns Hopkins University Press, 1977.

Spenser, Edmund. *Spenser: Poetical Works.* Edited by J. C. Smith and E. De Selincourt. London: Oxford University Press, 1912.

Steane, J. B. Introduction to *Christopher Marlowe: The Complete Plays.* Harmondsworth, U.K.: Penguin Books, 1969.

———. *Marlowe: A Critical Study.* Cambridge: Cambridge University Press, 1964.

Stockholder, Kay. "'Within the massy entrailes of the earth': Faustus's Relation to Women." In *"A Poet and a filthy Play-maker": New Essays on Christopher Marlowe,* edited by Kenneth Friedenreich, Roma Gill, and Constance B. Kuriyama. New York: AMS Press, 1988.

Summers, Claude J. *Christopher Marlowe and the Politics of Power.* Salzburg: Universität Salzburg, 1974.

———. "Isabella's Plea for Gaveston in Marlowe's *Edward II.*" *Philological Quarterly* 52 (1973): 308–10.

———. "Sex, Politics, and Self-Realization in *Edward II.*" In *"A Poet and a filthy Play-maker": New Essays on Christopher Marlowe,* edited by Kenneth Friedenreich, Roma Gill, and Constance B. Kuriyama. New York: AMS Press, 1988.

Summers, Joseph H. *George Herbert: His Religion and Art.* Cambridge: Harvard University Press, 1968.

Sunesen, Bent. "Marlowe and the Dumb Show." *English Studies* 35 (1954): 241–53.

Tambling, Jeremy. "Abigail's Party: 'The Difference of Things' in *The Jew of Malta.*" In *In Another Country: Feminist Perspectives in Renaissance Drama,* edited by Dorothea Kehler and Susan Baker. Metuchen, N.J.: Scarecrow Press, 1991.

Thurn, David. "Sovereignty, Disorder, and Fetishism in Marlowe's *Edward II.*" *Renaissance Drama,* n.s., 21 (1990): 115–41.

Traub, Valerie. *Desire and Anxiety: Circulations of Sexuality in Shakespearean Drama.* London: Routledge, 1992.

Urry, William. *Christopher Marlowe and Canterbury.* Edited by Andrew Butcher. London: Faber and Faber, 1988.

Vance, Eugene. *Mervelous Signals: Poetics and Sign Theory in the Middle Ages.* Lincoln: University of Nebraska Press, 1986.

Virgil. *Aeneid.* Translated by Robert Fitzgerald. New York: Vintage Books, 1983.

Voss, James. "*Edward II*: Marlowe's Historical Tragedy." *English Studies* 63 (1982): 517–30.

Waldock, A. J. A. "*Paradise Lost*" and Its Critics. Cambridge: Cambridge University Press, 1962.

Wallerstein, Robert S. "Self Psychology and 'Classical' Psychoanalytic Psychology: The Nature of Their Relationship." In *The Future of Psychoanalysis,* edited by Arnold Goldberg. New York: International Universities Press, 1983.

Waswo, Richard. *Language and Meaning in the Renaissance.* Princeton: Princeton University Press, 1987.

Weil, Judith. *Christopher Marlowe: Merlin's Prophet.* Cambridge: Cambridge University Press, 1977.

Wills, Garry. "*Oliver Twist* : Love in the Lower Depths." *New York Review of Books* 36, no. 16 (26 October 1989): 60–67.

Wilson, F. P. "*The Massacre at Paris* and *Edward II.*" In *Marlowe: A Collection of Critical Essays,* edited by Clifford Leech. Englewood Cliffs, N.J.: Prentice-Hall, 1964.

Woodhouse, A. S. P. "Nature and Grace in *The Faerie Queene.*" In *Elizabethan Poetry: Modern Essays in Criticism,* edited by Paul J. Alpers. New York: Oxford University Press, 1967.

Wraight, A. D. *In Search of Christopher Marlowe.* London: Macdonald and Co., 1965.

Wrightson, Keith. *English Society, 1580–1680.* London: Hutchinson, 1982.

Index

279

DATE DUE

FEB 2 6 2007		
APR 1 7 2007		